MW01297453

IN THE FACE OF FEAR

The True Story of the Weisz Family

by
Thomas Weisz

as told to Jeffrey Beal
Thomas Weisz MMVIII

authorHOUSE®

AuthorHouse™
1663 Liberty Drive, Suite 200
Bloomington, IN 47403
www.authorhouse.com
Phone: 1-800-839-8640

© 2010 Thomas Weisz as told to Jeffrey Beal. All rights reserved.

No part of this book may be reproduced, stored in a retrieval system, or transmitted by any means without the written permission of the author.

First published by AuthorHouse   9/21/2010

ISBN: 978-1-4389-4075-5 (sc)
ISBN: 978-1-4389-4076-2 (hc)

Printed in the United States of America

PREFACE

Practically all stories of World War Two, and especially those dealing with the Holocaust, are horrific to the point of being off-putting. So, yearly their audiences shrink, inured by the endless recounting of savagery. As a people, we seem to have become so intimidated by the horror of what human beings can do to each other that our capacity to respond has become overwhelmed. Perhaps that's why we do nothing about the Serbian slaughter or Tutsis or Darfur. And maybe that's why I can no longer procrastinate in sharing my story.

I was only five when the war began, so a lot of my memory of it has been reinforced by family members. Kids are too little to have anything to do with war other than be its victims. Wars are waged by adults. But there are some adults of good will, who struggle against the insanity. This story is about one of them, a man who looked in the face of fear, but showed none himself, someone so extraordinary I often have to speak with surviving members of my family just to remind myself that he was real.

It's been over six decades since that war in Europe ended, though it seems that every couple of years a new totalitarian gang takes power somewhere. But whether they're called Khmer Rouge or Hutus, they're all just Nazis. And I fear that, by the time this simple book is completed, even newer bullies will make their appearance. In any case, it suggests we've fallen short of our goal of 'never again.' So, my modest hope is that my story might inspire somebody else, somewhere, to do something to help at least one of its victims. It's a small blow against apathy, the ally of tyranny, the enemy of us all.

Thomas Weisz / July 28, 2008 / Aventura, Florida.

TABLE OF CONTENTS

CHAPTER ONE

A BRIEF HISTORY OF HUNGARY, FROM ATTILA TO MY MOTHER

My parents were squabbling again. The whole world was at war, but the bickering between my mother and father was a conflict that rivaled the best efforts of the axis and allied powers to capture the attention of the seven of us stuffed into that tiny apartment in 1940 Budapest.

My father was not an earner and my mother was. It was as simple as that. He had been a tin smith, a respectable enough trade for a Hungarian Jew in the first half of the twentieth century. His specialty was making pails, and the multitude of farmers in and around the village where we lived, before Hitler set his sights on the world, regularly bought my father's handicraft. But the industrial revolution, as late as it was in coming to farm friendly Eastern Europe, conspired to deny my father the sole source of reliable income he knew. Someone opened a factory in our county, and mass production relegated Dad to the dust bin of obsolete occupations. So, to the consternation of my mother, he now spent his time honing the only other skill he had heretofore developed, that of being a social butterfly. Long before the conveyer belt took root in our little corner of paradise he'd already had a great deal of experience hanging out, drinking, and playing cards with his pals, on a part time basis. So, he fell into it full time as comfortably as the Germans took to goose stepping. War is an extraordinary event, but ordinary life somehow survives even during a global conflagration, and my parents' arguing was still a persistent reality.

War isn't much good to anyone, but it's always been especially tough on Hungary. From the time of Attila right up to when our beleaguered family was forced to flee the tranquil rural village of my birth, the similarly set upon Hungarians defied the odds and came out last in nearly every armed conflict in which they had the woeful misfortune to become involved. Their one claim to fame, Attila, did manage to unite the barbaric Hun tribesmen, and earn a decent reputation as a fierce warrior, but after his death the troops fled eastward, abandoning to anonymity for another five centuries this as yet unnamed domain. Then, in the waning days of the Dark Ages, the Magyars swept into the Danube Valley, setting a high-water mark against which all Hungarian history would henceforth be measured.

The mysterious Magyars made some decent progress in their campaign through Europe, but having breathed the air of debilitating doom that seems to permeate this unique nation which would one day spawn Bela Lugosi and the Gabor sisters, their martial prowess had seen its best days. Any further attempts at raiding westward met with decisive rebuff from German King Otto, and so, the once mighty tribe reasoned that this fertile land, which would forever bear the name of their difficult dialect, was about as good as it was going to get. They hung up their stirrups, settled down for a few hundred years, and greeted the new millennium as good Catholics.

While the Magyars did not take a back seat to anyone when it came to sweeping through unsettled river basins, by the time the Mongol hordes arrived in the unlucky thirteenth century, they had long since become farmers, and were mercilessly overrun. Only the death from illness of the fierce horde leader sent the superstitious Asians back from whence they'd come, to live forever bereft of the benefits of a cuisine boasting that most pungent and mispronounced paprika.

Freed from the yoke of the oppressive though organized Mongols, chaos ensued, and no opposition could be mustered to prevent an Italian nobleman from coming in and taking over. He and his heir managed to marginally expand the borders, only to have them quickly reduced again. This set up a fateful pattern which Hungary would forever follow. Forces, anxious to expand our frontiers, like a second string offensive football team, marched again and again against like minded foes, with never a first down to their credit. But the hearty goulash nurtured hope in the breast of each new generation, and they continually came out of the huddle determined to give it another try. And each new campaign resulted in an even smaller homeland. One Hungarian noble, who was actually of Romanian noble descent, did manage to offer a brief respite of triumph, by stopping the Ottoman Turks' westward advances. However, the real victory of these nobles was to condemn most of the not so noble Hungarian population to eternal serfdom. Perhaps it was such a dismal fate, to forever be chattels of the crown, that made them less than enthusiastic soldiers, for they were subsequently defeated by the Turks, Hapsburgs, Russians, French, Italians, Prussians, Serbs, British, Germans, Americans, and, if you choose to believe the more xenophobic among my countrymen, the Hebrew Nation. All this history helps explain my father.

With imperial expansion left to the more successful European powers, landlocked Hungary settled into developing culturally from within, and by the time mechanized means of production overtook the rest of the civilized world our now peaceful population had evolved into a cabaret society. Scores of sidewalk cafes and bistros took root along ample tree lined boulevards, and generations of its citizens became bonvivants. Their carefree lifestyle suggested that Hungary was unconcerned with industry and progress, and that being a good mixer was considered by the general populace to be an admirable avocation, though you could not count my mother among their number. We were poor, and she resented my father's unemployment. She, and all my brothers and sisters, worked, but not my father. And not me. I was a kid.

I was only four when Adolph tempted Hungary with a chunk of neighboring Romania. Blissfully unaware of such political machinations I was born in and grew up happy about fifty miles northeast of Budapest in the town of Gyongyos. The population was only about thirty thousand, with a little less than ten percent of them Jews, yet enough to support a sizable synagogue in a poorer part of town. Status was defined by how far you were from water, and waterfront property, then like now, was more desirable. So we were a little proud to have our temple and adjoining cemetery, by a stream. It wasn't the Danube, but at least it was something. Of course, the axis eventually seized that synagogue and turned it into a warehouse, and by war's end it was completely destroyed. But Gyongyos was beautiful. Its very name, Pearly, reflected that beauty. It was at the foot of a winter ski resort and adjacent to huge vineyards. Years later that fact would help save one of my sisters, Yolie, and help our family. Yolie herself had saved me when I was only a week old. I was born at home in 1934, my mother attended to by a midwife. But when I was just a week old I developed a nasty boil on my neck, and had to be taken to the hospital for an operation. There my parents learned that their new baby boy had a rare blood type. Fortunately, Yolie had that same type and gave me a transfusion. This fact was always cited for my later success in business. Yolie was a financial whiz, and receiving her blood somehow gave me the knack.

My parents were especially relieved at my recovery, because they suffered guilt for having considered aborting me. We were terribly poor, and the thought of an extra mouth to feed was intimidating. But by the time they considered this seriously it was the second trimester, and the doctor told them that they had a choice of having a sixth child or maybe leaving five orphaned.

Back when the domesticated Magyars were off failing at expanding our borders, Hungary's population was itself expanding from an incoming tide of independent minded Slavs. Among them were some of us ever wandering Jews. Though the eastern province of Transylvania would later come to enjoy a reputation as a haven for vampires and other creatures of the night, back then it was famed as a refuge for religious freedom. Such sentiment spread, and by the time the twentieth century dawned Jews in Hungary enjoyed an existence relatively free of the harassment experienced in most eastern European nations. There were no pogroms, and hardly anybody batted an eye if they found out you were a member of Abraham's tribe. We could come and go as we pleased, and short of running the country, nothing was barred to us. If you could afford it you could go to fancy restaurants or popular places like the Gellert mineral baths in Budapest. We participated in all walks of life. The Weissman-Fried family was the country's biggest industrialist, manufacturing locomotives and other large machinery in their factory on an island in the Danube, and they were admired and respected. My brother Sandor won the county feather weight boxing title, and no special mention was made of his faith. And, while we all listened to the radio and were aware of Hitler's tirades, we thought that Hungary was different, and we'd be safe. And to their relative credit, the Hungarian government has the dubious distinction of being the last European country taken over the Nazis to take up the banner of anti-Semitism. But when they did they made up for lost time with a vengeance.

I was but a baby when the factory that buried my dad's tin pail business moved to town, so I absolutely never observed my father as a bread winner. He was there for us, and we had a loving relationship, but he was not the patriarch. My mother ran things. Both of my parents came from nearby villages in this area, the Tokay region, known for its wine. But in Gyongyos we had no blood relatives. There were aunts and uncles and cousins in nearby villages, but we didn't often see them. Travel between towns was not that easy. Automobiles were totally nonexistent in these outlying regions. Even later, when we had to flee to Budapest, we had to go in a horse drawn wagon. But convenient transportation that could have taken us to see family was out of the question. We had to rely on ourselves for our survival, as practically everyone else did.

My mother had no formal training or education, so, besides raising half a dozen kids, she had to be an entrepreneur. This was before the *Jewish Laws* came into existence, banning Jews from owning their own businesses. She opened a shop in the middle of the main marketplace selling used household goods. The farmers would weekly bring in their goods to sell, and they would buy knick knacks from my mother. A pot here. A lamp there. She worked such long hours she had to pay a maid to see to the house and take care of the younger kids, which at the time were me and my sister Anci, six years my senior, but still a year or two too young to work. She, like the other two brothers and two sisters were home schooled. I myself didn't start any studies until I was seven and we moved to Budapest. We had a series of maids, though I only remember one, the one who took baths with me. Anci, who had little interest in academic affairs, helped out our mother's business by taking the unsold items from the store and selling them for whatever she could get at the nearby flea market. Maybe that contributed to the one object of opulence that any of us kids had, her bicycle. The only other hint at opulence we could relish, which even the most bedraggled of our countrymen could enjoy, was lunch.

Whether you were in laid back Gyongyos, or hustle bustle Budapest, the pace of Hungarian life shared one trait, the noon day meal and nap. At twelve o'clock all businesses closed, and everyone -Jew and gentile, rich and poor, young and old- all stopped for lunch. It was the big meal of the day, and it was an event. We ate meager breakfasts and light dinners, but lunch was huge. Even though we were poor, Hungary was such a rich and fertile country you couldn't help but find enough to eat, even if it was just fillers like bread and potatoes.

A typical lunch might have pasta and salad. Potatoes were part of practically every lunch as well, smothered in succulent sauces. And no meal was complete without the heavy bread my mother made. Actually, it was the custom and financial necessity, for everyone to make their own bread. We weren't the only people in Hungary who couldn't afford the luxury of an oven, so we subscribed to the popular neighborhood baking method, which meant that mother made dough and carried it the local neighborhood bakery. The baker weighed it, gave you a number, stuck it in his oven, and you came back in an hour or two for your fresh bread. The man probably made more money this way than selling his own goods. My mother's dough weighed about three kilos, or six pounds, and one loaf lasted all week. Mom really knew how to stretch a *pengo*. During the war they changed the currency to *forint*, and mom stretched those too!

On this dense satisfying bread we smeared stewed green peppers and paprika, and chicken fat when available. Sometimes we had goulash, which is just a hodge-podge stew, and it usually had these little noodles in it called *csipetke*. One benefit from my father's socializing was the fresh vegetables and dairy products he got from his farmer friends with whom he caroused. Once in a while he even brought home a chicken for Friday night *Shabbos* dinner. And that chicken lasted all week, and not one part of it went to waste. Even the feathers were used to make pillows and the thick comforters that Europeans prefer to blankets. Chicken or not, we always ate at home, and never in a restaurant.

After Hungary eats it naps, or in our family's case, my parents fought, and then we napped. Most of the time they argued in German.

Hungarian Jews weren't inclined to speak Yiddish as so many other European Jews did. They considered it a bastardization of German, and we were very class conscious and didn't want to do anything that we considered vulgar. So, in order to keep things from the kids, my parents spoke German. They didn't formally teach it to us, but after a while we picked up on much of it. We did use some Yiddish, much like everybody does in America nowadays. Words like *schlep* and *goniff*. But when it came to insults we stuck with Hungarian, which suffers from no lack of highly descriptive and vile epithets.

Hungarian is especially effective for insulting outsiders, because it's a language that doesn't sound like any other. Romance languages are spoken in dozens of countries and have thousands of words in common. And the inhabitants of Slavic countries can practically read each others' newspapers. But the Magyars weren't imposing enough to spread their tongue beyond a trio of countries: Hungary, Estonia and Finland. The marauding side of the Magyar clan must have split up somewhere in western Russia, with half heading south to the Danube Valley and the other half north to frigid Finland. The weaker part of the northern bound band probably stalled in the future Estonia, while the hardier ones pushed on until the ensuing snows trapped them. When the frozen Finnish winter reached crisis level they probably ate their horses to survive, thus ending forever their chances of further sweeping through foreign lands. Finding the female companionship there exceptionally appealing, they embraced their fate, and stayed. They'd already eaten their horses, so they had nothing to offer these new conquests save their exotic language. It caught on, and the future field of linguistic geography would for years delight in tackling the riddle of this odd tongue. Stymied by the sounds of my native land, scholars had to invent a unique class of dialect, *Ungaro-Finn*. But to hide what you say from a Hungarian child you speak German.

Another thing that my parents fought over was the fact that my mother was financially helping a sister who lived in Budapest. Aunt Mariska was a talented musician, but suffered from some facial disfigurement. Mother felt particularly sorry for her and sent her whatever she could manage. I can't imagine how miserably poor she must have been that the pittance sent to her by my mother could have made much of a difference. But send it mom did, and it always vexed my father. Ironically, that generosity paid off for us in a most unexpected way a few years later.

So, we were living the lives of typical Hungarians. At least that's how we felt. Then Adolph started ranting and promised Hungary the return of some of the land they had lost, naturally, to neighboring nations in some all but forgotten previous conflict. The carrot was tempting, so once again our brilliant leaders exhibited their nearly infallible consistency, and picked the wrong side.

CHAPTER TWO

THE LIVES OF JEWISH HICKS

We were not even aware of the earliest impact of any anti-Jewish sentiment on our family. But it was there. It had to do with Sandor's boxing title.

It was not so extraordinary that a Jew would compete in an athletic event. After all, we were Hungarians and loved all the same things. When Sandor won the bout there was no anti-Semitic grumbling or envy, like when Max Baer became a boxing champion in America around the same time. It was a normal sporting event. Maybe some orthodox Jews with a Zionist fervor found some special gratification in it, but our family didn't feel any particular Jewish pride. We just felt proud of him as a member of our family. If we'd have thought about it at all we probably would have felt that everyone else must have felt the same. But there actually was anti-Semitic reaction to it. We just didn't know it then. It was dealt with far away on a whole other level. It never occurred to us at the time, because it was subtle, and a few years later it became clear to us why he was not invited to try out for the 1936 Olympic Games in Berlin. It was an unnoticed event, but things would escalate dramatically, and the atmosphere of coming war would soon become a lot more obvious and affect our lives profoundly.

Besides running her humble store mother cooked. And, like all European women east of the Rhine, she made strudel. I used to watch her make this pound of strudel dough and spread it paper thin over a large table. If we'd had a larger table she probably would've made it even thinner, though you could practically read through it as it was. She filled it with fruit and nuts or poppy seeds and rolled it all up. A trip to the neighborhood baker, and two hours later you got an unforgettable treat. It may sound like sentimental reminiscence to say this strudel was better than anything called strudel you may find today, but it's not. In Hungarian we called this heavenly pastry *rétes*. While we didn't speak a lot of Yiddish in our home there is one word that made its way into Hungary that can best be used to describe my mother. She was a *balabusta*. And like all such dedicated matriarchs, she lived for her family. She cooked, cleaned, worked, saw to our religious upbringing, made sure we learned a trade, and never harmed a soul. Naturally, the Nazis thought such a person unworthy to live.

In Gyongyos we lived in a small rented house. I remember Anci, my nephew John, and my parents being in the house. But my brothers Sandor and Josef, and sisters Rose and Yolie were already living in Budapest, studying a trade or already working at one. Due to the difference in our ages, and the war, it would be years before I'd get to know or, in some cases, even meet all of my siblings. There were the infrequent dutiful visits from the sons, though I hardly remember them myself. The sisters' visits hold a tighter grasp on my memory, especially those of Rose. Actually, this story is really hers more than anyone else's.

Rose was about fourteen years older than me, and already assuming all the responsibilities of a proper young lady. She lived in Budapest, working as a seamstress, and made occasional trips to Gyongyos. It was always a special treat for me to see my glamorous, grown up, older sister. She was like a celebrity, and she treated me special. To this day I can relive the wonderful emotions I felt the night she smuggled me into the local cinema under her overcoat.

They were showing a movie that had a scene with a naked lady in it, and naturally such things were barred to children. Then, like now, you had to be at least eighteen to enter such a movie. But for some reason I've never even considered, Rose thought it would be fun to take her kid brother to see it. Just going to the movies at all was special enough for me. We were poor, and such treats were rare. I really don't think

Rose taking me to that particular movie had anything to do with her wanting to initiate my sexual education. She just wanted to take me to the movies, and they just happened to be showing one that was restricted. Only in town for the weekend, and not wishing to miss either the movie or the opportunity to spend time with her kid brother, she merely did the needful. Such restrictions were of little consequence to her anyway, and ignoring them hardly seemed like criminal behavior. It was this facet of her character, not to cower before every imposed prohibition, that contributed to her ability to survive. Of course, no such lofty considerations figured into my part in it. I was just thrilled to spend time with my big sister. And being hidden by her under her coat made me feel warm and loved and protected. Eventually she would play the role of my protector on a much deeper level. This blithe flaunting of convention is a clue to that part of Rose's personality which let her defy the Nazis. For millions of Jews breaking the rules became a necessity of life. If you were a European Jew, and obeyed every legal invention imposed by governmental authorities between 1934 and 1945, it was suicide.

As I said, I spent precious little time with Rose. I was closest in age to the youngest of my three sisters, Anci, and we were close companions. She was ten years younger than Rose, while my other brothers and sisters were separated by no more than two years apiece. All the time that I spent in the country I was just a child, dedicated to playing. Like all Hungarian country kids, most of whom work as soon as they can, I did not attend school. We respected education, and most Hungarians are literate, but we were usually schooled at home, regardless of religion. And later we were sent somewhere to either learn a trade or pursue a formal education at *gymnazium*, which we in the west understand as a middle or high school, depending on the level. For the privileged few, that formality could lead to university. For Jews that door would soon close. But such things were a million miles away from my life in Gyongyos.

I was a poor country kid, more concerned with playing soccer than world events. I especially liked to tag along with my sister Anci, and she was always happy to take me everywhere she went. I was like her pet. But my main play mate was my nephew John. It might sound odd, for a kid to have a nephew, but it really wasn't out of the ordinary in Europe in the first half of the twentieth century. My sister Yolie, the oldest of the six siblings, married young, and had John. And he came to live with us in 1938, the year that marked many changes for the Weisz family of Gyongyos, and the Jews of Hungary.

Mom's business couldn't provide for us all, much less finance any big change in our lives, so it was decided that the family would sell the one thing of value they had horded for years, a diamond brooch. The brooch was given to us by my maternal grandmother, who lived in Budapest.

Hungary's capital is actually two cities. Buda is on the west side of the Danube, and is hilly, while Pest, pronounced *Pesht,* was built on its flat eastern plain. The extra expense involved in building on the uneven terrain of Buda meant that its citizens were among the more well to do. They enjoyed a more opulent lifestyle, frequenting Buda's nightclubs and other establishments of lively entertainment. The featureless topography of Pest is better suited to factories, train yards, and the populations that labor in them. While it had its better neighborhoods, Pest is decidedly on the other side of the tracks, or river, and was home to the middle and lower classes, including the Weisz clan. My maternal grandparents however, lived on the Buda side and ran one of its more popular cafés, *Mej Pince.* They did well, and did what they could to help the family. But it was a big family, and the wealth had to be spread thin. Our portion of it was the diamond brooch.

Like most of the western world Hungary had been in the grips of the great depression for nearly a decade, so on our home turf we didn't know of any potential customers for this piece of fine jewelry. The few Hungarians wealthy enough to be able to buy it would've almost certainly taken advantage of the widespread poverty, and we'd never have gotten its true value. So, to get the diamond brooch's much needed full worth, and to avoid dealing with strangers, it was determined that it was well worth the expense and trouble of traveling to Paris to negotiate the pricey bauble through Uncle Bela, mother's brother in the jewelry business there. The extra profit more than justified the trip, and practicality pointed a finger at Yolie as the most logical one to make the trip. She was the eldest of the siblings and the most worldly at that time. Of course, none of us had ever traveled even as far away as a hundred miles, what to mention a foreign land.

Yolie had left Gyongyos a few years earlier and married and settled in Budapest. Her husband Nick was the chief lighting technician for The National Theater, and though self educated, he impressed everyone as a cultured gentleman. Yolie herself had landed an important position as the national representative of the Hungarian wine industry, and it had been decided that she would represent it at The New York World's Fair that year. The combination of the family's need, and the need for Yolie and Nick to finance a trip to the fair, meant that Yolie would have to travel to the French capital where Uncle Bela would arrange for the sale of the brooch.

In an attempt to help the family, Yolie would be taking a harrowing journey through the gauntlet of a growing Nazi menace, passing through the borders of four European countries, all of which had one or both sides guarded by soldiers of, or allied with, The Third Reich. It all happened on the Orient Express.

CHAPTER THREE

TERROR ON THE ORIENT EXPRESS

$\mathbf{I}$t was the grandest adventure that any of our provincial family had ever made. For over half a century the Orient Express had linked Asia Minor with Western Europe. The train route had been the brainstorm of a nineteenth century entrepreneur whose main challenge was to convince so many countries, used to disputing every inch of land on any side of a border, to allow a single train to enjoy autonomy as it traversed two thousand miles, from Istanbul in the east to Paris in the west. The countries along the route all cooperated, but with the compromise that local locomotives would have to be changed at every international border. This industrial bureaucracy provided the guardians of red tape with a window of opportunity to exercise their authority. It was as satisfying and exhilarating to them as it was tedious and frustrating to the passengers. But once the Third Reich had risen to power, and its influence over various European countries cemented, those border crossings escalated from tedium to terror.

Practically our last pengo went into a second class ticket from Budapest to Paris. Second class meant no meals. So, mother packed some food in a box, and sewed the diamond brooch into the collar of Yolie's coat. Nick took her to the train station and saw her off. At that time Jews did not have to put the infamous yellow Mogen David, or Star of David, on their clothing. But by 1938 the European political scene made it clear that Hungarian Jews would have to make some drastic decisions to survive. Some countries had already enacted Jewish Laws, disenfranchising them, and restricting their freedom. Even if you thought that it couldn't happen in the freedom loving land of Bela Bartok and Franz Liszt, you couldn't turn a blind eye to the writing on the eastern wall, or the writing in Yolie's passport that identified her as a Jewess.

Europe had been paper happy for who knows how long. Everyone had to carry some sort of identification. If you didn't have a scrap of processed wood pulp on your person to vouch for you it was as if you didn't exist. And the more responsibility you took on, in your struggle to earn a living, the more complex your little scraps became. For example, many people didn't even require a photo on their documentation. But if you were lucky enough to gain employment in a large factory then you had to have a glossy black and white likeness glued onto your credentials. Yolie felt no particular apprehension over her papers. They were legal, correct, and up to date. But in 1938, being up to date and accurate meant that your true religion was a matter of record. It was a detail, but it could cause her inconvenience. Be that as it may, the family needed the income that was to be derived from the sale of the brooch, and we had no idea of the severity of the disregard in which the so-called Aryans held us. We knew about Hitler's speeches, but we hadn't felt their effect in far away Hungary and we had a classic false sense of security. So, she climbed aboard the legendary train, and settled in for a long journey. My parents prayed for her safety while Uncle Bela awaited her in Paris.

European trains divide their second class passengers into a series of small, cozy compartments on each coach. Yolie settled into hers, sitting by the window at one end of the two upholstered high-backed sofas that faced each other. Five others sat around her. The coach car was kept full the entire time, with four of the seats being used by a series of passengers, while one was occupied by the same woman the entire trip. Naturally, they were all strangers, and the politically suspicious climate of the times did not lend much credence to relying on their kindness.

First class passengers on the Orient Express had their luggage shipped in the baggage cars. But most of the second class travelers stored their small valises in overhead bins, like carry-ons of today. Yolie stashed hers, but sat with the precious parcel of food in her lap. She also kept her overcoat with the diamond brooch near her at all times.

The trip would take longer than a twelve hundred kilometer journey ought to take for a modern locomotive, because the celebrated rails were not laid in a straight line. The Alps made that impossible. Besides, such great European capitals as Vienna, Munich, and Zurich all craved access to the storied train, causing it to cross many politically sensitive borders. It would be three tense days of searches and anticipating them.

Looking out the window of any train traveling through central Europe does not offer a great variety of panoramas. It's mostly crop land. Yolie was facing forward and she watched the endless fields of grains, beans, vegetables, and grazing animals flying past. It's easy to imagine why the Magyars and Huns, coming from arid wastelands, found it so inviting. And it's no surprise to see why, if it wasn't the cradle of western civilization, it was a pretty good incubator. It is endlessly green, fertile and life sustaining. But at this time in history certain inhabitants of this nurturing land were not content to enjoy its fruits. Rather, they would plunder it and make it unfit to live. The Great War had already seen plowshares broken into swords, and the land sown with over a million artillery shells. At that time, if you were employed digging up unexploded cannon rounds out of the rich black earth, you had a job for life. But Yolie did not have the luxury of carefree time to consider such context. She was nervous about every detail of the trip. Would she lose anything? Would she be robbed? Would she be mistreated? Fortunately she was distracted from her fears by the frivolous conversation of her companions.

When not waging war against each other, Europeans can be a gregarious lot, and this group was no exception. Everybody was content to leave politics off the agenda, and enough common languages and topics were found to fill time. Film reviews, tourist anecdotes, and family photos took up the slack, and the sun went down almost unnoticed. But the crossing of the western Hungarian border into Austria brought about enough stress as to dampen everyone's mood. Here was a country openly in support of the Third Reich. And as Nazis always do, they smell conspiracy around every corner. The collective apprehension in the car, facing a potential common enemy, gave them all a calming camaraderie, and buoyed their spirits. Like her compartment mates Yolie was anxious, or at least annoyed, over the three hours of bureaucracy, far longer than it really took to change locomotives. And when your own papers were under review any imagined esprit d'corps evaporated. At that point you were on your own.

Nobody was exempt from the drill. Everyone's papers and valises were inspected. But Yolie's overcoat with the brooch escaped their vigilance. When the Austrian official reviewed Yolie's papers and saw that she was a Jew he regarded her briefly, but not so briefly as to not convey a momentary mixture of suspicion and disdain. But the official could just as easily have expressed condescension over her being Hungarian, which any Aryan railroad official would have considered below his station, so to speak. Next stop, Vienna.

After the anxiety of the search she could no longer endure the anxiety of hunger. So, once the train had resumed its normal rate of speed she decided to open her box of rations. She couldn't help but notice that nobody else had eaten either, and could only surmise that everybody else in her tiny coach car was in even worse financial straits than her. So, she opened the box and offered it around to her grateful companions. Particularly thankful was a lady who had sat silently opposite Yolie since departing Budapest. A blond, well dressed, worldly looking woman of about thirty years of age had quietly sat right across from Yolie the entire time with hardly saying a word. This was an extremely observant lady. With nothing else to do to fill the monotonous hours on the journey, and already having had her share of train trips and verdant panoramas, the woman devoted her sightseeing to the interior of the train, watching her travel companions. Yolie couldn't help but feel her gaze, yet there was nothing she could do to prevent it. She was a poor desperate young Jewish woman, sitting on a well worn public couch. She had no money, power or influence. But she felt that, as long as she minded her own business, she could make it to the safety of Paris and her uncle. If she needed anything beyond her limited resources, she would have to rely on luck and God. She prayed, as her forefathers always had on Friday nights, to be free of any risky contact with strangers.

Occasionally she would return her companions' looks. She was possessed of no guile, and her gaze was one of wide eyed innocence.

But it was an era of suspicion, and nobody could pass for innocent, not for all the beatific countenance of an angel.

Hour after hour dragged by, and the observant lady had much opportunity to assess this pilgrim from Budapest. Plus, there was the chance that she had a peek at the young woman's papers at the Austrian border, and had also learned that detail of her identity that could put her in jeopardy. Mere conversation failed to mask Yolie's distress, but whatever the woman thought or knew was a secret. Yolie could only hope for the best and keep calm.

When small town Yolie moved from Gyongyos to Budapest it was a heady experience. Grand buildings, automobiles, and finely dressed multitudes made her head spin. But even that did little to prepare her for the opulence of Vienna. Nestled between the Alps and the Carpathian mountains it was storybook lovely to young Yolie's eyes. Though unable to see very much of the city, due its flat topography, what she could see of the buildings from the windows of her rolling train car reminded her of fine doll houses she had seen in the windows of upper class toy stores in Budapest. The blond woman seemed to take some pleasure in watching the inexperienced young girl's fascination with her first taste of the big outside world.

Blessedly, they were already well within Austria's borders, so they didn't have to go through another search. Besides showing her ticket Yolie just had to sit still for an hour while the train loaded and unloaded passengers and baggage, and took on fuel.

Everybody but the blond woman got off in Vienna, so they passed the time chatting about things of little consequence. After half an hour a family of four, parents and children, invaded the compartment, exchanging pleasantries. The adults sat next to Yolie, while the children sat by the blond woman. This suited Yolie fine, as she found it less stressful to look at, and be looked at by, kids. No sooner had the well fed Wieners sat down than the Orient Express resumed its journey westward.

As the train was slow in picking up momentum Yolie had a nice opportunity to explore the streets of Vienna. There were many cars and trolleys, and more taxis than she had ever seen in one place. She took particular note that there were hardly any horse drawn conveyances in sight. But most impressive of all was the architecture. It reminded Yolie of Budapest, but it was so much grander and filled with greater detail.

The intimidation of a strange place and the familiar looking buildings conspired to make her feel terribly homesick. Her new travel companions were confidently boisterous, making Yolie feel all the more outclassed and vulnerable. This did not escape the analytical eye of the blond woman, who was as calm as Yolie was tense. Contemporary sophisticates would probably have identified a secret policeman behind that blond woman's reptilian simper, but Yolie grew up free of the hate and the prejudice which now permeated every westward meter she rode. That innocence protected her from further stress, so she napped. When she awoke Vienna was far behind, yet the haven of Paris was still an eternity away.

Hunger woke her. The jolly Weiner family had gone to the dining car, so she shared some more of her box of food with the blond woman. Taking advantage of their being alone together for the first time since beginning their trip the blond woman now leaned forward and spoke in a tone warmer and more serious than Yolie had any right to expect.

"I want to thank you for sharing your food with me," she said.

Yolie was a little surprised by the sudden simplicity with which her compartment mate now addressed her. But she also felt flattered and relaxed by the sudden change, and comfortably replied, "You're quite welcome."

In leaning forward to talk to Yolie the woman took on a humble posture. "I really mean it. These are hard times, and your kindness has made this trip far more bearable than I had anticipated."

Yolie sweetly smiled. A reply didn't come quickly, but she was rescued as the woman continued. "And it's delicious. Did you prepare it?"

Proudly, Yolie informed her, "My mother made it."

The woman could only respond with a genuinely warm smile. Clearly, here was a simple Hungarian girl out in the world for the first time. She leaned forward even more and looked around her to make sure the door was not ajar. Even more softly than before she gave Yolie a crash course on the realities of everyday life in modern Europe.

"They're going to search us again when we cross the German border."

"Yes, I know," said Yolie.

The woman looked at once disappointed and amused at Yolie's naiveté, and couldn't hide an ironic grin. "If you think Austria was thorough you have no idea what awaits you when we cross over into Germany."

The confused pupil openly asked, "What do you mean?"

The woman now introduced herself. "My name is Franci Luden, and I am a German citizen."

At this Yolie politely nodded, as she had long since assumed her nationality from her accent. But now the woman's gaze became more fixed, and Yolie felt truly concerned.

"I don't know how seriously you're taking things over in Hungary, but life in Germany has been changing very much over the last decade."

Yolie's whole being was now hanging on her new mentor's every word.

"Everything has political overtones. It's bound to affect your country soon enough. Anyway, the German guards will take this train apart and everyone on it. If they find anything that is being hidden, even if it's a legal possession of yours that you are hiding just for safekeeping, they'll confiscate it and maybe even arrest you."

Yolie couldn't speak. She was wide-eyed with terror as the woman continued.

"Better you have that look of fear now, and get over it! If it's plastered on you when you hand over your papers to a German guard he'll take it as a confession of guilt and take you in for questioning."

Agape, Yolie could barely breathe.

"If you have anything on you," counseled Franci Luden, "give it to me. I won't have to go through such a tough time of it as you will."

Yolie's education was brief, but it woke her up. What was she to do? If this woman was telling the truth she was doomed. If it was just a story to get something from her she was likewise doomed. But at least she'd be free. She stared at Franci for a long time, each moment growing worldlier.

"Why will you be safer than me? Because you're German?"

The ironic grin returned. "Being German doesn't amount to much."

She opened her packet of identification papers and showed them to Yolie. There, boldly and menacingly displayed, was a swastika. She froze at once and was paralyzed with dread.

"Get over that too. You're about to see a lot of swastikas."

Yolie could only stutter, "Are you a N-Nazi?" To see Franci shake her head caused her chest to heave and choke in relief.

"These are the papers of a member of the Nazi party." Now she spoke with urgency. "Look at me. I'm obviously an Aryan, and I have papers saying I'm a national socialist party member. So, things won't be so hard on me when we arrive. But a Hungarian? They'll search you down to your underwear!"

Now Yolie had to make what would sound like a confession. Why should it be? Was her religion a crime? But she was nervous about it, and needed to be fully prepared.

"I'm Jewish. And it says so on my papers. Will that complicate things?" Now it was the German's turn to be wide eyed.

"Are you serious?" Yolie could only nod sheepishly.

With pity in her voice, Franci whispered, "My dear." But her mission of gratitude was to educate this child. So she put the lesson back on track.

"What's your name? What are you doing on the Orient Express so far from home? And compose yourself. The happy Viennese troupe will be back soon. This may be your last chance to protect yourself before we hit Germany!"

She was right. She was far from home, with no options. Yolie knew she would have to obediently follow this Aryan's lead.

"I'm Yolie Weisz. I'm going to Paris to see an uncle who's going to help me sell a family heirloom I have with me, a diamond brooch. It's the only thing of real value we have left to help us finance our move to Budapest, and help buy our passage to New York."

"New York," Franci repeated. Now she was impressed with this little Hungarian hick.

Yolie finished her confession, "I'm going to represent our wine industry at the World's Fair."

Franci digested all of this. "Give me the brooch. Where does your uncle live?"

As Yolie contemplated the possible dire consequence of surrendering the brooch to a stranger, and member of the Nazi party, Franci continued, "If we get separated I'll bring the brooch to your uncle's apartment. Don't dawdle, Yolie Weiss. You must trust me."

Yolie was desperate. But she had no choice. None at all.

"My uncle is Bela Krausz. He lives in the *Morais* district, by the hotel Victoire on the north side of Paris. He has a small jewelry shop in the same neighborhood."

She didn't know if she felt relieved or foolish. She had just told her life's story to someone who could destroy her. She was numb. Franci continued to stare at her, exhibiting her impatience. Yolie retrieved her overcoat and fiddled with the collar. Slowly the diamond brooch emerged.

It was a dazzling four carat solitaire cut diamond, imbedded in an inch and a quarter long field of diamond pavé, all set in an eighteen carat gold bed. When people saw it for the first time they were always moved to use such words as exquisite or recherché. Franci was no exception

It was a painful surrender, and Yolie silently prayed that she was doing the right thing in handing it over. Franci meanwhile was all business, and didn't waste a second in cleverly hiding the brooch in the lining of her own overcoat. She was so adept at doing it, as if she'd done it many times before, that Yolie felt impressed. But she still begrudged surrendering it. Franci leaned back.

"Once we're safe in Paris I'll give it back to you. You'll make it to New York. Don't worry."

Yolie nodded, still numb. Franci breathed easier. She seemed calmer and self assured.

"Don't worry, Yolie Weisz. But it wouldn't hurt to pray."

It was true. She was little Yolie Weisz, far from home. But somehow she felt alerted, and a little more prepared, and braver for it. Now, it was her turn to show some gratitude. She put her coat away and brought out the box of food again.

"Here. Taste my mother's rétes. It's really good!"

Franci smiled, "It's not my first trip to Hungary. I love *rétes*. Even more than *krémes*, I think."

This made Yolie smile and calmed her down quite a lot.

"Yolie. The Nazis are going to search you. They might even bring in a female security officer to strip search you. It won't be pleasant. They'll ask you a million questions. They don't like Jews, and they don't like Slavs either. But at least Hungary has good relations with Germany. So, as long as they don't find anything out or order, like hidden diamond brooches in coat collars, you'll probably make it through okay. Try and keep your dignity. But don't seem confrontational. They're your superiors. Be humble. But not too lowly either. They're arrogant bastards. All policemen are. Anyway, like I say, as long as they don't find anything worse than the fact that your papers say you're a Jewess, probably nothing will happen to you. Don't act like we're together. What would a member of the Nazi party have to do with a Jew? I'm not going to look at you, and you're not going to look at me. Do you understand?"

Like a soldier Yolie dutifully nodded.

"And once our travel companions return keep the chit chat to a minimum. I'll act in a formal manner." Yolie firmed her jaw and resolutely nodded, practically with a military snap.

They shared another small piece of rétes, and she closed the lid. It had to last well into France. Slowly savoring her mother's morsel of pastry Yolie felt more tranquil now. She had an ally. Or at least felt she did. She'd also had a crash course in European politics, and felt better prepared for her first meeting with Nazis, if anything could ever properly prepare you for that.

If Franci hadn't tutored Yolie on German border searches she probably would have broken down crying. It was humiliating. They spoke to her as if she were a piece of stone. They didn't so much speak to her as at her, barking orders all the time. And they never really looked at her. They just looked at parts of her. Her hair. Her hat. Her feet. Different parts of her anatomy. They suspected everything. Every article of clothing. Her tooth powder. Her comb. The lining of her valise. Her food. She felt lucky that they searched through it but returned it in tact. Clearly, these people had done this a million times before, maybe ten times that very day already. She could see that Franci was right;

they would have found her brooch. For several minutes it seemed as if she would be in serious trouble, because they discovered the hole in the collar that the brooch had squeezed through. They looked grimly at the coat and glowered at her. They summoned a female guard, and she took a terrified Yolie into a small office for a strip search. But her education on the train paid off, and she managed not to display too much fear. Anyway, there really was nothing to be afraid of, as the one piece of evidence that would have condemned her was now in the possession of a trustworthy member of the Nazi party. They demanded to know why her coat collar had a hole in it, and Yolie played innocent, claiming not to even know that it did. After all, she insisted, she was poor and it had been her coat for several winters. That was not a lie. Actually, if she made it back to Budapest, the coat would in all likelihood become a hand-me-down for Rose.

As for her professor she was standing only a few feet away, calmly enduring a perfunctory search, never revealing any emotion. They never even looked at her coat, and Yolie was glad about that, though hoped it didn't show. After several hours of searches they were back on the train. Next stop Munich.

After the ordeal at the Austrian-German border the ride into Munich and the heartland of the Third Reich was one long relief. First of all, Franci was still there. So she hadn't fallen prey to an elaborate ruse to beguile her out of her jewel. At least, not yet. The happy go lucky Viennese family had gotten off in Munich, and was replaced by some grim elderly people who smelled. Once, Franci even shot her a glance as if to register her opinion of their hygiene. It was a much needed lighthearted moment.

Serenely rolling through southern Germany on the Orient Express Yolie couldn't help but ponder what she had heard on radio broadcasts from Germany, that Deutschland was supposedly *uber alles*. It looked just like Hungary to her. Actually, Hungary looked a little greener. Her demeanor now serene she occasionally regarded Franci. Was she for real? Would she make off with the diamond brooch when they reached Paris? Worse, would she keep Yolie from pursuing her after the theft by making up some story to her Natzi compatriots, and get her arrested? Her new German friend looked calm, and that made Yolie

24

feel even tenser. But, no! If she wanted the piece of jewelry she could have gotten Yolie detained in Munich, and had a free ride to Paris. Would she have been so bold as to even go to her uncle's shop to negotiate the sale of the pin? It was useless to consider such things. She had already crossed the Rubicon with Franci. Now, she should worry more about crossing the Rhine into France. She opened up the food, which was more than half empty now, and, polite as ever, offered it around. The old folks had no interest in it, and almost scowled at her in refusal. But Yolie didn't take it as a rebuff. That's just the way old folks are, she thought. Franci, on the other hand, was as delighted as ever to help Yolie honor her mother's simple cuisine. And it gave Franci an opportunity to allay Yolie's anxiety by graciously smiling and thanking her. Just that little gesture and scrap of conversation did indeed have a salutary affect on Yolie. It bolstered her for the final Teutonic inspection before exiting the Third Reich into Switzerland. To calm herself further she thought of Gyongyos.

Back home our days were as yet free from snooping Nazis, and we continued to live at our usual pace. John and I played, Anci helped mother, and father loitered with his friends, all of us blithely oblivious to Yolie's trial by fire. Only mother worried, but she was so distracted by her work routine she could do little more than occasionally cast her eyes upward and pray. But nighttime brought ominous radio transmissions that caused us all to think about Yolie.

Once, father broke the silence, "I hope Yolie's alright."

But mother rebuked him, "If you brought home the bacon maybe we wouldn't have to take such desperate measures." She switched to German. "Come to think of it, why didn't you volunteer to go yourself?! Or maybe you couldn't adjust your busy schedule?"

That was the first time I had ever seen father look really guilty. Usually, he seemed unconcerned that he was a professional social butterfly. But he certainly didn't want to put his kids in danger, and now he reflected that he might have, and fell shamefully silent. Mother, who usually displayed some satisfaction over winning their arguments, refrained from any such posture. She was worried for her eldest child. If she'd known at that very moment that the Orient Express was one kilometer from the southern German border she might have fallen to her knees.

The same dark night that had fallen on Gyongyos fell on western Germany. As the engineers uncoupled the locomotive in preparation for the change, Yolie steeled herself. Doubtless, Nazis felt it as important to inspect visitors leaving Germany as they did entering. Having already gone through it Yolie behaved identically, but she was careful not to make it look like routine. Franci had warned her that such a demeanor could be interpreted as arrogant, a temperament forbidden to all but the Aryan authorities. So, she endured the search with her eyes cast downward. Whenever the opportunity presented itself she glanced about for a sign of Franci. She didn't see her, but couldn't afford the luxury of exhibiting distress over it. After all, she was probably already back in their compartment waiting for a bit of rétes to celebrate crossing into neutral Switzerland. However, when she climbed aboard and sought the refuge of her little compartment little enough refuge awaited her. It was empty. She sat down and waited. Ten minutes went by. No Franci. Five minutes later some new travelers entered.

They greeted her formally, "Bon jour, mademoiselle."

Ill prepared for the moment she mumbled her own clumsy French greeting. Then the train shuttered and started to move. Would Franci dramatically appear, all out of breath? She tried not to look anxious, when she had the presence of mind to take toll of her bodily signs. Sure enough, her eyes were wide open in fright. She consciously reduced them to normal size. Had they seen? Could they feel her panic? Surely Franci would appear. Twenty minutes later and she felt as if all was lost.

After eating a morsel she sighed and leaned back while the train sped forward, crossing into Switzerland. Once inside she numbly went through another inspection, brief compared to what she had been through in Germany. She didn't even have to leave her compartment as the Swiss officials came on board. But her clothes were inspected, whereas the Frenchmen's were not. Years later she learned the reason for this. Before she left Germany the officials there had made a small mark in her passport, a capital J. This alerted the so called neutral makers of cuckoo clocks to the presence of a Jew, and some possible

26

wealth there to be gained. The Swiss were the Nazi's willing bankers, but would elude being identified as such for nearly forty years when international pressure finally forced them to return a portion of the Jewish wealth they had stolen. For now the prejudice was subtle; they searched Yolie, but left the gentile French alone.

It was night now, with nothing to see. Deeply depressed, Yolie blessedly fell asleep, and didn't wake up until crossing the French border. There the inspections were even less stringent than Switzerland. Her slumber was so deep she had to think where she was when she woke up. Her depression had transformed her into a numb individual whose lack of emotion would probably be misinterpreted by the worldly French as ennui. Being that she'd have to return through Germany, hounded by the same psychological state as she presently suffered, she might actually benefit from her apparent lack of concern for her surroundings. It might be perceived as indifference, and place her above suspicion.

Resigned to her fate Yolie feasted on the last of the food, and feeling full for the first time since leaving home, escaped again into unconsciousness, and stayed asleep until Paris. Waking up there only reminded her again of grim reality, that she was alone and had no diamond brooch. He trip was a fiasco. Her family depended on her, and she had failed them. She was miserable, and felt as if she would never be happy again. She was so distraught there was no controlling herself, and with no Germans to impress with stoic timidity she claimed the freedom to cry. She wept for what must have seemed like a solid hour before the gallant Frenchmen finally addressed her. *"Pour quoi triste, mademoiselle?"* She barely managed to mumble some German and a *"Pardonne moi."* Not even the sight of the Eiffel Tower in the distance changed her mood. Au contraire! It confirmed her fate. As long as she was on the train she was in a cocoon, insulated from having to face the world, and confess her sins. She had let her family down to an unfathomable degree. It was the worst day of her life. She was desolate.

CHAPTER FOUR

NOT SO GAY PARIS

The Orient Express reached Paris, France. A falsetto choir of squealing brakes, the release of built up steam, and the constant rumbling vibration of the past week stopped. Little Yolie Weisz from Gyongyos was in The City of Lights, the cultural capital of the civilized world. Paris was, after all, the raison d'etre for the Orient Express. For half a century it was a dream for millions just to go there. But Yolie wanted to die. She retrieved her valise from its overhead bin and, dragging it behind her like a wounded limb, left her home of the last three days. The most dramatic and dangerous events of her entire life had just transpired, and the only evidence of it now were some shallow dents in a sofa seat and back, and an abandoned box of crumbs. Yolie trudged slowly away like a prisoner on her way to the guillotine.

She waded her way through a mob of beckoning taxi drivers, and dragged herself to a nearby park, where she collapsed on a bench and released another torrent. Things couldn't possibly be any worse. Then it started to rain. It was only a light shower, but it jarred her enough to get up and seek some refuge. Once under the eaves of a building she searched through her pockets for her uncle's address. Then she remembered how she had recited from memory his address to a total stranger on the train, before voluntarily surrendering her family's entire fortune to her. Again, she was desolate. All around her were sights that graced post cards, yet she was oblivious to it all. She half jokingly told herself she should go to the Bastille and stay there. Not so half jokingly she briefly considered throwing herself into the fabled Seine. Finally, her mother's good sense got hold of her, and she stopped a Parisian to get her bearings.

By this time Yolie had no money left, having spent the few *pengos* she'd taken along on some meager liquid refreshment on the train. So, she'd have to walk to Uncle Bela's. She was told before leaving that she could take a taxi to her uncle's in case she was broke upon arriving, and he'd gladly pay the fare. But she accepted the long hike there as well deserved punishment for her stupidity, her naiveté, her sin.

Each step was torture. Not because her valise was heavy. Not because she was tired or hungry. Rather, each step brought her shame far worse than mere physical pain. She was in the most enchanting place on Earth, but she didn't deserve it. Like a zombie she schlepped forward, block after block of ornate palaces, regal cathedrals, art galleries and cafés. She saw the latest fashions in boutique windows and on the people. She smelled fresh baguettes and perfume. She should have been captivated and delighted. But the more wonderful the sights and sounds she encountered the worse she felt. She was angry with herself, and could not enjoy even the best Paris had to offer. She was anything but gay. And when she felt she could not be more desolate she arrived at Uncle Bela's whose merry greeting caused her to feel absolutely mortified.

The warm hospitality of her uncle was pure torment. After all, she deserved nothing. Seeing her uncle's concern she revealed everything. He sat patiently and listened.

"You told her about me?"

Now she felt even worse. If it had become dangerous just to be a Jew maybe she had put her uncle in danger.

But Uncle Bela filled her cup to fully half, "Then she knows where to bring the brooch!"

It didn't cheer her up. "Look, you had a tough choice. The Nazis would have almost certainly found the pin, and made up some excuse to relieve you of it. Then they would have interrogated you all day, and you'd have missed your train. You would have been stranded in Germany, penniless and alone. At least you're safe."

Frustrated, she blurted back, "What good is that? They depended on me, and I let them down! Now we have nothing!"

But Uncle Bela refused to let her suffer. He brought her something to eat, and invited her to make herself at home. He showed her a bathroom and a bedroom, and never stopped smiling and being merry the entire time. To him it was as if nothing had happened. His kindness was sheer torture to her. But after a warm bath, an even warmer bowl of French soup, and a change of clothes, she collapsed on her bed and escaped her torment into a long night's much needed sleep.

She awoke, listening to French robins twittering away like Hungarian robins. Her uncle had kindly let her sleep, and ten hours had transpired since she lay down on that deliciously soft mattress. It was already well into her second day on French soil. She was rested, so now her doldrums were fully alert, as opposed to the fatigued state of depression she had lived for the last two days. In the darkest mood of her life she padded off to the bathroom barely noticing her uncle and a guest sitting in the living room.

She mumbled *"Bon jour mon oncle."* When that greeting was returned by a feminine voice she stopped. She stepped back and looked in. Now the sun rose bright within her uncle's modest apartment and within her heart. Franci Luden was sitting, calmly chatting with her uncle.

Yolie ran to her and embraced her, kissing her cheeks over and over, tears flowing again.

She tried to speak, but couldn't manage a proper sentence, "I thought...where...what hap... why'd..."

Franci, ever the master, looked at her pupil seriously. "Sit down Yolie."

Uncle Bela, who had been beaming until now, also turned grave, and sat at the master's feet as well. You're never too old to learn.

"Yolie, they were watching me. They suspected we were together somehow. Of course, they suspect everyone, so by pure luck, once in a while they're right. Anyway, I told them I was only going as far as the border, and left the station."

Yolie was aghast. "You lied?! Couldn't you get in trouble for that?"

Bela piped in, "Big trouble with those galoots!"

Franci calmly continued, "But I'm one of those galoots. For now, party membership keeps you above suspicion."

Yolie was overwhelmed by Franci's bravery, and could barely contain her emotion. "They might have checked your ticket and known you were lying." This awareness impressed the German woman.

"You learn quickly, Yolie. You have a bright niece, monsieur."

Bela Krausz himself was no less impressed with both his niece and Franci. "Madame Luden, we are indebted to you for helping Yolie."

"And for helping us all," quickly added Yolie.

"That's right," said Franci, wide eyed, "I'd almost forgotten the reason for this visit!"

She picked up her coat off the back of the chair where it had been resting, and fiddled with the collar. Slowly, a diamond brooch gleamed forth. Yolie's relief brought back the tears again.

"You'll have to learn to control that," said Franci in her professor's voice.

Like a dutiful student she obeyed.

Bela filled the pause. "Where are my manners? Come to the table Frau Luden, and have some wine and lunch."

"French wine? French cooking? But of course. Merci beaucoup!"

"Well," corrected Uncle Bela, "half French and half Hungarian."

"Even better," she replied, as she strode to the table. Once Franci was attended to, the topic of food was forgotten, and Uncle Bela picked up his jeweler's eyepiece and examined the brooch. He turned it around and around and looked at it from every angle.

"Very nice. Very nice indeed. You know, I would never suggest you do such a thing again. But now that you have, I'd almost say that it was worth the risk! This is a very valuable piece."

Gravity seized everyone as Franci took control, "But she will have to do it again!"

Both stared agape at Franci. What did she mean? She looked at Uncle Bela.

"Monsieur Weisz. She's going to have to return to Budapest with the cash from the sale. And by the same route."

Again, Yolie's words got jumbled, almost as badly as her thoughts. Uncle Bela was observant, anticipating another lesson from their Aryan teacher. But Franci cast an aura of contentment around Uncle Bela's apartment when she proclaimed, "I think she'll be alright."

Franci explained that travelers heading west posed more of a threat to the paranoid fascist, because they were leaving their control. But eastbound sojourners, heading into the heartland of Europe, were cause for little concern, because they were committing themselves further into their sphere of influence, and that made them feel more powerful and at ease.

Relieved at the return of the brooch, and at the insistence of Uncle Bela, Yolie relaxed with a spot of tourism. Franci Luden was glad to be her guide while Uncle Bela arranged for potential buyers to inspect the piece. And while they visited Notre Dame, the Eiffel Tower, Montemarte, and strolled along the banks of the Seine, Franci tutored Yolie on how to act on her return trip.

How kind this woman had been to her. She lived in a country whose leader preached the most horrific things about Jews, yet she was unaffected by it. Surely, there must be other Germans like her. Maybe things weren't going to be so bad. There was hope, at least, in her heart, and when it came time to say goodbye she hugged Franci.

"I don't know how to thank you. You've done so much for me."

Franci demurred, "Not so much, really. I was coming to Paris anyway."

Yolie was enlivened by the humility of this German woman. Holding back tears she said, "If you're ever in Budapest come see us. I'll make sure you get all the rétes you can eat."

"Sounds wonderful," said Franci. "Who knows? Maybe I will. Adieu, Yolie Weiss." And she was gone.

Uncle Bela got the price we had hoped for. It was, after all, the reason for Yolie's long trip. They sewed the cash into the lining of her coat and enjoyed one last half French, half Hungarian meal together. Another uncle, Imre Krausz, came to see her before she left, and together they saw her off at the station. It was a gloriously beautiful day, and armed with a basket filled with dried fruit, cheese, baguettes, and a bottle of wine for the family, she boarded the train for home.

Being an experienced traveler now, she was well prepared for her return trip. She knew how to behave, and felt confident. She was well rested, well fed, and determined to see her husband and young son again. Having already learned that being nervous hindered instead of helping, Yolie relaxed herself by thinking of Franci Luden. Over and over again she thought of how kind she had been. It made her smile, and she wondered how many more Germans felt as she did. With such thoughts to comfort her, the trip went smoothly. A few times they looked at her coat, but she never felt any real cause for concern. Nobody bothered her, and before she knew it, she was back home in Budapest, presenting her mother with the bottle of wine her brother sent her.

Yolie's return was cause for celebration. We were all glad for her safe return, and hugged her and kissed her again and again. Yolie just wanted to hold her baby son John, and sat with him in her lap long after he'd fallen asleep. When she recounted her adventure we were all speechless. My parents swore that, if they had known the true political situation, they'd never have sent her. For one of the few times in my life that I can recall my parents prayed out loud to God, giving thanks for their daughter's safe return. But it was also a wake-up call.

Yolie had learned a lot from Uncle Bela and Franci Luden about conditions for Jews in the Third Reich. Clearly, Hungarian Jews were blind to the coming storm. While nobody wanted to consider the possibility of war, it was obvious that they needed to come up with a plan to survive.

For centuries the Jews of Europe had become accustomed to being uprooted. Enlightened rulers would, upon occasion, invite Jews to their lands, only to have their heirs reverse that decision and force them to migrate somewhere else again. Or some backwoods bigot, on his tenth vodka of the night, would begin chanting 'Christ Killer' and the Rabbi would have to grab the Torah and flee. But in Western Europe the last hundred years had seen a renaissance of tolerance towards our tiny nation, and Jews finally came to experience a measure of security unknown to them for too long. Eastern Europe Slavs, on the other hand, still clung to their established ethos of hatred. Even if fickle potentates periodically relaxed their prejudice there was scant protection afforded us from pogroms or disenfranchisement. But Hungary had long been a haven. You could be a judge or a boxing champ. It never seemed to be an issue. There were the occasional anti-Semitic comments from some sectors now and again, but it was never government sanctioned. But all that was about to change. And it wasn't going to do anybody any good to pretend otherwise.

Cultural anthropologists have been so bold and objectively cold blooded to apply, by way of explaining Jewish success in cosmopolitan societies, Darwin's theory of natural selection. They analytically suggest that only the smartest Jews survived two thousand years of constant harassment and persecution, and each successive generation was thus better prepared to access new situations, confront hostile conditions, and cut to the heart of the matter, faster than their complacent gentile neighbors who had never been in a situation requiring clever tenacity to insure survival. Most Europeans had fought droughts, harsh winters, and economic hardship, but such circumstances are gradual in their onslaught, allowing time for preparation. Jews, on the other hand, had to learn to flee with less warning than a flash flood affords. It could be peaceful one moment, and the next a screaming mob with torches is at your door. You grab your family, and anything of value that you can carry, and beat it out the back. You must be quick, in both decision and movement. Then, you must find refuge and establish yourself in new surroundings. And the whole horrible process could repeat itself at any moment. And if it doesn't happen for a decade it's still anticipated. Now however, the dispossession of the Jews wasn't going to occur in just one village, but over an entire continent. And all the warning in the world wasn't going to help at all.

The first members of our family to leave were Yolie and Nick. They were already slated to attend the New York World's fair that year, so it wasn't long before they were packing for the long train trip north to Hamburg. There they would take boat passage to New York. And once there they would send for John. This trip would not be as hazardous as Yolie's, because they had official papers from the Hungarian government vouching for them as representatives of their wine industry.

They chose a route that would take them through as little of Germany as possible. They would go through their traditional enemy Czechoslovakia, then continue heading north through Poland. Once in northern Poland they would turn west to Hamburg.

Their papers made for a relatively relaxed trip. The Czech officials treated them with the usual disdain reserved for their traditional rivals, regardless of religion. And the Nazi officials looked down their noses at them without exception. But their papers held, and they made it without incident. The Hungarian wine industry had even given them travel expenses, but they were frugal, opting to save as much of their money as possible for unforeseen expenses in America. They timed their arrival in the northern German port city to catch their boat. Though they had excellent papers they knew the atmosphere, and weren't eager to test it by parading around as tourists. They boarded ship and sailed to New York and safety. Shortly afterwards Uncle Bela bought a visa and escaped to Cuba, while Uncle Imre fled to Chile.

Early the following year American immigration quotas selectively relaxed enough to let in celebrity Jews, like Hungarian classical musicians George Szell and Georg Solti. And some Jews made it to Argentina and Palestine. But by year's end Germany invaded Poland, and the door to the west, and freedom, slammed shut. And whoever was left now faced a nightmare not even the most evolved of Abraham's tribe could comprehend.

CHAPTER FIVE

BUDA & PEST

𝕱or over twenty years prior to the official outbreak of hostilities in Europe, Hungary had been ruled by an exadmiral named Miklos Horthy. At first glance it seems odd that a landlocked country such as Hungary needed admirals, but for a period during and prior to the First World War we were part of the Austro-Hungarian Empire, and had access to the Adriatic, lending Horthy the opportunity for naval combat and two victories that forever brightened his résumé. After a brief takeover by communism the great patriot Horthy stepped into the void and assumed the reins of power by convincing everyone that he would return Hungary to a monarchy and its former glory. So, the landlocked admiral took the reins of leadership and within a year lost over two thirds of Hungary to its neighbors. Still, for lack of anyone to defy him, he managed to retain his power. Hungary was now supposedly a monarchy, though it had no king, and never would again. But bigger things were afoot, and two decades later Admiral Horthy, now calling himself regent, was recruited by a ranting German Chancellor, dangling the carrot of Czechoslovakian land in front of him. The Nazi despot promised to restore to Hungary a chunk of it, along with Transylvania in Romania, and the landlocked admiral fell for it. And in spite of the fact that Horthy had been a dedicated failure the Hungarians tolerated him as their leader for two and half decades. He was a colorful figure, often seen riding around Budapest on his beautiful white stallion, and it cannot be said that he did not have the best interest of Hungarians at heart. But eventually an impatient and mistrustful Adolph Hitler would have him imprisoned, and take over himself. When he did it was fatal for the Jews of Hungary.

Before Nazi atrocities came Nazi bureaucracy. The officious Aryans always made the enactment of laws their first step. After all, they didn't wish to appear uncivilized. Ultimately, from their bureaucratic point of view, they never did anything that was against the law. They simply made it illegal to be a homosexual, a Gypsy, a Jew, a communist, a mentally retarded person, or anyone else they found objectionable. Despite the fact that their hostilities sprang from *der Fuhrer's* seemingly uncontrolled hysteria, they applied a veneer of method to their madness. Every subsequent aspect of their aggression was conducted with precise calculation, and under strict bureaucratic approval. It's a fact! If some prospective victim found a loophole through which to escape liquidation the Nazis would allow it, albeit begrudgingly. For example, the citizens of neutral countries, such as Sweden and Spain, were exempt from the usual persecutions. Theoretically, a bearded Rabbi, bearing a Spanish passport, could have safely approached Hitler, addressed him in Hebrew, and lived to talk about it, such were the established guidelines. They adored rules and regulations so much they even followed those they made up. Their dehumanizing devotion to rules, no matter how abstract, was their ultimate defining characteristic. They observed sentient beings as mere objects, only differentiating humanity from stones with a small grammatical prefix, making them animate objects, as opposed to inanimate. This analytical perspective allowed them to tattoo numbers onto their victims, eliminating the need to consider them as anything more than ciphers. Once categorized, their victims' deaths were no more than entries in a ledger, numbers crossed off a list. And the adherence to proper bookkeeping procedures filled them with pride for a properly administered procedure. They flattered themselves with the glorious title of human, while decrying the supposed subhumanity of those they oppressed. Yet they were so devoid of the unique qualities that actually define humanity that they could coldly calculate the cost of the minerals found in an individual and declare it to be its worth. They could behave like rapacious jungle beasts, just so long as they kept count.

Along with exporting politics to their comrades in arms, such as Hungary, the Nazis also imposed their laws. Thus, they expected the descendents of Attila to enthusiastically implement the anti-Jewish regulations. They did so, but it was a rather quiet affair. These laws were passed in 1940, with few people even aware of it at the time. The first laws stated that Jews could no longer visit public places, such as parks and theaters, but they were not actually enforced in Hungary. We still lived in Gyongyos and led our lives as always. We even went to this large beautiful public swimming pool just down the road from our house. So, things looked normal. But my folks knew something was coming. Long before then we'd learned of the fate of German Jews, how they'd lost their jobs, and even had their pets exterminated. So, the most logical thing my folks could think of was to blend into the general populace, and stay unnoticed. My grandparents had been in Budapest for almost ten years, and it seemed like a safer place to be. We needed to be where nobody knew us, and everyone knew everyone else in or out of the general populace of Gyongyos.

Back in the days before the hypnotic distraction of electronic media people actually knew their neighbors. And though we might wax nostalgic about those quaint times, it was also a fact that such familiarity bred contempt. With little to complicate our own lives the lives of neighbors became the sum and substance of daily life. Everyone knew what you did for a living, when you were sick, and what your religion was. And this was especially true in rural Europe which was studded with thousands of villages. They say that God made the countryside, man made the cities, but the Devil made the small towns. Everyone had their noses in everyone else's business, and Gyongyos was no exception. We all got along fine, but if it was going to come down to getting into trouble for not pointing out the Jews you can be sure that the Christian population of this hamlet was not about to rock the boat. The people who loaned us their shovel today with a smile would dutifully identify us tomorrow as enemies of the state. So, it was decided that it was far easier to hide in plain sight, becoming yet another ant in the massive anthill of a big city. The four oldest children were already in Budapest studying and working, and nobody seemed to know or care if they were Jewish. With their experience, as well as the decade of invisibility for Grandma and Grandpa, it was decided that we too would live in Budapest.

Having a plan, and getting beyond your inertia to implement it, are two different things. So, for a while we were blithely complacent. Even when the new Jewish law was put into affect we were willing to accommodate it with an arrangement. The law said Jews could not own property or businesses. We rented, so the first law did not apply to us. But mother owned her household goods shop, and we needed it to survive. So, mother put the name of the business in her Christian employee's name. For the first few weeks everything went smoothly. The woman paraded as the owner, and passed along to mother her due earnings. Shortly though, the woman's true nature surfaced, and she threw mother out. That's when we knew we must act decisively to survive.

Later, another Jewish law would make it mandatory to move to one of the three big cities of Hungary. Jews would not be allowed to live in the countryside. Those who stayed were easily identified and shipped directly to the camps. Centralizing us like this was always the first step to putting us in a ghetto, which led to efficient organized deportation to the camps. It hadn't yet gotten to that point, so we decided to act before it did.

Father went to a Christian friend and borrowed a wagon and two draft horses. With no farewell to neighbors we loaded everything and everybody into the conveyance and took off for the big city of Budapest. I was six.

As mentally and emotionally stressful as Yolie's trip to Paris was ours was physically worse. The wagon lurched and bumped along at about four uncomfortable miles per hour, and we had to stop frequently to give us all a rest from the constant rocking. The trip was fifty miles long and it took three days. We lived, ate and slept in the wagon. It was our temporary home, and after reflecting on it, of all the cramped living conditions we would come to endure, it was the worst.

After three days of hell we made it to Budapest. It's regarded as one of the great cities of Europe, but we were too fatigued from our trek to feel the exaltation of its urbane sophistication. We arrived at Uncle Marton's apartment, and the owner of the wagon and horses was waiting for us. He'd made it there in just an hour on the train. As awful as the trip was we were grateful to him for the use of his wagon and animals. We thanked him and he left for Gyongyos at once. We never saw him or anybody else from that place again. All of my brothers and sisters were born there and it would never be anything again but a memory. We knew our neighbors would turn on us, so we had to abandon its gentle rural rhythms for the tumult of big city life, or die.

Before coming to Budapest I'd never seen a building up close that was taller than two stories.

Here there weren't any that short. I even thought the stores were three stories high or more. It took me a few days to figure out that the shops and restaurants were just on the street level, with residential apartments and an occasional office taking up the rest of the floors. The first time I ventured out I only explored one or two streets and came back quickly, because I was afraid I'd get in trouble. On my third foray I thought I had retraced my steps accurately, but I still managed to get lost coming back. I was actually standing in front of Uncle Marton's building, but it looked like all the rest to me, and I couldn't tell his from the others. My father came out and found me with a worried look.

"Why are you dawdling out here so long," he demanded.

I was too embarrassed to confess my confusion, but I think he realized it.

"Just get inside. It's the third floor in case you forgot that too!"

I scampered up the steps, red faced. A few more days though, and I felt right at home. Dad's brother, Uncle Marton, was glad to help us, but it meant another five people in his small space. So, after just two weeks of familial hospitality tested to the breaking point we found our own place. Once installed Sandor, Josef, and Rose joined us. We were now eight: mother, father, all the sons and daughters but Yolie, and John.

By now John was four years old, and wanted to know where his parents were. Yolie and Nick had gone to New York with every intention of sending for him, but war broke out, and it was now impossible. John felt abandoned and never truly got over it. He became a bit of a problem child, rebellious and argumentative. It would even eventually threaten his safety. We just attributed it to his feelings of abandonment, and were patient with him. His parents regularly sent gift packages from New York, but he was still inconsolable. For all of us though, those packages from America were like gifts from paradise. Cans of pineapple and other unknown delicacies fueled our desire to likewise flee westward. But that was not meant to be. No more train rides or boat trips for the Weisz family. In order to survive we'd have to keep a low profile and avoid exposing ourselves to the system. But at least the eldest Weisz child was safe. And that made mother happy. And I finally got to know my brothers and sisters. But I barely got to know Josef before he disappeared.

Josef was the second child, the first son. He had studied watch making, and did so well that he was the official clock setter for city hall. That fact probably lulled my parents into another phase of false security. If they were still letting a Jew tell them what time it was, maybe things won't be so bad after all. Also, being surrounded by family contributes to that illusory sense of safety. We were in the big city, but we lived in a microcosm that offered little confrontation or reminder of any alternate reality. Sandor had joined Josef in the jewelry store, Rose was already working as a seamstress, Anci was studying to do the same, and I finally started formal schooling. And though father might have been from the sticks he fell into the pulse of big city life as if he had been born to it. With a thousand times as many taverns, and innumerable potential pals, Papa Weisz was in his own element at last. War or no war, he continued to drink, play cards, and cultivate friendships. This made mother even more furious, and their quarreling took on new proportions. And the familiar ring of domestic hostility only reinforced the sensation that everything was status quo.

A normal life was so desired that we relished each rite of passage, like a marriage or a new baby. We should have asked ourselves each time if this was the last such event for us, but we kept up the pretense that routine life could still go on. So, when Josef found a bride we celebrated in our humble way. He married Elizabeth, and we joyously welcomed her into the family. And when Elizabeth gave birth to Vera we likewise rejoiced. But behind each smile mother added into the equation another soul to protect.

Mother enrolled me in a Jewish elementary school. At that time she still could have placed me in a regular Hungarian public school, but she chose the Yeshiva. She was not what you'd call an observant Jew, but she made sure we always celebrated all the holidays. She also had us go to Synagogue on Saturdays, though she herself always worked that day, her busiest. It was a ten minute walk to school, and I enjoyed exploring Budapest on the way. My routine brought me home for lunch, and I enjoyed making new friends, both at school and in the neighborhood. The entire reason we were in this city was due to our religion, but I was more interested in secular activities, especially soccer. I played every afternoon after school, and my ability at the sport made me popular with all the other kids, Jew and gentile alike. Hitler was on the offensive in France, Russia, England, Holland, Belgium, and Denmark, but all I cared about was soccer.

Whatever Dad lacked in sobriety and earnestness was more than made up for by my brothers. If anything, Sandor was almost too serious. He was a good provider, but a real disciplinarian. Whenever he came home and found John and I clowning around, he went berserk. He wanted order but found precious little of it at home. Maybe it was the stress of the war, coupled with the responsibility of having to earn for the family, but he was always strict around the apartment. He was undeniably mature beyond his years, and he lived for the family. For all that, he was mother's favorite

Eldest son Josef was also a good earner. But early in the war he would have to cede those responsibilities to younger brother Sandor, because he was drafted into the Hungarian army. Hungarian soldiers were axis soldiers, and they were soon to fight face to face with Hitler's newest foe, the Russians.

CHAPTER SIX

AS ADVERTISED, WAR!

When I was still a tyke back in Gyongyos, lusting for a bike, Hitler's more considerable avarice prompted him to make a pact with Stalin that assured peace between the paranoid powers. A mere year later, however, the number one Nazi reneged and sent a five hundred mile wide blitzkrieg across Mother Russia's western frontier. I confess that these events in no way mitigated my obsessive desire to acquire a bicycle.

Germany's closest ally in the neighborhood was Hungary, and she was called on to do her duty and join the fight against the heathen Godless Bolsheviks. No stranger to war, Hungary had always maintained a draft, with Jews participating on an equal footing. But now the descendents of the Magyars were officially Aryans, and they wanted the expendable portions of their population solely as front line cannon fodder. The front line Russian soldiers were themselves chosen from among the ranks of their nation's own surplus humanity, country bumpkins, short on sophistication, and long on grit. Naturally, Soviet generals rewarded these brutes' naïve patriotism by sending them in as first wave bullet takers. War production was so behind in the workers' paradise that there was only one rifle for every two soldiers. The Red high command reasoned that one of those troops would get killed soon enough, and voluntarily bequeath his weapon and bullets to his comrade. The exadmiral who ran our own army had the same low regard for his starting team, and considered them good for being little more than human targets on which to expend their enemy's precious fund of munitions. It was suicide to be in the front lines, so Jews were considered ideal for the position.

When you're drafted you have no choice. So when Josef got his letter to report mother made him a wonderful farewell dinner. Two days later he was marching in the army. With a minimum of training he was given a loaded rifle and sent to the front lines to give all for admiral and country. Previously, Hungary had always identified itself with a maternal designation, just as Russia always had, but being officially affiliated with the Germans, we now had to defend someplace called the Fatherland. Of course, any parental affection he might have ever felt for the land in which he and his ancestors had all been born, collapsed under the weight of the knowledge of his true current status. Josef was determined to surrender to the first Russian unit he came across.

My big brother's first day of fighting was far more terrible than they had prepared him for. Too much of his training had consisted of propaganda lectures and films about how subhuman his enemies were. They'd be fighting Slavs, and the less than human Slavs were only fit to serve the Aryan Third Reich as slaves. And if they couldn't be slaves they were useless and deserved to be annihilated on the spot. Much to his chagrin, Josef soon discovered that subhumans were pretty good shots. His fellow soldiers were dropping all around him at a frighteningly efficient rate. And the friends he had made in the barracks were lying on the ground all around him, screaming and bleeding. The Hungarian troop's immediate superiors, sergeants and an occasional officer, had the utmost confidence in their new conscripts, and to show their staunch support they positioned themselves behind their brave boys, threatening to shoot anyone who didn't exhibit the required level of valor. Any reticence in manifesting one's courage was construed as cowardice and addressed with far less hesitation. So, Josef prayed and advanced. Keeping his head down and pulling his trigger enough to make him sound dangerous, but not so often as to expend the limited amount of ammunition he was issued, he crept forward. Every inch he crawled toward the Russian lines was another inch further from the Axis that would sacrifice him and imprison his family. The mud was cold and claylike, and his uniform too thin for the conditions. He slogged on, Elizabeth and Vera in his thoughts.

Before long he was out of range of his superiors who would shoot him in the back. And they weren't the sharpshooters they'd have to be to pick off a deserter across enemy lines. If the Russians didn't shoot him first he might actually make it! So, he crawled and prayed until he found a foxhole. It must have been the nest of some forward scouts who reconnoitered the battle field and then reported back. Sliding down its muddy slopes he felt safe for the moment. The buzzing bullets were now high over his head, and his back was as safe from the retribution of the Hungarians as his front was from the volleys of the Russians. The hole was too far for anyone to lob a grenade, so he decided he'd just wait until nightfall, then surrender. He lied on his back and gripped his rifle to his chest, hoping he'd soon be using it against his odious sergeant, and strike his own personal blow for freedom. He envisioned himself as part of the liberating army that would forever free Hungary from the grip of Nazi tyranny. He'd make it to the Russian front, wave a white flag, surrender and introduce himself. The Russians would hang on his every word, eager to learn any tidbit of intelligence about the enemy position, and the dreadful situation in Hungary. They'd give him a new uniform, a shot of vodka, a slap on the back, and call him *tovarich*. Night would fall soon, and Josef would feel safe enough to cover the hundred or so yards that now separated him from his soon to be comrades in arms.

Unfortunately for my brother, the front line Russian soldiers considered anybody coming their way in an Axis uniform to be the enemy. These troops were bullet takers, just like Josef. But unlike Josef, they were not in the least bit inquisitive or intellectual. Nobody spoke Hungarian, and Josef didn't speak Russian. His smiling and yammering merely annoyed them. They took away his rifle and forced him to sit down in the cold mud. Josef tried to explain to them that he was a Jew and forced to fight, but they wouldn't listen. It's true that there had been situations when a willing Hungarian or Czech deserter was greeted into the Soviet ranks by a more educated officer, eager to have a clever motivated Jew join them. But Josef's situation was more routine. He was taken prisoner and sent to the Siberian salt mines. In that frozen tundra he would be a slave, with about as much chance for survival as an inmate in a concentration camp. We, of course, knew nothing of any of this. Simply and sadly, Josef was gone.

When we were alerted that Josef Weisz was reported missing in action Mother and Elizabeth became despondent. But Josef had shared his plans with us, and we reasoned with them that there was every chance that he'd survived and made it over to the Russian side. We became convinced that he'd one day return with his Soviet allies and liberate us. It was consolation, but mother was depressed just because her son was gone.

With the eldest out of the picture, and father dedicated to cards and drink, it fell to Sandor to be man of the family. But it was a task to which he was equal. Of course, father did occasionally work a few hours in the store. He just didn't make it a habit.

Now that the war was on full force we received no more word from Yolie. America was not technically in the war, but the Axis powers knew she was far from neutral, and was sending ship loads of supplies to both England and Russia. So, now there were no more cans of pineapple postmarked New York. But such products were sought, so Sandor added black market to his résumé. Between that and the jewelry store we were actually making a decent income. Of course, we had to. There were the seven of us, as well as grandma and grandpa, plus various cousins. So we struggled on. As in Gyongyos the sole luxury was again a bicycle. This time it was mine. So, 1941 was a mixed blessing for me. I missed a brother, but I got a bike.

For all I knew at that time, maybe my bike was a black market item. There were so many common household things that were not readily available. If you had a contact for coffee or sugar, you could always find a customer willing to pay the higher than normal price you asked. Everyone did it. Kids, the elderly, Christian and Jew alike. It was as commonplace as buying something in a store. Except the stores didn't have what you wanted, and the black market did. However, it was not the opulently lucrative field one imagines. In movies about black marketers they're like war time Mafiosos, conducting clandestine meetings, and reaping huge profits. And while the post war era did eventually evolve into that, for now the reality was far less romantic. Basically, you could make a few extra cents as a middleman if you happen to know someone with tobacco. There was a higher profit to be sure, but in the end, it was only slightly more profitable than legal buying and selling. But as slight as it was, it was needed and welcome. And if a pound of coffee defined us as criminals it was a moot point. We already knew we would have to defy the authorities to survive. With that in mind we always kept our eyes open for any chance to make a little extra money.

With Yolie in America, and Josef vanished into the abyss of the Eastern Front, it fell to Rose, Anci and Sandor to maintain the family. Sandor pressed on with the jewelry store while Rose and Anci continued to work as seamstresses. But even in war, some things in life cannot be denied, and romance found its way into the Weisz household. Rose and Anci had suitors.

Rose was like having a celebrity in the family. She was a phenomenon! She had the beauty, poise, and charisma of a movie star. When she walked into a room she caught everyone's eye, and it was a rare week when a cadre of eligible bachelors wasn't kicking down the door. Who could blame them? She was warm, charming, and intelligent. And she looked like Ingrid Bergman. That's not the exaggeration of a sentimental family member. You only have to see a photograph of her to agree. But whether or not you noticed the striking similarity, she was possessed of the same radiant natural glow. Her eyes, hair and skin all exuded health and vigor. And when she aimed that beautiful broad smile at someone they were captivated. Not that she thought of herself as an enchantress, nor did she employ her feminine charm to any selfish end. She was completely without guile. And everybody, from little children and small animals, to adults, were attracted to her. She brightened all our lives. In short, she was just the sort of person the Nazis liked to kill.

Rose was engaged several times, but always broke it off. I can't remember their names, or why she ended things, but by the time she got engaged to Nick Spatz we didn't take it seriously. At least not until she married him. Anci was also growing into womanhood, and had no lack of male attention. At fourteen she was practically a woman. Of course, back then Europe considered the midteens to be as good a time as any to get married.

As for us kids, John and I continued to play soccer in the street. Ordinary life was still somehow going through its cycles, despite the fascism creeping into our society. The year ended with America getting into the war, and that gave us hope. To us America was a fantasyland, populated by cowboys and Indians and movie stars. If Yolie and Nick hadn't gone there we probably would have never even considered it real. But one thing that did appear real about it was its invincibility. We really had no knowledge of its industrial or military capabilities, but it somehow seemed mighty. Its movies dominated the planet and they always broadcasted images of victory. The buckeroo in the white hat always got the bad guy. The love struck lothario always won the girl. There was nothing buy happy endings, so it was unimaginable that any endeavor that involved the mythical Americans might end in defeat. If the handsome and healthy citizens of New York or California got into the war then it must be to win it.

CHAPTER SEVEN

SURVIVAL PLANS

The Nazi grip on Europe in 1942 was wide spread and tight. But Hungary was not overrun, due to her alliance with them. Of course, Hitler's intentions for the descendents of the Magyars were no less onerous than his plans for the rest of the non-Aryans. But our kingless monarchy drifted along, thinking itself safe from that frustrated artist. After all, they were allies. What had they to fear? Their comrades were Teutonic knights, nearly invincible. Content on having her borders expanded, Hungarian hopes were high for a little piece of the coming world order. The only fly in the ointment was the Russian army. But surely that ragged collection of peasants was no match for the German juggernaut. Hadn't the communists bid for control of Hungary died after just a few months back in 1919? They had no staying power. And having had their own Magyar forebears driven back by the Germans, the pragmatic leaders of Hungary decided that, being unable to beat the Nordic warriors, they would join them.

Equally eager to jump on the racist bandwagon they started up their own fascist party, called *Nyilasok*. They even came up with their own threatening symbol, a cross with arrows at the ends of each stem. A Nazi wannabe named Szalesi ran it, and he was determined to impress the landlocked admiral, ruler of the kingless kingdom. Horthy had the naiveté of a child, while not quite the brains.

Little children will learn quickly enough in the playground to shy away from a traitorous playmate. If little Bobby picks little Billy to be on his team, then pushes him down, the rest of the gang will have enough sense to beware. Little Adolph spit in his hand and shook hard with little Joe. They were on the same team, and the European school-yard was divvied up fair and square. A year later, when that German scamp caught Joey off guard with Operation Barbarosa, it still didn't occur to little Mickey Horthy that the same fate might await him and his pals. America's allies had beaten Hungary twenty years earlier in the Great Game, and now, in Great Game number two, they were lined up against each other again. If that wasn't an omen for Hungary she must have been as drunk on the early successes of the Nazis as the Nazis were themselves. She wasn't occupied yet, as were France, Holland, Poland, and others. She could still switch sides, and join Joey and his mates. She could be smart for once, be a winner. Any child with a lick of sense could look at a world map, compare the vastness of Russia and America with Germany, and draw the inevitable conclusion. But, like children who experience early success with their aggression, they were turning into bullies. And like all such belligerents they live in the ephemeral here and now, blind to tomorrow's uncertainty. Hungary's prospects appeared to be on an upward trend, but it was just hoisting itself higher and higher upon its own petard. And, in fulfilling that in-famous Shakespearean metaphor, it would manage to abet the murder of half a million Hungarian Jews.

Four tense years had passed since Yolie and Nick had found refuge in America. Sandor was making money at the jewelry store, while Rose and Anci still sewed. The Third Reich was expanding its empire, and hardly paying any attention to the café society of Hungary. While my parents battled on so did the Russians with the Hungarian army, whose leaders daily polished their blinders. But we had already lost Josef, and had no allusions. We knew that we had to do something to protect ourselves, but didn't know exactly what. We considered the choices.

There were two basic alternatives. One was to stay and hide, and the other was to flee. Fleeing meant going to a neutral country by either boat or ground transport. Hungary is a landlocked country, so there was no thought of escape by sea. If we did want to consider that then the closest body of water is the Black Sea to the east. From the Black Sea port of Odessa hundreds of thousands of Jews had immigrated to America at the turn of the century. But that was a Russian port and they were now the enemy. Traveling on a Hungarian passport would surely have meant enslavement in the Siberian salt mines. Besides, we had to go through Romania first, and they were antagonistic toward Jews and Hungarians alike. So, being Hungarian Jews we would have met with rebuff at the border anyway. To the north was Czechoslovakia and Yugoslavia lay to the south, both already in Nazi hands. Austria was to the west, a Third Reich stronghold. If we had passports we would've had to have gone through Austria to get to neutral, landlocked Switzerland. Of course, the not so neutral Swiss could dispossess them, if they let them in at all. The only other neutral European countries lie in Scandinavia, and on the Iberian Peninsula on the Atlantic, both on the far side of the impenetrable bastion of Nazi held territory. Spain was a desirable destination, because they did not cooperate with Axis anti-Semitic policies. A Jew with a Spanish passport was safe. It was hands-off, but it was impossibly far off. Also sympathetic to Jews was Bulgaria. But it was technically an Axis power, and beyond our reach, being respectively south and east of Romania and Yugoslavia. We later learned that, even if we could have gotten to a European port to escape, there was nowhere to go. Most countries had already met their Jewish immigration quotas, and despite international awareness of the Nazi's treatment of Jews, short of knowledge of the death camps, they did not relax their quotas. Simply put, we were surrounded and trapped. The only other alternative was to hide.

Hiding required the cooperation of a Gentile who was either sympathetic to the plight of the Jews, and willing to defy the Fascists, both German and Nyilasok, or who simply needed money. Whether you had sympathy for the persecuted victims of fascism, or were motivated to help for purely mercenary concerns, the fascists discouraged such displays of empathy through brutal repression. If you were caught helping you would be shot, if you were lucky. If you were unlucky you would be tortured first. Then your body would be hung from a lamppost or tree, decorated with a sign proclaiming 'Jew Lover.' You might also be beheaded. So, it's no surprise to learn that the percentage of the population willing to help was small and diminishing daily.

So, leaving Hungary was impossible, and hiding offered slim opportunities at best. Basically the plight of the Jews of Hungary, like most of Europe, was hopeless. The only other glimmer of hope was a quick win by the Russians on the eastern front. The British were never going to make it this far east, and the Americans were still a dream. So, for now, we saved money, a commodity that we reasoned might help when it came to hiding.

We didn't just save any kind of money. We saved gold. If we knew nothing else we knew that people always wanted and accepted gold. Whether you were Jewish or Christian, or even a Nazi, gold was universally desired. So, since our move to Budapest we had been converting whatever wealth we could get our hands on into small gold coins called Napoleons. They were about the size of a dime, and easy to hide. If anticipating an inspection a woman could hide them in that hiding place exclusive to her gender, and men could hide them in that place universal to both sexes. Mother was the keeper of the exchequer, and in anticipation of the future need, she hid Napoleons all over Budapest. In our apartment, in the basement coal bin, and in the apartments of relatives. It gave us the only hope we had. It wasn't for travel, because we already knew we couldn't pay our way through a thousand miles of war torn Europe. The gold would have to go toward bribes. Bribes to escape arrest. Bribes to buy false identity papers. Bribes to pay for a hiding place. Our family was a large one, three generations worth. The Weisz clan had fled the countryside for the anonymity of Budapest, and we now numbered around forty. We couldn't imagine how many Napoleons it would take to hide us all. We just had to collect as many Napoleons as we could and stash them. Time was growing short, and the noose was getting tighter every day.

CHAPTER EIGHT

HUNGARIANS CAN BE GOOD LITTLE NAZIS TOO

By the end of 1943 we had to wear a yellow Star of David on our clothes. It had actually been a law for two years, but now the Nazis insisted the Nyilasok get tough and crackdown. Regretfully, they were ready, willing and able to comply. The Hungarians, indifferent for so long as to whether or not you were a Jew, now embarked on an industrious campaign to make up for lost time. They were keen to show their Nazi masters what reliable partners they could be when it came to hatred. So eager were the Magyars' pathetic descendents that they would come to surpass even the Germans. In their attempt to kill every Jew in Hungary they would commit more murder in a shorter time period than any other country involved in the Final Solution. Hungarian leaders became more obsessed with an internal aggression against a small and defenseless sector of their own population than with the external war threatening their existence. If they could not prove their metal on the field of combat then they would at least demonstrate how fierce they could be as bullies. In 1943 things started to get bad. 1944 fell on the Danube valley like a shroud.

Everyday we heard new stories of Nyilasok terror. They beat up Jews. Neighbors turned in their neighbors. People disappeared. Life was cheap and getting cheaper. It was at this time that mother sat me and John down and explained how our lives were going to be from now on. I remember it as if it was five minutes ago.

She looked at us a long time without breaking away. She sighed and began.

"Boys, you know who the Nazis and Nyilasok are. Yes, they're mean. Yes, they hate us because we're Jews. No, it doesn't matter why. They just do. It doesn't matter if you're nice or pretty or play soccer good. They hate us all, and they're going to arrest us and send us somewhere, or do something terrible to us right in the street. That's right. If they can they'll kill us. Yes, even women and old people and children. The Russians might beat them, and even America is fighting them, and I think they'll lose. But maybe not for a while. So we got to take care of ourselves for now. Listen to me. Stay close to home. Don't go out without the star on your clothes. Don't give them any excuse. Don't look them in the eye, because when you look at someone you make them look back at you. So don't. Just don't! If they don't notice you it's better. If you got any Christian friends don't go to their houses any more. Only go to two places, school and here. Go straight to school and come straight back, always on the same street. Don't stay and talk with the other boys after school. Just come straight back. If you're late we'll go crazy."

All the while John and I were looking straight at mother and sometimes at each other.

"Boys, we might have to move soon. They'll make us. They're going to make special buildings just for Jews. It could be tomorrow. But listen. Listen carefully. We got gold. Maybe we could buy our freedom from some soldier if we have to. I'm hiding little bits of it all over. I'm going to show both of you. If something happens to me you got to know where it is. We can't buy a ticket on a train or go nowhere. We can't travel. It's too dangerous. We got to stay here in Budapest and become invisible. Do you understand? And if we tell you to do something you got to do it. It's not like before. Don't ask questions. Just do it! Understand?"

We shook our heads and looked at each for a long time. Then mama opened her arms and we both fell into a good long hug, her kissing the tops of our heads. Finally, she lifted our spirits. "Be smart, and we'll make it."

After mother's speech John and I were officially adults. Clever ones at that. If we were anything less we wouldn't last a week. We became feral, and cunning, and developed a sixth sense for dangerous situations. Any encounter with authority could be our last. We had to be one step ahead of anything that came our way. We weren't big and strong. We weren't the offspring of the rich and influential. We weren't blessed with blue eyes and blond hair. We were the poor and poorly fed prey of giant sadistic beasts that hovered outside our door. They owned the street and the air we breathed. Like minnows in a shark tank we had to become survival experts. Only by cunning and luck would we make it through this war.

With gangs of armed murderers roaming the streets, hot for your Jewish blood, there is no time to consider their motives. You just hide. But I can certainly tell you that when you're being hunted you tend to take it personally. All I could wonder was why did they want to kill us? We had never done anything to them, or anyone else. My brothers and sisters were nice. So was my mom. My father was a little lazy, but did he deserve to die for that? And what was all this crap on the radio, that the Jews had all the money? I grew up poor and so were all my friends. It was all a bunch of lies. We didn't kidnap Christian children. We weren't in league with the Devil. I didn't even know what they meant with that talk. And we sure as hell didn't start any war. That kraut Hitler did. Why were they trying to kill us? It didn't make any sense! But after a while you even stop thinking about things like that. Contemplating their motives was a luxury we didn't have. There was no time to ponder any of it. It was now a full time job just to stay alive. And before long the stories of brutality became reality before my eyes. On the way home from school one day I saw a gang of fiendishly laughing Nyilosak punks beat up an old man. He had a long beard and the yellow star, and they kicked him and hit him until he managed to flee.

Soon we didn't bother with school any more. It was just too dangerous to go out. Anyway, a week after we renounced our formal education the authorities boarded the school up and took all the people there away to the ghetto. At any second our own door might come down and we'd be dragged off to the ghetto ourselves. Or worse, they might skip the ghetto, and just load us on a truck bound for the train depot and a concentration camp. Or we could be just walking down the street, and some Nyilasok gangsters would shoot us and throw our bodies into the river. Not long after quitting school I had an occasion to go out, and I witnessed two hoodlums beat a boy of about twelve to death. I'm sure he was dead. They beat him, laughing all the while. But once the boy stopped screaming I was certain he was dead. There was blood everywhere, and I realized that at any moment my own blood could mingle with that poor boy's. I was only a kid, but I had already seen more than most adults see in their lives. I was ten, going on fifty.

We had serious choices to make. One of those choices was not to wear the yellow stars any more. We figured that our neighbors already knew we were Jewish, so what was the point? If they were going to point us out what did it matter if we broke the yellow star rule or not? We'd be goners anyway. And outside there was no advantage to wearing them either. With a star you were telling the world you were Jewish, and could be killed for sport, or deported to a camp. But without it there were two possibilities. The first was that you'd be arrested or killed for breaking the rule. But the second possibility was that nobody would think you were Jewish and you'd make it through another day. It seemed like a fifty-fifty bet, and I found those odds to be the most favorable. Though I did hedge my bet for a while, wearing a star on an article of clothing a few layers down, just in case it was needed. But the decision to parade without stars only applied to me and my sisters, because our appearance was not perceived to be as overtly Jewish as my parents. So they stayed home, and my sisters brought them food. Sometimes I would go out on that mission too. Life had turned into a series of commando missions. Day and night, with no vacations, we walked a tight rope with no safety net or end in sight. It was hellish.

By mid 1944 Jews were no longer accepted as regular Hungarian soldiers, not even as bullet takers. Instead they formed a work brigade from among those sectors of the population considered unfit to serve alongside the master race. Naturally, it was mostly made up of Jews, and we anticipated at any moment to be recruited into it. Would they be as merciless as the old czarist recruitment, which took eleven year old Jewish boys away from their families for years? Would it include the women and old folk? We heard on the radio that Jews were being sent to work in camps under the slogan *'arbeite macht frei'*, work makes you free. Was that the plan for all Jews? Were we to be slaves? We were all existing in a state of anxiety that was unbearable. For the present all we could do was horde gold and pray for allied victory. It's no joke to state the obvious, that the war now took precedence over domestic quarrels. The older generation of the Weisz family, my grandparents, put their hopes in their children for finding some way out. But it would be their grandchildren who took the first bold step.

CHAPTER NINE

ALL TOGETHER

𝔄 letter came to our apartment. Sandor Weisz was to report immediately to the Work Brigade.

To not report would mean certain imprisonment. And if they sent us a letter that means that they must know where we are. They must know where all the Jews are. That was part of the old established European system of identification papers. Every time you moved you had to report it to the police department, who issued new papers with your new address. For example, back when we first arrived in Budapest we stayed with an uncle for a few weeks. But then we moved to 57 Harsfa Street, and dutifully reported it to the police. Then they gave us new papers stating our new address. Only a European writer, like George Orwell, could have envisioned Big Brother. No American could've ever imagined it. It was forty years ahead of its time, but it was in full swing in 1944 Budapest. So, Sandor reported and he was taken to a camp at the east end of town. They sent him and his fellow inmates out to clean up the rubble created by the bombing raids. By now the Americans had joined the Russians in intense bombing raids. The Americans came from the west, while the Russians continued their raids from the east. Together they ravaged Budapest, and kept Sandor and his comrades busy.

Though Sandor and the other inmates were not soldiers they still lived like them. They wore uniforms and slept in barracks. And like regular troops they were constantly ordered around. But instead of carrying guns they carried shovels. Instead of moving caissons they pushed wheel barrows. But, unlike soldiers, they could never leave their encampment except to go to work, and always under the watchful eyes of their commandants and guards. Any attempt at escape meant death. It was harsh, but compared to a concentration camp it was a vacation. They were allowed visits from family members at the fence and even received food packages. And if you had money to bribe the guards you could even make an occasional phone call. But it was not without peril. They constantly worked in the most unstable and dangerous sites. More than once Sandor witnessed entire walls collapse on his fellow workers. It was dirty and arduous, and the Nyilasok worked them from early until late, allowing them little rest. But the visits and food from home bolstered their spirits, and like their family and friends on the outside, they prayed for the allies to rescue them.

We knew the Russians weren't far off. If only they could make a small advance we might be saved. We didn't believe the Reds would persecute Jews. After all, the communist founder, Lenin, had preached that anti-Semitism was a counter revolutionary notion. Of course, we didn't really think of the Russians in a political sense. It was immaterial to us if they were communist or Bolshevik or any other persuasion of socialist. They were fighting the Nazis, and that's all that mattered. Their ground forces were on the offensive, and we prayed for the atheists to come and save us.

It's unimaginable that any routine occurrence would appear in our bleak midst, but Anci got engaged to a young man named Andrew. He was a shy boy who was too timid to visit on his own, always stopping by accompanied by his friend Robert. It seemed incongruous to have any sort of love life, and the Russian heroes we awaited would have considered it oddly bourgeoisie. But life snuck in anyway, and Anci got engaged.

Anci's main task now was to bring food to Sandor. At first his situation seemed better than Josef's. Once Josef was sent to the eastern front we never heard from him again. At least we knew where Sandor was. And seeing him on our trips to bring him food made it seem almost normal. So, every few days, mother prepared a food package for him and either took it to him herself or sent it to him with Anci. They took the trolley to the end of the line, and walked one block to the camp. There, they could easily hand the package through the barbed wire fence, and briefly converse with him. My mother knew Sandor was alive and being fed. It was a great relief.

Just three months earlier I had been playing soccer and attending gymnazium. Now, I was like some cunning foraging animal, maneuvering through rubble strewn streets. But it was still a big city, and afforded the protection of its vastness. My camouflage consisted of three things: a not too Jewish face, a lack of identifying yellow star, and the confusion of a metropolis. It was one of the foreseen advantages of moving to the city for which I must give my parents credit. The Jews who had remained in the countryside could be easily identified, with or without a star, and they were all rounded up and sent to the ghettos or camps. Their neighbors whom they had known for years, even generations, turned them all in.

The first step of the Hungarian cooperation for the Final Solution was the same as every other European country with a Jewish population, to isolate them. First, a move from the country to the big city was mandatory. After some time certain buildings in the big cities were designated as either Christian or Jewish. Finally, the inhabitants of the Jewish buildings would be herded into one neighborhood called the Jewish ghetto. From there it was easy to load them onto trains and transport them to the concentration camps for slave labor or liquidation.

For now, our family was mostly intact. Anci continued to bring food to Sandor, and mother was kept busy hiding Napoleons. She wanted to have more of the gold coins at the ready, so she hid them behind the boards of our coal bin and those of our neighbors. She figured that as long as they didn't know to look for them they'd be safe. Only a bomb could expose them, and if a bomb hit what else mattered?

The coal bins were also used as air raid shelters. And when the allies bombed you had to find shelter. The only public ones were the subway stations. But neither afforded anyone protection. I actually used to roam the streets during raids, preferring to be able to see where the bombs were coming from, and having the mobility of escaping to different places. If you were in a shelter you had no clue what was happening, and had no chance to escape if the bombs got too close. There was actually a maze of ancient tunnels under Budapest, which might have made great shelters, but we didn't know it at that time.

Now the Nazis were more visible on the streets. We heard radio broadcasts, but had long since stopped believing them. The Nazi ministry of propaganda told Hungarian radio what to say and their newspaper what to print. And according to these two sources the Axis never lost a battle. But some news trickled back from the eastern front, and we took courage from reports that the Nazis were retreating from Russia. Perhaps they'd met their match after all. Maybe the communist totalitarians would defeat the fascist totalitarians. We hoped so. Meanwhile, we horded gold and thought of a plan.

It's hard to even recollect specific days, because they all drifted into each other. It was like one prolonged agony. People were starting to disappear off the streets. But one day became fixed in our minds forever, the day Anci was taken away. It was June, 1944. The bombing had intensified and we were encouraged that the horror might end soon. It was in the middle of what should have been a lovely summer, with clear blue skies, too beautiful for war. Mother and Anci took the usual box of food to Sandor. They boarded the trolley, wearing their yellow stars. About halfway there the air raid sirens went off, and fearing for the lives of her young son and nephew, mother jumped off the trolley and ran back to our neighborhood. Anci went on alone. When she got there she stepped off the trolley and started to walk toward Sandor. He had been waiting, and actually watched as she got off. But she never got to him. As Sandor looked on in horror Nyilasok officials stopped her. As they led her away she craned her head around and looked back at Sandor in desperation, her eyes wide in terror. Helpless, Sandor could only stare back, his hands clenching the barbed wire fence. Yearning replaced the fear in Anci's eyes. Yearning to run to her brother one last time. To be free. But she only managed to mouth a goodbye. Then her face fell in resignation. Sandor watched as she turned her head back around, her shoulders drooping in surrender. Her form became smaller and smaller as she receded into the distance. He watched his little sister until she was just a dot on the horizon. Then he couldn't see her at all. And he never would again. Little Anci had never done anything to anyone. She was just sixteen.

Sandor had some money hidden, and he bribed a guard at the camp to let him make a phone call. He called our apartment and informed us of Anci's fate. Father, who had made acquaintances in all levels of society, ran to a friend who was a policeman. The man wanted to help, and he even went so far as to go to Gestapo headquarters to see what he could do, but he was impotent to change anything. Anci was sent to Auschwitz. If mother had not gotten off that trolley to come back to us during the air raid she would have certainly gotten arrested along with Anci. Women her age were immediately gassed upon arrival at the camps.

It was agonizing for mother. Father got up the courage to go out, but his failure to get her released caused mother to take her frustration out on him. It was the last time I saw them fight during the war. After that father stayed close to home. Besides, bigger events now dominated our lives. Not long after Anci's disappearance Rose's husband Nick was also stopped in the street and arrested. It was a mere two weeks since they had been married. He was put in the Jewish Work Brigade, but his particular group was sent to a combat zone, so nobody could communicate with him as we did with Sandor. He was gone from our lives, and after some time we practically considered him dead. Anci's fiancé Andrew vanished next.

Almost as quickly as mama had told us, they started designating buildings as either Jewish or Christian. Taking stock at that time things looked dismal. Josef had disappeared. Sandor was in a forced labor gang. Our brothers-in-law were gone. Who would be next? Everyday the Nyilasok were getting more brazen. They had issued guns to teenage hoodlums, and gave them the power to stop whomever they wanted. They could arrest you if they wanted, shoot you and toss your body into the Danube. It was in the midst of this mayhem that Rose took the first step.

They hadn't come to our building yet, but Rose didn't want to wait for that. She had saved some money and decided to approach a Christian she knew with the idea of buying her ID papers. The woman was in desperate need of money, and agreed. After the transaction the woman simply went to the police station and reported that she had lost her papers.

The papers were not hard to forge. The actual paper itself was routine bond, not like the stock used for printing currency. There were no watermarks or secret threads imbedded in it. It was just a matter of having the will to do it. Under the circumstances Rose found it. She swapped her photo for her friend's and learned the signature. She was now Maria Willem. And after passing the first inspection she implemented the second part of her plan, to move Maria Willem into a Christian building. She told the family, and they were very nervous for her. But they admitted they hadn't a better idea. Shortly after that Rose heard the bad news about Sandor.

The Jewish Work Brigade had to clean up after bombing raids. There was a lot of rubble and dead bodies. Even though it was still red hot from the incendiary bombs Sandor and the rest had to go in and clean up. First, they had to clear the street. As they were doing so they had to neatly stack whatever rubble there was. Bricks in one stack, wood in another, and chunks of cement or concrete in yet another. The rare pane of glass that was still in tact had its own repository. And whenever they came across a cadaver they had to stack that too. If they were caught relieving a body of any valuables they were shot on the spot. It was dangerous work. There were entire walls that remained standing, only to collapse without warning. Sandor had been clearing up some rubble when a brick fell off the top of a wall onto his head. He died almost instantly.

By the most horrific of coincidences, a friend of Rose actually witnessed it. She called her, and Rose came at once. But there was nothing to be done. His evil task masters had no need of a dead Jew, so they let her cart him off in a wheel barrow. She had wrapped her beloved brother's cadaver in a sheet and pushed the barrow ten miles to the Jewish cemetery. There she paid some people to bury him. She returned home with the bloodied sheet and hid it under a bed. It was a full two weeks before my mother happened upon it. Until then Rose had kept the truth from my mother. Sandor had been mother's favorite, because he worked so selflessly for all of us. He had been a boxing champ, and an ideal son. Certainly the Nazis would be glad to hear of his demise.

Rose, now Maria, made a promise to herself to fight to save us all. It was a vow she meant, but even then she knew it was more bravado than common sense.

CHAPTER TEN

TRUST NO ONE!

Rose rented a bedroom in an apartment in a Christian building. A Mrs. Barna rented a five bedroom apartment there, and sublet four of them. She didn't bother looking very closely at anyone or anyone's papers. She was a quiet woman who just wanted to rent out her rooms, and be left alone. So, Rose took off her wedding band, put on a cross and moved in, passing for Catholic. She didn't have what the Nazis called a typical Jewish look, and there were no questions. It was a good idea and it worked. She felt safe, at least for now.

Mrs. Barna also rented one of the bedrooms to a Hungarian man who was the representative of an Austrian shoe company. Even in the midst of war people needed shoes, so he still held his job. It was a little disturbing for Rose to have a man in the next room in the same apartment, but it was a wartime situation, and nobody found it risqué or made any mention of it. Any man's presence would have made her feel uncomfortable, but this particular man frightened her to death. They had yet to be introduced so she had only his appearance by which to assess his threat to her.

He dressed as if he were a fascist official. He didn't actually wear a uniform, but his civilian clothes conspired to give him the look of a military man. He sported a full length leather trench coat over a suit cut similar to a uniform, and tall boots, shined to a mirror finish. He was tall and handsome, with his hair elegantly slicked back, and when he arrived on his motorcycle with sidecar he was an intimidating presence. People averted their eyes, lest they incur his suspicion or wrath. German soldiers always regarded him with respect and admiration, assuming his slight limp to be the result of heroic service on the Eastern Front. Josef Cséh was an Aryan Adonis.

His countenance did not inspire any such feeling in Rose. She was simply terrified of him. Why was a shoe salesman so well appointed? Was he a retired military officer, or even an active one? If so, why did he rent a small room in a modest apartment? Nothing about him made any sense. And she absolutely dreaded that he might speak to her. How would she respond? Was he spying on her? Was he following her? All she wanted to do was disappear among the Christians, but now she was beginning to see that it was going to be the most complicated life she could imagine. And having a mysterious man in the next room made it an anxiety ridden hell.

Hell, on the other hand, was not what came to mind for Josef Cséh when he saw Maria Willem for the first time. It was a Saturday. There was still some semblance of routine infrastructure in Budapest, and intercity mail was often delivered. To keep our live appearances on the street to a minimum we occasionally wrote cryptic letters to Rose, and one had arrived just as Mr. Cséh was pulling up to the building on his motorcycle. Mrs. Barna was busy on the ground floor, so she asked him to bring it up to Maria. As he was already going up there he agreed.

His limp on the wooden stairs heralded his coming, and Rose dreaded it. Worse, when the apartment door opened he called out for her.

"Miss Willem? Miss Willem, there's a letter here for you!"

She braced herself, plastered on a fake smile, and went out to retrieve the letter. For all her bravado she was visibly shaken by his presence, and felt utterly vulnerable. Mr. Cséh was likewise dumbstruck, but for a different reason. And he wasn't lying when he said, "It's a real pleasure to finally meet you."

Rose weakly smiled and excused herself. The man remained standing until she left the room.

Alone in her bedroom all Rose could think was that she was grateful he hadn't clicked his heels. Judging from his appearance she would have bet he would. For a moment she regretted being Maria Willem.

But there was no going back. Anyway, the alternative was too grim to imagine. Actually, the alternative was totally unknown. All we knew was that once someone was taken away they weren't heard from again. Nobody at that time imagined such horror as was the reality, but not knowing anything at all was in itself terrifying. Rose and the uncounted thousands of others, living similar lives as Rose, were quite happy to not have to consider the alternative. But she could not turn a blind eye to Josef Cséh.

Whenever he found the chance he tried to engage Rose in pleasant conversation. She couldn't afford to raise any suspicion, so she spoke briefly with him, and then excused herself to go to work. She told herself not to be afraid. After all, she was a Hungarian girl in Hungary, working as a seamstress. What was suspicious? But every time she came into the apartment there he was. Didn't the man ever go out selling his shoes anywhere? And then, one day the inevitable happened. He asked her out.

"Miss Willem, I was wondering if you might not like to go to the theater with me this Friday night. They are presenting a very nice dance recital. Do you like dance?"

Rose nearly swooned from the panic, and prayed it didn't show on her face. But at once she realized that such anxiety was not only intolerable for her, it would eventually betray her. The turmoil within had to be tamed, so she gave herself a pep talk to get through the moment, and swore to herself in silence never to allow Maria Willem to be nervous again. Rather, she would embrace Maria Willem and imbue her with the soul of Rose Weisz. And, as the best defense is a good offense, a composed and relaxed Rose sounded her trumpet and charged forward.

"Oh, that sounds absolutely charming, Mr. Cséh. But I'm replacing another girl at the shop this Friday night. She must visit her sick aunt, and frankly I'm happy for the extra income."

Maria Willem was now totally at ease and even effusive, flashing Rose's smile, tossing Rose's hair, batting Rose's eyes. She was a perky explosion of glamour and allure. By comparison, Scarlet O'Hara was an introvert.

"But it's very kind of you to invite me. Fact is, I adore dance. I just adore it. What a pity. Perhaps next time. Now, if you'll forgive me. It's been a long day. Good night!"

If Mr. Cséh had been merely smitten by the demure Miss Willem, he was now absolutely shaken to his very soul by her real personality. He hadn't made a sound during her short rejection speech, because he was literally speechless. He bowed ever so slightly from the waist when she excused herself, his eyes watering, his breathing labored. He actually had to sit down from the overwhelming charm of this creature. Josef Cséh had just met Rose Weisz and he was one hundred percent in love.

Rose hoped her rejection would make him aware of her unavailability. Anyway, she reasoned he'd have to go back to work in Austria, or travel to another city to sell his shoes. But it was not to be. A week later he asked again, this time to dinner. He even summoned up the nerve to jest.

"You do eat, don't you?" He was trying to be charming, and it caught her off guard.

She had to make a decision. She could reject him again and again. But maybe it would be quicker if she went out with him just once and behaved in such a way as to make him aware that nothing but a platonic relationship would ever be possible. He was being very polite in waiting for her response. But she knew how Nazis were. They were polite right up the moment they pulled the trigger.

Finally, she erupted with, "Why not?"

Joska stuttered with delight, "I, I, I..how about eight?"

"Very well. I'll meet you there! I'll come straight from work."

"F,F,Fine, he stammered."

"Where?" inquired Rose.

"Where?" Joska quizzically parroted.

"Where are we going to dine Friday night?" mocked Rose.

"Oh!" Joska had to actually shake his head to come to his senses. "Maxim's. Do you know it?"

"I adore it," she lied. "I'll see you there at eight." And Rose waltzed away.

Mr. Cséh mopped his brow. He'd never met anyone like her.

Rose came to visit us to discuss the mysterious shoe salesman. She wanted our opinion on what to do about him. Hearing the name of Josef repeated over and over again made mother depressed, because she thought of her lost son. At least this man was Hungarian and not a German. Maybe he wasn't a Nazi after all? Nothing was cleared up for Rose. We all had the same speculations about him. One thing was certain. He was probably not going to give up. Rose had attracted more than her fair share of suitors before marrying, so it was no big surprise. There was another thing for certain, however. She had nowhere else to go, and she was going to have to deal with it. She was also going to have to find out where Maxim's was.

At dinner he was a perfect gentleman. It was the first time that Rose had eaten in a restaurant in so long she couldn't even remember. And she felt guilty about it. So much so, that she fell oddly quiet. The vivacious blond he had fallen for was gone, replaced by this morose girl. So, now she was mysterious as well as charismatic.

A week later he asked her out again, and she had no good excuse. But in all this time he was a gentleman, never pressing his advantage, even though they lived in the same apartment. For most men of the time it wouldn't have been so hard to try and take their relationship to a more intimate physical level. But Mr. Cséh's thoughts were on a much higher plateau. After three weeks of platonic dates he proposed marriage.

A charade was a charade, but Rose couldn't go that far. Or could she? Could she pretend to love him and even sleep with him if he was the enemy? But was he? He was always respectful of her. Could a Nazi be so sensitive? What were his politics? He never said anything about the Germans or any fascist that would suggest he was in sympathy with them. Maybe he even felt empathy for the victims of the Nazis, but was afraid to say anything about it out loud for fear of being accused of being a traitor. After all, Maria Willem was a Christian. Maybe she'd turn on him if she knew his true nature. But he professed true love for her.

Was Mr. Cséh's confession of true love a rouse meant to gain her confidence? But why would she merit such lavish fascist guile? Certainly, they couldn't be after her. Anyway, if they were, it would be simple enough to just arrest her and shoot her and dump her in the river. Why the big act with wooing and a marriage proposal? So, she made a decision. She wished that she could have consulted with her parents first, but she was alone. She would have to decide for herself. And it was going to be the most difficult and dangerous decision of her life. If she was making a mistake it could mean her torture and certain death.

She had told Mr. Cséh that she would have to think his proposal over, and he generously agreed to give her the time she needed. This reserved patience of his fortified Rose's resolve that she was taking the right path. The next time they were together in the apartment Mrs. Barna was out. She invited Mr. Cséh into her small room. He entered and found a tense Maria, standing and subconsciously wringing her hands. She looked at him for a few moments to confirm her decision.

"Sit down, Joska. I have to tell you something."

There were two chairs placed so that they faced each other.

"Alright Maria." Mr. Cséh felt worried. Was she going to end it? As long as it wasn't that he could stand anything. But she had used the familiar form of his first name, so perhaps it wasn't going to be so bad. Obediently, he sat down, and looked up at her with an almost beatific innocence.

No Nazi could act this well, thought Rose. She pulled up her own chair and sat down, and took a deep breath. "Joska, I can't marry you, because I'm already married."

He didn't flinch.

"My husband was taken to a concentration camp months ago. Actually, just two weeks after we were married."

Still, he didn't answer or move. He just looked at her squarely, barely nodding. So far, so good. He now knew that he was talking with someone whom the fascists considered less than ideal, yet he was still sitting there, staring innocently at her. There was no going back.

"I'm not Maria Willem. I was born Rose Weisz. I'm Jewish. I'm hiding here to save my life, and trying to see if I can save my family too. My sister was sent to a concentration camp, and one of my brothers died when he was in the forced labor brigade. My older brother disappeared fighting the Russians. My parents live in Budapest with my little brother and my nephew. So does my entire family. We fled here from the countryside about three years ago."

Still no sound from Joska.

"There," finished Rose, "that's everything. Now you know. Still want to marry me?"

Joska looked serious. During her entire talk he had not broken off his gaze from hers. He had listened intently. He never looked shocked. Perhaps he had heard such things before. Rose was starting to feel she had made a terrible mistake. Panic was whelming up inside her when he finally spoke.

"I understand." He seemed earnest, even empathetic. Maybe it would be alright.

Without changing his expression he added, "Let me think about all this and tomorrow night we'll meet again and talk." He stood up, never taking his eyes from hers.

"Good night," he hesitated, and then added, "Rose."

In the morning Rose came to our apartment and revealed to us that she had shared her secret with this man. John and I were asleep, or at least pretending to be so in order to hear the adults' conversation. So, it was just Rose and my parents discussing our fate.

"How could you?" chastised my mother. "He sounds like a fascist." He's probably turning you in right now."

My father, usually argumentative, agreed with mother and added, "What if he followed you here? We'll all get sent to a concentration camp!"

Rose, who had felt confident about her decision, now was completely demoralized. "Mama. I don't believe this man is a Nazi or with Nyilasok. I believe he really cares for me, and won't turn me in."

Mother shrugged her shoulders. "Well, you can't take it back. That's for sure. Whether you're right or wrong it's already decided. But tell me, if he loves you and would never turn you in, then why didn't he just say so at once?!"

"I don't know," admitted Rose, and fell silent.

Mama had a point. If we moved we'd have to tell the police where we lived anyway. Even under normal circumstances it'd be illegal not to. But now that the police were affiliated with Nyilasok someone worse would come for us. Mama's point held. There was nothing we could do about it.

We ate a not so grand lunch in silence. And we were way too worried to nap. That night mother and father didn't sleep, or squabble either. They just sat there, too afraid to discuss what might be transpiring at that moment between their daughter and her acquaintance. At the same moment that I was falling asleep Rose sat in her humble room, waiting for the arrival of Mr. Cséh. The fact that he wasn't there yet made her nervous. She fully expected the door to get kicked in and Nyilasok to drag her out. Finally, at eight thirty he walked in.

"Hello, Rose."

The fact that he used her real name filled her with hope. But then he seemed grave.

"Sit down. I need to talk to you."

Now Rose was terrified that he would confess that he was a Gestapo spy and had no choice but to turn her and her whole family in.

"Alright, Joska," she whispered. She was so frozen with panic she couldn't manage to speak any louder anyway. The next moment would decide her fate.

"You know, when Hitler started making those speeches, saying that the Jews started the war, and that everything was the Jews' fault, all I could think was, 'Those poor people. I feel so sorry for them.'"

The degree of relief and elation that Rose felt at that moment was incalculable. All her fears evaporated, and she wanted to run and tell her mother. Clearly, this man wouldn't turn her in. He couldn't. But what he said next made her nearly faint.

"So, I'm going to do everything I can to help you and your entire family."

Her heart rose to her throat and her chest heaved as she took in little gasps of air. Her ecstasy was such that she was light headed. Too rapturous to speak, she took Joska's hands in hers and looked at them. Choked up she whispered, "Thank you."

Her gratitude was so solemn it was almost religious. He was embarrassed by it and tried to calm her by getting down to brass tacks.

"Tomorrow, I'd like to meet your family. There's no time to lose."

Openly weeping, she nodded her head up and down jerkily like an obedient child. She lifted her hand up and gently touched his face. He looked at her benevolently, still too much of a gentleman to press any advantage. Rose lifted up her other hand to his arm and gripped it. Pulling him toward her she kissed him tenderly, and then leaned her forehead against his chest. They stayed that way until she regained a semblance of composure. Finally, she spoke in a hushed voice.

"I don't know if my husband is alive or not. I don't even know where he is, or if I'll ever see him again. When I know for certain I'll marry you. For now..."

Her voice trailed off as normal life again insinuated itself into the lives of people desperate to escape the hell around them even for a minute.

Joska Cséh's mother was Hungarian, and his father Austrian. Since the two countries had shared a common destiny, members of a united empire since 1867, it was commonplace for citizens of either country to visit the other. In 1913 Joska's father came to Hungary to take charge of some coal mines. He met a woman, fell for her and her country, and stayed, settling in the southern university town of Pécs. One year later Joska was born. And a few months after that a Serbian student shot the imperial archduke and World War One began. When the conflict ended the empire was dissolved. Hungary had lost yet another war and some serious real estate. Joska was raised speaking Hungarian and perfect German. He knew everything about Austrian culture and traveled there often. He was Hungarian, but could pass for Austrian or German with ease. He had all the physical traits of an Aryan super-man of 1940, but the benevolent consciousness of a citizen of the Age of Reason. He looked like he should goose step, but wouldn't hurt a fly. He was perfectly equipped to pass as a Nazi, and was determined to use that against them at every opportunity. But there was no fooling anybody. Even with his best intentions it was a daunting task. And the threat to him was as grave as it was for Rose.

CHAPTER ELEVEN

HOPE

The next day I took a rare foray outside to buy some food for the family. As a nine year old, I was a real prize for the Nyilasok. I was only a block from our apartment building when I saw the motorcycle with a sidecar coming toward me. It looked like some policeman, and I was afraid. I glimpsed it for a moment, and then turned nonchalantly away, so as to avoid drawing attention to myself. In that half moment I could've sworn I saw Rose in the sidecar, though I knew I shouldn't look back. However it was too compelling to see my sister, and I calmly glanced her way again. It was Rose! But this was too unusual. Something must be wrong. Had my sister fallen into a trap and got tortured into revealing our whereabouts? Maybe a neighbor complained about us. It didn't take much. Every comment was taken as seriously as witch sightings in Salem. One day a person was your neighbor, and the next your accuser. I was terrified, excited and relieved all at once. At least she looked alright. But then I thought she might've been followed. I just didn't know what to do. In any case I didn't call out. Both Rose and mama had told me to keep quiet. Maybe this policeman was bringing her here to investigate us. Then she called out to me.

"Little boy."

I followed her lead and answered as if I didn't know her, "Yes, Miss?"

When she pulled up close she leaned forward and whispered, "Tommy, don't talk. Just listen. We're not in any trouble. Everything's alright. This man's our friend. Go up and tell mama I'm alright. We'll be along in a few minutes."

I had been too afraid to look at the man when they were approaching, but now I gave him the once-over. He gave me a little wink and a quick smile and they sped off. Now I really lost control, and bounded to the building and up the stairs to our apartment.

I burst in. "Mama! Papa! Ro...Maria's alright!"

They immediately shushed me, lest the neighbors hear my frantic banter. I lowered my voice.

"She's here with a man who's going to help us!"

"Who?" demanded mother.

"What man?" added my father.

"I don't know. He's got a motorcycle. He looks nice. Ro...Maria says he's our friend!"

My parents looked at each with concern, and then stared around, unable to express their apprehension. John, who had been sitting there quietly, broke the tension.

"What happened to her? Is she alright?" I told him what little I knew.

"Yes, I think so. Anyway, they're coming up here right away!"

My mother's eyes opened in horror. She looked around as if there were something to hide.

"What do you mean," asked father. "Right now?!"

Before I could answer there was a timid knock at the door. It was our secret knock. Three quick knocks, a short pause, followed by three more. If we didn't hear that knock we prepared for the worst. Trembling, mother opened the door. Rose entered while the man patiently stayed back. He saw me and winked again. I smiled, but gave him the once-over again, this time in detail. While Rose and mother hugged my father invited the man in.

"Please, don't stand in the hall. Come in."

Rose wiped her eyes and pulled the man in by the arm. Mother was a little taken aback by the familiar gesture, and father narrowed his gaze at the tall handsome stranger.

"Mama, this is Josef Cséh. Joska, these are my parents."

Joska spoke to them in a warm tone, "A pleasure to meet you Mr. and Mrs. Weisz. Rose has told me so much about you I feel I already know you."

He didn't talk like a Nazi. He seemed nice. Rose continued with the introductions.

"This is my nephew, John. His parents are already in America."

John liked the attention, but the reminder of his parents made him at once melancholy. Joska noticed it and empathized with the little boy at once. My father took it all in, and was totally won over by the stranger in our midst. Rose proudly presented me last.

"And this little devil is my kid brother Tommy."

Joska seemed delighted to meet me and shook my hand like a peer. "Great to know you, Tommy. I hope we'll be good friends."

I shook back, but couldn't manage a sound. He was friendly but kind of overwhelming at the same time. It was this charisma that was his, and our, saving grace. He looked like a poster for German army recruitment. He had blue eyes, light brown hair, was tall, and clean shaven. Just a boy, even I could tell he was good looking. He had perfect posture, and always looked you in the eye when he spoke. And the way he spoke left no doubt that he was an aristocrat. Added to that, he had a slight limp that testified to his experience on the battlefield. All he lacked was a monocle and a dueling scar on one cheek to evoke images of a Prussian military academy. Then we learned of one of his greatest assets. Under her breath, mother made a comment to my father in German, and father quickly shushed her, aware of her paranoia and rudeness in front of a guest. Then, to the wonderment of all, Joska responded in the same language. My God, he spoke German! Not just German, but *hoch deutsch,* the language of the elite.

For a moment we all thought we had been tricked by this clever Aryan who was now going to spring the trap he had so cleverly laid. But he continued to speak German to my parents in a calming and reassuring tone. The little bit of German that I had picked up on during my parents' frequent fights told me he was Hungarian, but had a an Austrian father, and spent a lot of time in Vienna. And his limp had nothing to do with combat, but was the result of a short bout of polio as a child. He said that he hated the war, and considered Nazis and Nyilasok vermin. Finally, he said he would do everything he could to help us and our entire family, including trying to bring back Anci. Without breaking his rhythm he turned to John and me and said, "You kids want to go for a ride on my motorcycle?"

My parents' mouths literally hung open. All the while Rose had been standing to the side with her hands clenched together under her chin, looking through teary eyes from Joska to her parents and back again. My mother and father slowly turned to each other, and then to Rose, who could no longer control her joy. She rushed to her mother's ready arms and hugged her, with her head sobbing on her shoulder. Even my father, ever the ready wit, was speechless. Joska preferred this silence to embarrassing gratitude. Perhaps to avoid it he swept John and me up, and we were out the door, headed for our first motorcycle ride. As we all plodded downstairs Rose and my parents wept with joy, then celebrated with a little drink from a bottle left over from Sandor' days in the black market. Father had hidden it.

Joska said little until we reached the street and were out of earshot of our neighbors. "Ever been on a motorcycle, kids?"

John spoke up, "Motorcycle? I've only taken two rides in automobiles!"

It was true. In Gyongyos we never so much as saw a single car. And though we had lived for over two years in the big city, we had scant personal experience with them. We had taken our share of trolley rides, but on only a couple of occasions did Rose or father arrange to give us rides in the private autos of friends. And the thought of going for a ride now in a motorcycle couldn't have excited us more if we had been invited to take off in the space ships we read about in comic books. We were beyond giddy.

Joska straddled the black machine and invited John and I to plop down in the side car. Being just kids we fit snuggly together, one behind the other.

"Don't stand up. You might fall down." That was our only warning before he roared off.

Stand up? We practically wet ourselves at the speed he went, and ducked down even lower. It was the biggest thrill I'd known since my sister Rose smuggled me into the cinema. After going a few blocks without crashing we slowly peered up over the edge of the side car. Joska's laughter at our trepidation caught our attention, and we glanced up at him. He found our uninitiated fright hysterical, and beamed down on us with a benevolent and protective gaze. He was like some movie hero, and we felt as if nothing would happen to us while we were with him. What happened next only reinforced that premonition.

He pulled the side car over to the curb in front of a bakery. "How about a little strudel, kids?"

Strudel? He invited us to strudel? He told our family that he would fight to protect us from the Nazis. Then he took us for a ride on a motorcycle. And now he was going to buy us pastry? He was not merely a hero. He was a God! John and I just stared at each other and broke out laughing. We had to, because no words could describe our joy. In a minute Joska emerged from the bakery and handed each of us a piece of warm fragrant strudel.

"Thanks, Mr..." Joska stopped me, "Just call me Joska." Then, with comfortable gusto, he bit off a man sized chunk of his own crispy delicacy.

"Thanks, Joska," we both obediently chimed, and dug in.

"I'll bring some back to your folks," said our pal, and he disappeared inside again.

Just as we were finishing our opulent snack some uniformed Nyilasok hooligans walked by. Although we were with our new protector we must have exhibited some uneasiness at the sight of them. As wild animals can, they smelled our fear, and stopped to save civilization from the onslaught of carefree children.

"What do we have here? What are you doing parading on a public street? Papers!"

John and I froze and looked at each other wide eyed. Our look of fear only fed their bravado.

"Are you deaf? Stand up when spoken to by your betters!' One of them reached out and grabbed John's arm.

"Get your filthy hands off those children!" Joska was now standing next to us.

"You can't go out for a simple piece of strudel without being harassed by you hoodlums?! Look at you! Your uniforms are a mess. Don't either of you own an iron? Did your parents never teach you to

78

stand up straight? And why are you bothering my nephews? I have a good mind to report you. What are your names?"

The Nyilasok punks stammered before the Aryan Adonis and hurriedly tried to improve their posture. "I'm sorry, your honor. We only thought..."

"Thought?" Joska fired back. "I doubt if thinking is something either of you has any experience in at all. If you did you'd see these are two decent Hungarian Christian boys."

The two young fascists could not even manage to stammer now. Joska pressed his advantage.

"Are you deaf as well? I asked you a simple question. Can you not see that they are decent Hungarian Christian boys?"

They snapped to attention. "Yes sir. I'm sorry sir. Yes, of course. We have made a terrible mistake. By all means, go on about your business. I hope you enjoyed your strudel, sir. Good day, sir."

They gave a fascist salute and walked away as quickly as they could, arguing between themselves about whose fault it was.

"Let's go home," said Joska.

John and I nearly threw up our strudel from the mixture of fear, shock and relief. I never told him, but two layers of clothing down we both had on yellow stars. Joska was God!

Joska had saved us. But when we got back to the apartment and recounted our harrowing adventure mama made us aware that it was also Joska that would have been to blame had anything happened to us. So, mama sat Joska down and let him know in no uncertain terms that we were already in harm's way, and didn't need to go around tempting it any further. A sheepish Joska promised to save his performances for when they were needed, and to meanwhile keep an equally low profile as the rest of us. But it was headier air we were breathing now thanks to him, and for the first time since Anci's arrest we felt hopeful.

I've relived that first motorcycle adventure many times in my memory. I was a child when it happened, but as an adult it's motivated no end of philosophical reflection about Joska, the war, and human foibles.

Joska Cséh's success was based on creating an impression in the minds of people that he was someone to respect. And half that performance rested squarely on his looks. If he'd had a big hook nose and black wavy hair, his histrionics might've accomplished nothing but getting him shot. But he looked like an Aryan, so his performance was convincing. It was an act made believable by a fair face and blond hair. Over the years that has made me think a lot about how shallow humankind can be. Someone can make an argument, but we might ignore its content, preferring to base conclusions on the deliverer of that argument. The classic example is when John F. Kennedy beat Richard Nixon in the first presidential debates simply because he was handsomer. People love beauty, and will vote for it every time. Would Hitler have been so successful had he been ugly? Certainly, he was not good looking like a matinee idol, but he did have even features, clear skin, decent teeth, a full head of hair and blue eyes. Perhaps he made more than one *fraulein's* heart race. What other charismatic leader cultivated his looks toward the end of swaying hearts and minds? Mussolini, minus the hair, can claim most of the Fuhrer's aforementioned physical attributes. Stalin's moustache gave him a virile and competent countenance. Without it he might have been labeled homely, and not have enjoyed his inexplicable success. And Saddam Hussein appeared to have daily dedicated a good hour at least, in front of a mirror, flossing and combing. White power advocates often cite what they deem as the black man's plainness to justify their views. Had the quarry of history's white slavers all resembled Denzel Washington and Halle Berry I wonder if we would have even had slavery at all. The men sent to capture the slaves would probably have fallen in love with the women, and then been too jealous of the men to bring them back, fearing serious competition for the attentions of lonely colonial females. Though we're always taught not to judge a book by its cover it seems to be a losing battle, as if it were part of our nature. After all, who goes to an art gallery to see an ugly painting? It is primordial and without any logical explanation. There's even a passage in ancient Indian scripture that says that God has unlimited perfect qualities, but it's His beauty that attracts us most of all. In *Mein Kampf* the first critical thing that Hitler says about Jews has to do with their appearance. So, the holocaust was about ridding the world of people who have more than their fair share of bad hair days? One group of people has the right to rule over, or even kill, another group based on who's prettier? People do judge books by their covers! When I was nine years old I did not reflect quite so deeply on the whys and wherefores of our situation. But if we could be saved because I had a sister who looked like a movie star who motivated a handsome Christian to bluff everyone with his flawless features, we were glad to live in such a shallow world. And we felt sorry for anyone not in close proximity to such impressive physical beauty.

In gratitude, appreciation, and fairness to Joska, it must be recognized that he was not merely motivated by love for a pretty face. For us that would have been enough, but to him it was more than that. Actually there were two reasons besides ardor.

First, Joska had not been swept up in the rising tide of fascism, as were so many of his countrymen. He just didn't buy what the Nazis were selling, and knew they were evil. Helping us was his way of fighting them. The other reason was odder, and more difficult to comprehend. Upon hearing it one might even think him crazy. But Joska Cséh had an adventurous streak. It's that simple. When you hear mountain climbers brag that they ascend the snowy peaks because they're there, that's Joska! Of course, mountain climbing is a lot safer than defying the Nazis, but that was part of it, just the same. However, we were hardly inclined to consider Joska's deeper motivations. He was our angel of mercy, and we trusted him completely. In her famous diary Anne Frank says she feels that all people are basically good. I confess that I cannot agree with her. I saw too much on the streets of Budapest. But I do know that some, maybe many, are good. Joska Cséh is proof of at least that much.

CHAPTER TWELVE

WE TAKE ACTION

The plan was to emulate Rose's modus operendi for every member of the family. That meant Christian papers and residences for everyone. The two things that could make this work were the very things upon which we had based our hopes from the beginning, being a tree among the vast human forest of Budapest, and gold.

In 1944 Gyongyos it would have been staggering to report forty-two different lost sets of identity papers. It certainly would have been investigated by the authorities. Of course, having papers in a small town was just a formality anyway. Everyone already knew who and what you were. Rose's plan could only work in a big city. And before she met Joska, it depended on finding forty two Christian citizens of Budapest and buying their papers. If forty two citizens out of half a million report their papers lost it's a low percentage, and not likely to cause suspicion. You could even go to forty two different police stations around Budapest to report the loss. What Joska had in mind was faster. He went home to Pécs where his family lived. Everyone in that town had known them forever, and knew they weren't Jews. They were never stopped, and probably never would be. They had no urgent need of their papers, so they all willingly surrendered them to help the persecuted Weisz family. Joska was not only an angel himself, but he had apparently been raised by them as well.

Joska Cséh could rely on his family for all of their papers, but he was still short a few sets if he was going to save the entire Weisz clan. So, he'd have to buy more. Two factors figured into the wartime identity papers equation. First, most people were desperate for money to buy food and other basic necessities, so there was no alternative but to take such a risk. Secondly, by this time it was impossible to close your eyes and pretend you could avoid involvement in the conflict. Full raging warfare had already been brought to the doorsteps of civilians. There was no longer such a thing as a noncombatant. And helping a victim of the bad guys was one way of fighting back. If you weren't prepared to do something overt to the enemy, like joining the partisans and using violence against them, at least you could do something covert, like help prevent the killing of one of their victims. And if you were paid for doing something subversive, better yet.

By now, breaking the law was an accepted norm. The war had already made everyone a potential criminal, and thousands were willing to profit from those little scraps of life and death papers. One of the many things you learn when trafficking in false identity papers is what happens when someone dies of natural causes. It's eerie, but dead people have an address. The cemetery. But they don't come and go, and don't need to show any proof of being deceased to anyone. And Budapest had more than their fair share of deceased people who no longer needed their papers, but whose family members needed money. Add to that the fact that the majority were Christians, and you have a very favorable equation for locating the necessary papers. Joska just had to find them, and then use the second thing upon which we had always depended, gold.

Mother had horded the little gold Napoleons and now they could possibly save our lives. It wouldn't be the first time such a scenario took place. On various occasions a Nazi storm trooper would kick in the door of a Jewish family and discover them cringing, but also offering their jewelry to allow them to hide their infant son with Christian neighbors before being taken away. A few Nazis possessed a tiny portion of the heart with which they had been born which, when mixed with a normal amount of greed, could result in a kind act. In our case we weren't planning on bribing any Nazis with residual heartbeat, but rather normal Hungarians who needed money enough to take a chance.

The gold that mother had hidden by now added up to about two pounds. We actually didn't know how much we had, because we couldn't take the time to count it. The slim coins were so small that spreading them all out to tally them would have been inconceivable. It was imprudent to have them all in one place as well. If someone broke in we'd lose everything. And having them out and exposed for the length of time needed to count them would have been equally unwise. So we were satisfied with their weight. Hopefully, it was enough to finance everyone's papers. Joska had some money too, and was willing to invest it in us. He had good contacts in Vienna, and had been trafficking in the black market since the start of the war. He could get tobacco, chocolate, coffee and sugar, and had steady customers in Hungary. Actually, his shoe salesman job was little more than a front for his more lucrative activities. He did sell shoes wholesale to a regular line of stores in Hungary, and he needed the position to explain his frequent trips to and from Austria. But he made no endeavor to be salesman of the month, when his time could be more profitably spent on the black market. So, between Joska and the Napoleons there might be enough to buy papers for everyone. Besides, there was no set price. Every case was unique, depending on the needs or demands of each potential seller. Just having the money though gave us an advantage. Financial times were tough in our country, and many people were desperate enough to consider such a brazen offer. But consider the offer.

War torn Budapest was an atmosphere of tension and terror. Nobody trusted anybody. Over the slightest suspicion you could get arrested, tortured, or shot on the spot. Then, out of the clear blue sky, a total stranger approaches. He looks like a Gestapo officer. He asks you if anyone in your family is recently deceased. He wants to know if there are any old identity papers in the household, even going back years. He says he wants to buy them. Is it a trick? A trap? Has somebody spoken to the authorities about you? Some lies? Have you been mistakenly identified? Do they have you confused with someone else? You must refuse them. You have no papers. You deny having any knowledge about anybody with such papers. You never have. You are law abiding loyal citizens. You know nothing. If you hear of any papers you'll tell them. You're happy to help. *Sieg Heil!*

But Joska was prepared for dubious receptions and sales resistance. He could not be discouraged. After all, he was a traveling salesman. And if you're good at that it doesn't matter if you sell shoes or anything else. You sell yourself, and overcome objections. He took it in his stride. Because, when Joska wasn't doing his Nazi act, he exuded a carefree aura. Authentic totalitarians are not noted for emitting good vibrations. They don't need to respect anyone's Miranda rights, gain one's confidence, or beguile anyone into a confession. They don't play good Gestapo agent, bad Gestapo agent. They just beat it out of you. Joska didn't come off like that. He had a relaxed demeanor, which suggested to whomever he met, that the woes of the day would pass. This carefree image was one shared by the nobility, whose blithe character always suggested to authorities that they were of true Aryan birth, and transcendental to searches and interrogations. And to the average civilian of Budapest he came off as harmless, and someone you could trust.

But it must be appreciated that Joska, despite his relatively unassailable appearance, took his life in his hands from the moment he met us. For all his calm exterior he knew he walked in harm's way. Anglo-Saxons enjoyed preferential treatment, but if you were discovered to be something other than what you seemed to be, you were a dead man. As dead as a communist, a Gypsy, or a Jew. Being gentile was no guarantee of safety from anything. Actually, the Nazis were more sadistic with Christians who helped hide their victims than they were with their usual prey. They hung them, beheaded them, and adorned their bodies with signs identifying them as 'Jew Hiders' or 'Jew Lovers.' And Joska was a candidate for a Nazi necktie party from the moment he started helping us. But he appeared calm in all circumstances. And if you could keep your head when all around you are losing theirs in war torn Budapest, you had a fighting chance. What posed the most real threat to Joska was the possibility of betrayal. But if someone did turn him in he was ready to go into his act and deny it. After all, who were you going to believe? And to garner that trust Joska had one more weapon in his arsenal to guarantee it. It was something he chose not to reveal to anyone until it was absolutely necessary. Tucked snugly in his wallet was a brilliantly forged set of German military papers, identifying him as Lieutenant Josef Cséh, veteran of the Eastern front, and on special assignment in Budapest.

Whether it was Joska's own family or a stranger, he had to be careful to always obtain papers that matched someone in the family. Identity papers had a birth date, and we had to be careful that each set of papers matched or approximated the person's age. Once we had the papers we had to affix a photograph of the matching person. Identify papers, in and of themselves, were not that complex. They were printed on standard paper, using a variety of different typewriters, depending on which city printed them. They displayed embossed seals, much like notary publics, and also ink stamps. The stamps were coveted and closely guarded. But they could be imitated, and probably were a thousand times over during the war. As long as the papers looked original, had a matching photograph, the proper seals, stamps, and signatures, you might pass. Another detail we had to be careful with was the look of the pictures. We had to be careful not to use recent photographs. If you were forty years old, for example, like my mother, your photograph should not look as if it was taken yesterday. Real papers had photographs that showed a younger you. To get around that, we carefully removed the pictures from our old papers and applied them to the new ones. But that wasn't always easy, because there might be a red or a blue stamp that was half on the picture and half on the paper. Each document took time to prepare. The commercial art market was practically nonexistent, so talented artists plied their craft in this new high demand field for pay. They could paint the mark of the stamp well enough to pass most inspections.

Since the outbreak of war it had become routine to have your identity papers inspected. At first it was annoying, and you didn't feel afraid to let the policeman, whom you had known most of your life, know it. But as the military tightened its grip on our lives nobody dared question the ubiquitous invasions of privacy. And it seemed as if there was no limit to the number of people who could demand to see your papers and go over them. It was no longer just the same old cop on the beat that you'd grown up with. He was soon reinforced by the Nyilasok and all manner of Hungarian soldiers. And once hostilities reached their zenith the Nazis came in, all eager to have a peek at our paperwork. There were S.S., Gestapo, and unlimited ranks of German soldiers. In no time we became fluent in *papieren bitte,* papers please. And to go outside without identity papers was suicide. You were immediately arrested and detained until a family member showed up at the police station or Gestapo headquarters with them. It was actually now a crime not to carry your identity papers. If you left them at home you might have to undergo prolonged interrogation. It could even lead to being sent to a concentration camp. And you didn't have to look Jewish for this to happen. Everyone was suspected of being involved in some subversive activity. Fascists saw cosmic conspiracies everywhere. Life was one big witch hunt, and everyone was eligible quarry.

Presenting your papers was an art in itself. You had to appear calm and unconcerned. If you exhibited any lack of ease it aroused suspicion. But it was also dangerous to act too blasé. Idle chatter made you appear nervous. If you looked away it was also suspicious. But looking them too squarely in the eye was confrontational and dangerous. You had to find a happy balance. We learned that looking at the papers along with the official was the safest bet. It was no guarantee of safety, but it was the least suspicious and confrontational. Of course, it always depended on who was doing the inspecting. The least threatening were the old fashioned policemen. They were just doing their job and weren't looking to complicate their lives by having to drag you in and fill out endless paperwork of their own. If you were clean and decently dressed, and didn't look overtly subversive, they just wanted to ascertain if you even had papers. They looked at them, and as long as it didn't actually say in bold black letters that you were a spy or a partisan, they were inclined to go on about their business and let you do the same. Regular soldiers were the next least threatening. Most average German soldiers were farm boys, and in over their head when it came to acting as policemen. This made him similar to the Hungarian policeman. As long as you seemed normal they were too. They were not specifically trained as such, but they did as they were ordered. After all, German soldiers always obey orders.

The strict adherence to the military chain of command was an integral part of the German soldier's character. It was key to his success, but ironically it also contributed to his eventual defeat. He acquiesced to the orders of his superiors, and did his duty. But his mindset was of a submissive nature, and not prone toward taking any initiative. Military analysts have even suggested that it was this tendency to obey, at the cost of self determination, that made him less of a soldier than the American GI. If a German platoon leader were killed in combat the *soldaten* waited for orders rather than act on their own. American soldiers were also trained to obey orders, but, if left on their own, the indomitable American spirit of independence won out. A GI sergeant could get killed, and a private would not hesitate in assessing the situation and doing the needful. Not so for a German foot soldier. He would wait for orders. On D-Day German panzer divisions were within reach of Normandy, but they stayed put, waiting for the Fuhrer to wake up and give the order to attack. So soldiers were threatening, but not the most terrifying. That distinction was competed for by the politically tinged segments of the military, the Nyilasok and Gestapo. If you were stopped by one of them you had no idea what could happen. They might whimsically arrest you for the fun of it, or capriciously kill you, if they so desired. It was the tendency for the master race to feel superior, so the Gestapo prided itself on being more professional than the Nyilasok. They wore shinier boots and were charged with the specific agenda to seek out subversives. Naturally, they never missed the chance to arrest Jews, but they were obsessed with searching for members of the underground. Hungary didn't have the organized nationwide resistance that many Nazi dominated countries had, but there were many independent cells of partisans. The Germans suspected everyone of being a member, and they were far more thorough than farm boys when they stopped you. Not content to merely peruse your papers, they would immediately start an interrogation. Right off, they had to know where you were going. Or they would test you, asking you details that were on your papers, like your address. Or they might observe that you were far from your neighborhood, and demand to know why. Less than credible replies led to your arrest and more formal interrogation. The Nyilasok were even worse. Not standing on a pretense of Prussian formality, they shot first and asked no questions after. The one formality might have been to take their victim around the corner before pulling the trigger. They found it especially convenient and satisfying to shoot people by the river. They just pushed the bodies in. One horrific method of mass murder was to bind together the hands of a line of people, maybe twenty or thirty in a row, like a human chain. Then they shot the first few and pushed them into the river. The weight and momentum carried the rest to the bottom. From 1943 to 1945 the Danube had more bodies floating than the Ganges.

As the intensity of inspections became greater so did the need for better forgeries and artwork. This meant an increase in expense. Forgers and document artists charged whatever the market would bear. And why not? If they were found out they were dead too. Regardless of the risk, there was a whole world of possibilities if you had the money. And mama had hidden gold Napoleons everywhere. But now we had to risk bringing it all together in one place. Before, if we lost one hiding place, we could survive. Now, we had to consolidate it. Against everything she believed we had to put all our eggs in one basket.

Joska returned from Pécs with twenty two sets of papers for our family. There weren't enough matching members of Joska's family to cover us all, but he'd deal with that later. For now, we had to get to a safe place. Joska found us a nearly empty apartment building in the eastern suburbs of the city, which is where the rail yards and train stations were. It was an industrial zone, with most of the buildings being either warehouses or factories, with a few apartment buildings for the lower classes that worked there. Joska took me out there on his motorcycle just to see it, even if it was only from the outside. It was a good thing he had removed the side car, because the rubble from the Russian bombing would have made a trip in a car impossible. I sat behind him, hanging on to him, and we went around and in between mountains of smoking debris. At times there was no more than two feet of clear road. It was a challenge even for the motorcycle. Joska kept reminding me to pay attention to landmarks, in case I had to make my way there. Finally we got to the outskirts of town, and the perimeter road that circled it. We had gone due east almost the entire time.

"Okay, Tommy. All we have to do now is find number sixty three. Remember, the address, sixty three Hungaria Korut. That's where your family is going to be. If we get separated that's where we can look for each other. Remember the number, sixty three Hungaria Korut."

It didn't look like a typical Hungarian building like the ones I was used to seeing in Budapest. It was flat and ordinary. But it was our haven, and I took a good long look at it. Then Joska spoke to me in a very confidential tone.

"Tommy, we'll be able to put your parents and sisters, and your aunts and uncles and cousins here next week. Everyone with papers will live here. But it might be harder right now to get papers for you and John, so just for now we might have to put you boys in the Red Cross. But it's only for a few days. I have my eye on a Christian family for you, and this lonely old watchmaker for John. Okay?"

That was another reason I loved Joska so much. He treated me like an equal. Here, we were, two men discussing important matters of life and death, and he even wanted my opinion. Naturally, I agreed with him. "Yes, Joska. I understand."

"Remember the address," said Joska. I repeated it and he was happy.

Joska took me back to Harsfa Street, and then took my parents on a trolley to show them, so they could get their bearings too. The following week they would all be shuttled out there while John and I were dropped at the Red Cross Orphanage. Meanwhile, Joska would carry on with his mission to find more papers. The plan seemed simple enough, but that very afternoon we found out that our building was going to be turned into a Christian building in two days.

That's how the Nazis worked. With no prior notice one building at a time got purified of any Jewish presence. So, little by little, the Jews would be herded into the ghetto to facilitate their deportation to a concentration camp. The information that our building was going to be Christianized was classified, and the Gestapo only shared it with Hungarian police authorities for logistical purposes. One of the police captains was a friend of my father's and he got a warning to us. Finally, my father's social gallivanting paid off! Even my mother had to give him credit for that. While this information was heaven sent we still all had one day to find shelter for a week. John and I could be dropped off at the Red Cross easily enough, but my parents would have to find a haven from the Nazis for seven days that felt like an eternity.

That night, our last in the apartment, Rose stayed with us. While our parents were busy discussing temporary refuge she busied herself changing the photographs on the identification documents. She affixed the photographs of Ignatz and Riza on the papers of Joska's own parents. For now, if any asked, Joska was their son. That was no great challenge, because my mother already felt that way. When she was done falsifying documents John and I got ready to sleep in the bedroom. John dropped off immediately, but I was too nervous to sleep. Rose looked at me with a sad smile and sat down next to me.

"Tommy. They all hate us. The Germans. The Hungarians. Maybe even the Russians. Who knows? So, we can't count on anyone. Just us. And Joska. We have each other, and we all care about each other. You know, I love you very much."

I just stared up at her wide eyed, and nodded my head earnestly. I knew what she was saying.

"You have to be smart Tommy. Listen to what we tell you to do. Joska is going to find a place for you and another for John. It's just not possible to put all of us together. But wherever Joska puts you just stay inside. Okay? Anyway, we're going to be Christians now. You know how Christians act?"

I leaned back and crossed myself. She laughed softly and took me into her arms.

"That's right. And if your Christian family takes you to church, be enthusiastic. You should probably even ask your Christian family how to act the first time, just so you don't look strange and attract any attention. Joska's even bought some crosses for everyone to wear."

I moved my head to let her know I understood. She took a big breath and held me at arms length, looking into my eyes.

"You're going to be fine. Just be a good little Christian boy, and before you know it, the Russians or the Americans or the British or somebody will come in here and kick these German bastards back to hell where they came from. It won't be too long. You know?"

All I could manage was a soft, "I know."

She held me in her arms, and softly sang, *"Es geht alles voruber. Es geht alles verbi.."*

It was the refrain from a song that was known all over Europe. It was in German, but everyone sang it. It said, *"This will not go on for-*

ever. Everything has an end." It was just a pop song, but it became an anthem, promising a brighter tomorrow to Europe's oppressed. It gave hope to us that the Nazis would be defeated and there'd be peace again. Everyone sang it except the Nazis. She sang until I fell asleep. I had sought refuge, and being in my sister's arms was it. Not to this day, regardless of sleeping in luxury quarters in deluxe hotels or condominiums, in any country in the world, have I ever felt as protected and safe as that night, falling asleep in the arms of my big sister.

CHAPTER THIRTEEN

GOLD AND THE RED CROSS

With only one day to find temporary refuge my parents came up with a risky solution. Aunt Mariska, who had for years received a tiny monthly stipend from my mother, married a Gentile, and lived in an apartment in Budapest. We never saw them, because marrying outside the faith was still anathema, even for assimilated Jews like us. Of course, Rose' pledge to marry Joska after the war was an exception that even the Grand Rabbi of Jerusalem would approve. But these rarely seen relatives were not of the intelligentsia. The husband was a drunk, and when he fell under the influence of schnapps, which was more often than not, he revealed an attitude that was less than completely sympathetic to the victims of fascism. Considering Mariska's facial deformity it was considered a miracle that any man married her, so she tolerated everything just to avoid the stigma of living out her life as an old maid. Anyway, there was no time to come up with an alternate plan. There was only one full day remaining before the building became Christian, and with curfews for Jews, that meant they had mere hours to go. So, they packed up and prayed the estranged sister would let them in.

Curfew for Jews changed daily. The Nazis posted the changes, as well as any other edicts, on posters around town. If you didn't happen upon a freshly posted new regulation, or know someone who did, that was your tough luck. Disobey and you were dead. An old rule that was now being strongly enforced was the order for all Jews to wear the yellow star. And if that star was spotted on the street after curfew arrest or death awaited. Of course, I was already going out without the star, but my parents were nervous that they looked too obviously Jewish, and would get us all caught if they tried it. Their state of panic could sound an alarm, but if we had to be out after curfew we had no choice but to eschew the emblem. Of course even their departure, being at night, could attract undue attention. But powers beyond our control had already shaped our destiny, and we were committed. What we had feared since leaving Gyongyos was now at hand.

First things first. Joska had to get me and John to the Red Cross Orphanage. We didn't have far to go, because it was only five or six blocks from our apartment. Joska gave them some story about our parents dying in a bombing raid, and left us there, promising to return for us in a week.

While we were being enrolled at the Red Cross Orphanage Joska had my parents pack one suitcase apiece. Mother sent my father down to the coal bins to collect the Napoleons hidden there while she dug out the rest from the other secret caches. Meanwhile Rose removed the yellow stars from all their clothing, and quizzed them on their new names. She also ran them through the basics of Christianity, like who was Jesus and how to cross yourself.

That afternoon a gregarious Joska and his best friend, Stephen Seredy, showed up with some cans of paint, and ladders, making a racket. Joska told curious neighbors that he was going to move into the soon to be ex-apartment of some Jews, and he wanted to paint it first. He had brought the ladders in Stephen's car. When night fell it was arranged that my parents would go down the back stairs and use these ladders to climb over the ten foot fire wall out back, and down to the street. Once outside Joska would arrange for transport. Rose went back to her room in her own Christian building. If they would be caught they wanted to reduce their number even if it was only by one.

"See you in a few days, Rose," said mama.

"Mama, papa. Just do as Joska says, and you'll make it."

They gathered up their suitcases and whatever family heirlooms they could carry, and waited.

At exactly seven thirty that night, like a military exercise, they headed for the back stairwell as planned. If anyone heard them it might raise the specter of suspicion and they'd be caught. My father was nervous and sweating, but mother was confident. She loved Joska immeasurably and followed his plan. In her heart he replaced her dear son Josef, who had long ago disappeared into the void of war. And, just as she would have trusted her son, she blindly trusted Joska.

Though they had walked these halls a thousand times they now felt foreign and threatening. And they'd never noticed the creaky floor boards before either. Every time they brought one to life they froze and looked at each in horror. They waited to see if there was a reaction before continuing. The faint moan of those boards was probably not audible to anyone inside their apartments, but to them it sounded like an air raid siren. They expected an army of neighbors to burst forth from their doors demanding to know the cause of such a racket. When that didn't happen they gave sincere thanks for their momentary deafness, and pushed on. When they got to the rear of the building they climbed out through a small door. Mother stoically clambered through, though without any hint of deftness. Father, not in the least athletic, had to make several attempts. He was indecisive about which leg to lead with, and started and stopped what seemed like a hundred times before electing the right. When he finally stood straight up mother shot him a glance that spoke volumes, none of it repeatable.

When they stepped through that portal to no one's surprise Joska was waiting with the ladders. By now we all knew that if Joska Cséh said he was going to do something, or be somewhere at a certain time, it was a fact. He had already set a ladder against each side of the wall, and quickly demonstrated how to negotiate the obstacle. He scurried up and down the wooden devices as a silent blur, then brought their possessions over just as quickly. Mother, determined not to be a burden, bravely broke the record for climbing ladders in the middle aged matron class. Dreading a repeat rebuke from mother, father somehow matched mother's athletic feat. Down on terra firma again they picked up their things, and looked at Joska as to what to do next. They were outside after curfew, Jews without stars. It was the riskiest moment for my parents since the war began. They were in the shadows, and probably not visible from even ten feet away. Joska told them to be still and disappeared for just a moment, returning in a moment with a car he had hired for the occasion. In record time they loaded the trunk and poured into the car for their third car ride in as many years.

The driver asked for their destination, but mother didn't know the exact address of her sisters' apartment. She only knew the area and how to get there. As they drove off into the night Joska gave everyone a warning, "If we get stopped go along with whatever I say."

This declaration only made my father more aware that their situation could elevate to a predicament, and he became more nervous. He knew a lot of things could go wrong between here and the estranged sister's place. Mother, on the other hand, felt more assured. If Joska was in charge she was fearless. So she gave the driver commands en route, "Left here. No no, right! Make another right. Now left."

They drove through the streets of Budapest, praying that their only chance for refuge had survived the Russian bombs, and would not turn them away. Meanwhile, mother was focused.

"We're getting close. I recognize the area. Make a right at the next corner."

The driver followed mother's directions and turned down a dead end. The street was completely black, and only the car headlamps revealed the rubble in the road. Mother looked this was and that, but the moonless night made the buildings indistinguishable against the dark sky.

"Are we here, Riza? Cause this is a dead end," asked Joska.

Mother almost hit herself, 'No, go back. Must be the next…"

She froze at the sight of the three Gestapo agents at the end of the dead end, and stopped talking.

"That's exactly what not to do, Ri…Gertrude," admonished Joska.

"Everybody, listen. We're coming from visiting your dying mother, my grandmother, and we got lost on the way back, looking for some gas. Remember, you're my parents now, Gertrude and Klaus. And speak German! Hoch deutsch!"

Then, without a break in the conversation Joska got out of the car, and walked straight toward the Nazis. There was no doubt in his mind but that these fellows were about to do the same. He was also certain that a car turning into this street, suddenly breaking at the sighting of authorities, then retreating, was far too suspicious for any representative of the Third Reich to ignore. Rather than escalate things Joska wanted to level the playing field by mounting a subterfuge. He believed that the best defense against fascism was a strong offense, and he was already launched into that mood full throttle.

"Excuse me, sir," began Joska in perfect German, "I'm terribly sorry to bother you. But we were coming back from a last visit to my grandmother. Poor dear passed away not an hour ago. Ninety years old! And…er…well, this is a little embarrassing. I should have planned things better. Really. But we're dangerously low on gas, and someone near here indicated the presence of well…you know, somebody with some gas for sale. You wouldn't happen to know anything about this, would you, mein kapitan? The kids are asleep in the back seat and I was hoping to make it home without waking them up. I'm sure you understand."

The Nazis looked at Joska as if he was from another planet. This guy was yammering about social visits and gasoline as if nothing more important were going on. One of the Nazis calmly asked for Joska's papers, and the others assessed him as foolish and harmless, and went back to their conversation, probably having something to do with the following day's planned round up of Jews. After briefly shining their lights on the car they let Joska go with the mildest of Gestapo rebukes.

"We don't know anything about any gas. We have more important things that concern us. Now go home, please. Schnel!"

Joska shrugged, disappointed at not finding any gas, and came back to the car. He kept up the charade by starting an argument with the driver over how stupid he was for not tanking up earlier in the day when he had the chance. They kept up the argument until they were out of the street.

My mother thanked Joska profusely, but she knew they were not out of the woods yet.

"There it is," blurted out my mother. They all looked up and saw a light on in the window of a second story apartment. They parked as close to the door as possible, and piled out and into the vestibule of the building. Mother pulled Joska aside.

"Joska. Wait here. Ignatz and I…."

Joska corrected her, 'You mean Klaus. Get used to it, Gertrude. Please!"

Mother apologized, "I'm sorry. It won't happen again, I swear. Klaus and I will go up and speak to my sister. She is my sister, after all. She has to take us in. If we're not down here in five minutes just leave. But please, check on us tomorrow, because if her galut of a husband has two drinks he'll throw us out."

The ersatz Klaus and Gertrude quietly went upstairs. When they reached the landing they turned down a hall until they came to number 207. Mother knocked as softly as possible.

"Who is it?" asked the voice of a nervous woman. Mother practically pressed her lips to the door and speaking as softly as possible without actually whispering, said, "It's Riza. Open up."

Inside we could hear the muted conversation of a frightened woman and a bitter man. Bits and pieces of "What do they want? I don't know. Tell them to go away. It's late. She's my sister. Oh, now she's your sister? Some family!" Finally the door opened a crack, and they could see the terrified bulging eyes of Aunt Mariska.

"Mariska, let us in. We have nowhere to go."

My aunt turned around and repeated the obvious to her antagonistic spouse. She was clearly terrified of this man, and though it makes you wonder why she stayed with such a hard hearted person, the only thought was to see that door open more than ajar.

From within they heard, "Tell them to go away. We're not bothering them. Why should they bother us?" Mariska begged, "Please. They must be in terrible trouble or they wouldn't be here."

The man countered, "And we'll get into the same trouble if we let them in."

"My sister sent me money for years just to help me. We can't refuse her now. Please. Just for tonight."

Finally the masculine voice relented, "Just for tonight. You hear? One night and they're out!"

Blessedly, the door opened, and my parents went in. As soon as he was inside my father said, "Thank you, sir. Thank you for letting us in." Mariska's husband made a sour face and nodded begrudgingly. "I'm going to sleep. I have work in the morning."

Mariska was not alone with this sourpuss. She had a grown daughter who also lived there, who was equally intimidated by her father. But once he went to the bedroom they relaxed and greeted their long lost relatives more warmly. They brought out blankets and made some bedding on the floor. They offered some morsels to eat, and bid them good night. And for now, it was a good night. Tomorrow would be another ordeal.

While my parents were talking their way into Aunt Mariska's flat John and I were assessing our new home at the Red Cross Orphanage. It was wall to wall kids just sitting there talking. There were no activities. Not that these kids needed any. Most of them were happy just to be alive, having lost their families hours, days, or weeks before. We looked at their faces and wondered if they were all really Christian. Some looked Jewish, but I wasn't about to quiz anyone. We had to pretend to be Christians at any rate, and the less discussion about it the better. John and I knew precious little about gentile beliefs, so we were grateful for the don't ask, don't tell policy that seemed to pervade the atmosphere. We were in a totally alien place, but we were not alone. Mostly, we were grateful to have each other. John and I were not just family, but closest playmates. We were quite accustomed to spending time together, finding our own amusement. So, we explored our new turf, curious to learn how to exploit it.

When Klaus and Gertrude, nee Ignatz and Riza, awoke in the morning, their gentile host was blessedly absent, having already gone off to work. The more relaxed atmosphere allowed for a reunion of sorts. But after the perfunctory updates on everyone, the conversation came around to the situation at hand. Try as she might, my mother could not open Aunt Mariska's eyes to the reality of their plight. She didn't see the threat to Jews as fatal, and was blind to her own precarious position and that of her daughter. Marriage to a gentile afforded no immunity, and a half Jewish daughter was in as much peril as well. Mariska begged them to find another place, for she knew that her husband would have a drink that night when he came home and become belligerent. Clearly, there would have to be a Plan B.

When Joska came around to check on my parents he realized that they'd have to move. This was a challenge even for Joska, and he was pained to find himself at a dead-end. Seeing Joska's furrowed brow brought forth another miraculous declaration from my father, at least in the eyes of my mother. The very same police official who told my father of the coming Christianization of our apartment building might very well let us stay in his own place of residence. But to find out meant that the newly Christened Klaus would have to go out in the daylight to speak to his old friend. So, despite the mortal danger he acutely felt, he steeled himself enough to mount himself in the sidecar of Joska's motorcycle. Once he had taken this huge first step he was able to relax enough to survive the ride over to the police station. Ignatz regretted that all of the yellow stars had been removed from their clothing. He felt that going out in public in broad daylight was still acceptable, provided he wore the Mogen David. But the stars had been removed in anticipation of moving into their new Christian life at Hungaria Korut, and he now lacked that shield. So, he would truly have to forget Ignatz and become Klaus for real. No more time for rehearsal. The curtain was up.

They did not go quite all the way to the police station, but rather just short of that destination, timing their arrival to coincide with the usual time his friend took lunch. A creature of habit, he emerged from the station at precisely the noon hour. Joska and Ignatz left the parked cycle and followed the policeman into the café. He still had not noticed his old Jewish friend Ignatz, so Joska approached him first, and laid the ground work for their clandestine interview. The last thing they needed was for somebody to innocently blurt out my father's real name, especially when it differed from his new identity papers.

The policeman, it turned out, was every bit the true friend that my father claimed him to be, and welcomed him and my mother into his home. However, the circumstance was a repeat of their present predicament. For, while he was loyal, and no friend of fascism, his wife could not be counted among his rank. She was not really a Jew hater, but like so many Hungarians, she was not about to risk her life for them either. A day or two there would tax her tolerance for Abraham's tribe, and my folks would have to find yet another place to ride out the remainder of the week until Hungaria Korut opened up.

Our third day at the Red Cross dawned as uneventfully as the previous two. We were a little skinnier, and a little dirtier, and more consumed than ever over my parents' fate. The false sense of security we had at the orphanage gave us the liberty to worry over others, so I spent some time describing the building Joska had shown me to John. He was a little jealous over my tighter relationship with the heroic Joska, but he was glad to hear about Hungaria Korut just the same. As we had little else to discuss he asked endless questions about it, and I had to remind him over and over again that I never went inside, and that I was only there for about one minute, outside the whole time as well. But even these redundant conversations filled us with hope and confidence. How many other kids in this place knew there was a refuge out there for them? How many others had living parents on the outside? How many others had hope?

As anticipated, the policeman's wife threw my folks out after two nights. Actually, the cop might have made a more receptive home for my parents had he not been so forthright about their real identity. He could have said that their building had been bombed and that they needed a place for just five nights until their new place was vacant. But it was too late. The cop's innate goodness, consisting of an honesty sadly misplaced for this time and circumstance, had revealed too much and forced my folks out into the street with three nights to go.

It was a strange new universe for my mother, who had long ago given up expecting anything worthwhile from my father. But the man had actually facilitated their salvation for two whole days. And now the miracle would be repeated. While his years of socializing had produced mostly ephemeral acquaintances, he had made a couple of sincere friends. Now he would find one of them.

He selected Zoltan Fischle. He and his wife were Jewish, so he hoped they were still in one piece at their old place. And being Jewish it also seemed reasonable to anticipate refuge there, unless of course, their flat was already crammed with others in hiding. But once they got there Zoltan greeted them as warmly as hoped, and the next three days would be spent in relative peace. What's more, my father repaid them by inviting them to Hungaria Korut at the end of the week. It was an emotional invitation, because the Fischles were in the same boat as us, and our arrival was the miraculous salvation for which they had been praying for since the war began. When the third day expired Joska came and started the shuttle process to Hungaria Korut with Klaus and Gertrude.

Rose was waiting for her parents on the ground floor apartment. Joska had also reserved apartments on the second and third floors for the rest of our family. Like most of the city there was no electricity, but Rose had lit candles. They entered their faintly lit refuge, the light shedding just enough illumination to let her see the smiling faces of her family, while casting the meager quarters in a flattering light. The morning would reveal the plainness of the room, but for now it looked charming. As soon as they were inside Joska excused himself and drove off. There was some water in the bathtub and they washed their hands and face. Then they ate the simple meal that Rose had prepared while trying to get their bearings. Being in a new place is always a little disconcerting, but this was not just a usual moving day. They had sought refuge and found it. They were joyous. They went to bed that night crying tears of happiness. They were safe, or at least felt so, and the next day they would bring their entire family there, God willing.

In the morning Joska showed up with some food. While my parents ate Joska outlined their day. Regretfully it involved one last risky venture into the outside world. But it was necessary for two vital reasons. First, in their rush to flee the old apartment there hadn't been time to collect all of the Napoleons that were hidden around Budapest at relatives' apartments. Secondly, they would have to round up those relatives and bring them back a few at a time. At least they would be killing two birds with one stone. So, my parents returned to central Budapest with Joska, while Rose waited behind.

For now they had to make the rounds of the Weisz clan. At each stop mother introduced Joska, and explained the plan. The gratitude got so embarrassing that after two stops Joska waited in the car and let mother explain things. Anyway, if the plan worked, there'd be time enough later for all the appreciation in the world. Plus, time was short and there was much to do. Each brother, sister, uncle, aunt and cousin had to be profiled for suitability for using Cséh identity papers. Those who were a reasonable match were told to pack up for a move to Hungaria Korut at once. The others had to wait until the following day. Also, at each apartment mother dug out the gold Napoleons she'd hidden there. After the last visit had been made, and the last coin unearthed, Joska and my parents took off again for their new residence. But first they decided to stop at a small restaurant for one last meal in freedom. Once they'd get to Hungaria Korut they'd be in hiding there, and not go out again until a Russian tank drove down their street.

Joska parked about a hundred feet from the Postolok Café, and they strolled over to the modest restaurant with confidence. Joska made them feel safer than they had been in years. They walked in, and were glad to see it was mostly empty. They took a table in the back and slid in, placing the bag with the precious coins on the floor at their feet. They gave their order to the blasé waitress, and Joska tried to make small talk. Almost at once, another small group, two adults and a child, came in and sat down a few tables away from them. This made father noticeably nervous. They nodded their heads formally in our direction, as cordial strangers do. Mother and Joska politely returned the greeting. Actually, mother was a little giddy at being in a restaurant for the first time in memory. Also, she was in a celebratory mood, having just given so much good news to so many members of her family. Besides, she didn't feel as if anyone was looking at them. After all, they were just a Christian family looking for a little lunch. Then the Nazis came in.

There were four of them. They were just soldiers, and Joska didn't bat an eye. But mother and father reacted by lowering their eyes. It was what we had always trained ourselves to do, but was now the wrong reaction. The soldiers found a table and sat down. Father immediately felt lost and was agitated. He got up, and mumbled, "Oh! We're going to miss mass!" And before they knew it they were out of the restaurant and halfway down the street. Joska was stern.

"Klaus, we must keep a cool head. You could have attracted attention."

Father realized he had acted impulsively. "I'm so sorry. It won't happen again."

Mother suddenly gasped. "My God! Oh, dear God! No! We left the bag with the gold in the café." Mother started to weep. Joska was emphatic.

"Gertrude! Control yourself. We must not attract any more attention! Wait here." And before they could say anything Joska was on his way back to the Postolok Café.

Joska entered the café and made a limping beeline to where they had been sitting. An old man was now sitting there.

"Excuse me sir," said Joska.

He knelt down and felt around for the bag, but it was gone! Joska felt sick to his stomach.

"Looking for this?" The old man had the bag in his lap. Joska didn't know what the man's intentions were. Was this a game of finders keepers? For an eternally long five seconds the old man said nothing. Joska kept calm, and innocently replied, "Yes, I'm so glad you found it."

Finally, the man broadly smiled and said, "Here it is. You should be more careful!"

A very relieved Joska said, "You're so right. Thank you sir. Thank you very much!"

The old man kept smiling. "I'm happy to have the opportunity to help someone."

"Bless you," added Joska, and he rose to go. As he did so he glanced over at the soldiers' table. But just as he did one of the soldiers happened to fix his gaze on him.

At a moment like this the average person would have felt panic in his heart. And that panic could have been the first step on the way to doom. After all, avoiding the authorities had by now become a full time job for ninety percent of the people in Europe. Even if you were clean, with presumably nothing to fear, it was best not to confront the system. The potential for problems was too great. So everyone had long since developed a system of self preservation that began with avoiding eye contact at all costs. Once that rule was broken there was no going back. But whatever Joska now felt inside was his own business. Without the slightest hesitation he cocked his head to one side and narrowed his stare on his new uniformed friend. He straightened his head as if he had figured something out, and looked plainly at the

German soldier with bemused curiosity. The soldier was caught off guard. Joska advanced on the table, all good spirits and jubilation. In his perfect German he began his assault.

"Is your name Mueller? I think I know you! No no! Don't tell me. Vienna. Right?"

The soldier was flummoxed. "My name's not Mueller," he said.

"I can't believe it," continued Joska. "Then you must be related. Do you have any relatives with that name? A cousin? A second cousin? You are the spitting image of this corporal I met there. Rolf. Rolf Mueller. He got me some pictures."

By now all of the soldiers at the table were interested in this gregarious Austrian.

"Pictures?" marveled the soldier.

"You know! Pictures!"

The soldiers laughed at their slow to comprehend comrade. Joska raised his eyebrows. Then all of the soldiers laughed out loud. Joska forged ahead.

"They made my eyes pop out. I think a few of them were Jewish bitches, but what tits!"

Now the soldiers were rolling in laughter.

"If you're ever in Vienna you should look this Mueller up. It'll be like looking in a mirror I tell you."

All smiles, the private answered, "If I ever make it out of this stinking shit hole of a country I will. Thanks." Joska clicked his heels and had the last word, "Heil Hitler!"

He made it out the door and down the street where we my parents were waiting.

My mother was moved to tears, "You got it! God bless you, Joska!"

It was decided to forego lunch in a restaurant. Instead, they stopped at a market, and brought food back to Hungaria Korut. If mother had adored Joska before, now she absolutely worshipped him. The man had his hands on a small fortune and he dutifully brought it back to her. It's safe to estimate that ninety nine percent of the people in Budapest, nay, in Europe, could not have borne the temptation of that sack of gold. But Joska did. It was never forgotten.

Back at the Red Cross it was not gold that was on my mind, but food. They fed us twice a day in their cafeteria on the second floor, and there was no chance of going outside to scrounge for more. We were stuck there with absolutely nothing to do but wait for those meals.

The building was five stories tall, and there must have been two hundred kids on every floor, covering every inch of furniture and floor space. We got in there on the pretext of one of Joska's little white lies, that we were recently orphaned in a Russian bombing raid. But most of the kids there were not liars. They really had been orphaned in bombing raids, and they really were Christians. John was nervous, but I was too preoccupied looking for a way out to worry. I trusted Joska absolutely, but I had also learned not to count too heavily on just one person. He himself taught me that. Anyone, regardless of their charm or brains, could be killed in a moment. After all, Joska could be shot for what he was doing, or killed in a bombing raid like so many thousands of others. We couldn't just sit there and wait. We had to keep our eyes open for any other chance. Mine came along on my sixth day there.

I was sitting at the edge of a bunk with several other small children, shaking the sleep from my head, when a young Christian couple came in with a boy who was about my age and size. I didn't look directly at them, but I listened to them with all the focused energy of a spy.

"Now Thomas, daddy and I have to move all of our things to our new apartment."

Thomas?! This kid's name was Thomas?! Now, I was hanging on their every word.

The woman continued, "As soon as we're settled, just a day or two, we'll come back for you. Now here are your papers. It's your birth certificate. It says you're a Christian, so don't lose it. You don't want them to think you're a Jew. Don't worry. They'll take good care of you while you're here. We'll see you tomorrow or the next day. Give mummy a hug. Be a good boy. Bye-bye." And they were gone.

This was too good to be true! His name was Thomas and he was nearly the same age as me. No doubt. As soon as his mother mentioned his birth certificate I knew I was going to swipe it.

Upon hearing of the birth certificate my knee-jerk reaction was to steal it, but that doesn't make me a character out of Oliver Twist. It was a decidedly Dickensian atmosphere in which I was living, but there's no justice in comparing wartime survival tactics with routine civilized morality. Any semblance of normal social order had already been as soundly overcome by the Nazis as was the Polish cavalry in 1939. If you were going to live you had to depend on much more than manners.

From the moment I learned of this boy's birth certificate he was my new best friend. Actually, he was sad being left alone, and grateful to have someone who knew the ropes. Anyway, after the horrific story I told him about how my parents had been blown to bits in a bombing raid the week before he didn't feel so bad. At least, his parents were alive!

As soon as I decided to dedicate my time to this new boy I had to stop hanging out with John. He'd be on his own, but I knew that Joska would be coming back for him soon. He had food for now, so I didn't feel bad about it. Anyway, war had already molded him and everybody else into a survivalist. And John was no retard. He'd take the first chance he saw too. As for this boy Thomas, he was a Christian. If they doubted his Christianity they could pull down his pants and check for circumcision. It is true that there were some gentiles who were circumcised, having subscribed to the belief that it was cleaner. It was done at birth, and not after a week, like it was ritually done with Jewish babies, but the foreskin was missing, just the same. Generally though, gentile kids weren't circumcised, so he'd probably be okay. Of course, I say this in retrospect. The truth is, I didn't give him a second thought. I was focused solely on getting my hands on that birth certificate. Survival meant thinking about Thomas *numero uno*. If I didn't I was a goner. Don't get me wrong. I wasn't a complete animal, ready to steal food out of my own mother's mouth. But, short of that, I was ready to do anything to survive. By then Hungary was one big survival course.

After a day of hanging out with Thomas *numero dos* I knew everything about him, including in which pocket he kept his birth certificate. Having the same name as me was a real bonus. Too many people with false papers had had been tricked by clever Gestapo agents. If they suspected you had false papers they'd let you go on your way, only to calmly call your so-called name after about five seconds. If you didn't respond, as many people were not used to doing with a new name, it was your death sentence. But I would automatically answer to Thomas or Tommy. Kids were always called by their first names, so I would be safe. Another advantage about this kind of document was the lack of photograph. Birth certificates never have photos, because practically all new born babies look alike, wrinkled and bald with their eyes shut. So, with no wrong picture or name to react to, I'd be totally safe if I could just make it out of there.

That night I went to sleep in the bunk next to *numero dos*. I pretended to sleep, but after about two minutes I opened my eyes to make sure Thomas was still there. He was, but I thought it best to wait a little while to make sure he was sound asleep. After what I figured to be another half hour it was perfectly quiet except for the occasional cough.

Just pretending to be asleep was a talent I had perfected. It's really quite difficult. You lie down among a thousand sleeping kids and it's normal to fall asleep yourself. But I kept thinking about my parents and Joska and his motorcycle. I also thought about that movie Rose had snuck me into back in Gyongyos. I kept my mind active, and my eyes open. Finally, I decided to test things. I reached my arm out toward his sleeping form, and held it out in the air. Nobody noticed me. I drew my arm back. After a minute I did it again. Nobody said anything. I kept my arm in the air and immediately reached and slipped my hand into the pocket with the certificate. It was there and I withdrew it quickly and quietly, and stuffed it down my pants. I continued to watch him sleep. He was totally unaware. I got up, and went to the bathroom on a different floor. I unfolded the birth certificate and took a look at my new name. I was Thomas Molnár. Molnár! What an easy name to remember! Thomas was my own real first name, and Molnár was the last name of Hungary's most famous author. Even with my scant formal education I'd heard of him, so it was an easy name to remember. With no need to doctor photos or signatures, I was home free. This piece of paper was my passport to freedom, and worth its weight in gold. I committed to memory my place of birth and the exact date of my new birthday, then lay down for real.

Earlier that day Rose paid one last visit to Mrs. Barna's, where she had first met Joska. She needed to pick up a few last personal items. The building was remarkably intact, still officially Christian, and she had no trouble going directly upstairs. Even though she had a key she didn't feel she had the right to use it, as she no longer resided there. She knocked, and almost at once she recognized her old landlady's clopping gait coming toward the door. When she opened it she was delighted to see Rose.

"Maria Willem!" She hugged Rose. "I thought something had happened to you. Thank God you're alive!"

Rose looked around cautiously. "We're alone," said Mrs. Barna. "Sit and we'll chat."

Once seated in the little drawing room Mrs. Barna began, "So, what happened to you? One day you're here, and the next you disappear. Such a girl!"

Rose smiled at her concern. So far this apartment had proved itself the cradle of her family's liberty, so she felt just as confident as ever to tell Mrs. Barna the truth.

"Mrs. Barna, I left because I didn't want to get you into trouble."

"Go on, my dear," coaxed Mrs. Barna, half expecting what came next.

"You see, this is a Christian building, and…" Rose slowed for just a second, but Mrs. Barna picked up the slack.

"Because you're Jewish passing for Christian."

She didn't ask it, but stated it. What's more, she seemed delighted to know it.

"How did you know?"

Now Mrs. Barna stayed quiet, just looking at Rose with an affection that enveloped her. Rose stared back curiously until it finally dawned on her.

"No," Rose blurted out so suddenly that Mrs. Barna had to shush her and put a finger to her lips. Rose felt alarmed and ashamed, and momentarily went wide-eyed in horror.

"You too?"

Mrs. Barna, or whatever her name was, just nodded.

"But how did you know I was?"

The older woman just shrugged. "Takes one to know one!"

Then they both laughed and hugged. Rose told her old landlady all about Joska and her family.

"Such a mensch. If only all Christians were like that…" She trailed off and fell silently melancholy, remembering who knows what unspoken horrors of her own family.

Rose took the woman's hands in hers and whispered, "I'm Rose Weisz. Who are you?"

"Abigail Unger."

They stared at each other for several more moments, then Mrs. Unger spoke in a regular voice,

"Don't be a stranger, Maria Willem."

Rose promised, "I won't."

She took out her old key, held it up for her new friend to see, and placed it down on the table. Abigail nodded knowingly, and Rose left.

CHAPTER FOURTEEN

THE STENCH OF DEATH

The Hungarian Red Cross in 1944 had a very restricted schedule. There were only two activities, loitering and eating. The first activity was not an activity at all, chiefly composed of waiting around most of the time for the second activity. We hung out day and night, thinking of a way to get someplace better, and anticipating one of the two meager meals. We got an early breakfast and mid afternoon dinner, neither of which, under normal circumstances, was worthy of anticipation. The more you looked forward to it the bigger the disappointment. Anyway, I decided not to wait for breakfast. I was hungry, but I had to get out of there before that kid discovered his missing papers and made a stink. People came and left all the time, so my departure would hardly be noticed. It wasn't jail, so I just walked out.

I got down to the street and walked away as fast as I dare, lest I attract attention. After a few blocks I figured nobody from the Red Cross was running after me, so I slowed down to a more leisurely pace. I was Thomas Molnár, born in Budapest, a Christian, and just one year younger than my actual age. As I walked along I repeated my vital statistics over and over again in my head. The orphanage was in Pest, so at least I was on the eastern side of town where my family was. I'd have to walk about five miles to get to the eastern outskirts of town and the Hungaria Korut beltway. Once there I only had to find number sixty-three and I'd be safe. But between me and my parents were five miles of bombed out train yards and factories, partisan fighting, Nyilasok punks, and allied raids, all in Nazi controlled territory. Plus, it was winter and I only had on a jacket. When you add it all up, I was starving, freezing, and scared out of my mind.

Though I'd lived in Budapest for five years I was now seeing more of it than I ever had before. Block after block I walked through alternating cityscapes. One moment there was an aristocratic looking building, and the next a mountain of rubble where another had been. I saw buildings with its sides blown out, still occupied with its tenants clinging to the pathetic remnants of their former lives. People sat in easy chairs as if it were normal not to have walls, like a people zoo with humans on display in their natural habitat. There were the dead and dying on the sidewalks and streets. People walked by pushing wheel barrows piled up with corpses. The bloated bodies of dead cats and dogs, long since abandoned by masters too hungry to share with mere pets, were feasted on by swarming maggots. Women and children, desperate for warmth, stripped corpses of their clothes. Two women, not ten feet from me, were fighting over a scarf both found at the same time. A man collapsed next to me, and I heard his retching and coughing as I moved on. I didn't look back. I never looked back. I only wanted to get to safety. Stopping meant dying.

Liget Park offered me a safer route. The zoo was closed, and no electricity meant no rides, not that anyone visited in winter anyway. It was like an abandoned Central Park. I'd be alone for a good mile, so I veered in that direction. It meant a slightly longer journey, but a safer one.

Every step I took was to the soundtrack of gunfire. There was the distant report of small arms and artillery, and the droning of the bombers. They sounded far off to the north, and ahead of me to the east.

A family came out of nowhere and was now walking along my route.

"Have you seen any Krauts?," the man asked.

"Uh-uh," was all I gave him in response.

I didn't want to get involved in a conversation, nothing to sap my energy. One of the kids pried further.

"Have you got anything to eat?"

I just shook my head and kept going. The park was straight ahead. The other kid chimed in.

"Where you headed?"

I allowed him one syllable, "Home!"

I wished they'd leave me alone. I was practically running, almost as much from them as toward the park. The trees would hide me. Just let me get there. I was a little kid, so maybe nobody would notice me. And then we were there. The two kids seemed delighted to see it.

"Oh Daddy, the park!"

I didn't even bother to stop and look at the big statue at the entrance. It's a monument to the great heroes of Hungary, with Attila the Hun and whoever else they considered worthy of being cast in bronze at the time. But I was completely unconcerned, both for the heroes of Hungary and for the family that insisted on traveling with me. The glee of the children at entering the park was cut off when we both observed the next family. It was a man and wife and three children. But they were as lifeless as the heroes of Hungary. The Nazis had strung them up from some trees. Signs hung on all of them. 'THEY HID JEWS!' 'TRAITORS!' My travel mates stopped in horror. I stopped for a moment too, but realized I'd better keep moving if I didn't want to join either of these families.

Alone now, I ran through the park. I passed the still Ferris wheel and roller coaster. I went right by the merry-go-round without as much as a sidelong glance, and past the ice cream and sausage kiosks. I had to keep going. I got off the paved path and ran through the woods. I started to think there might be wolves among the trees. How crazy it would be if I was afraid of people, but an animal would kill and eat me. The thought only made me hungrier myself, and I refocused on getting to Hungaria Korut and my parent's apartment. I was almost crying now with desperation. What if my parents were caught? Would they be there when I got there? But they were with Joska, so they must be alright! I would get there and they'd be glad to see me. I'd see Rose. Just thinking of seeing her made me happy and excited. I started going even faster. I thought about Joska and our first motorcycle adventure and it made me laugh out loud. The sound of my own laughter startled me. I sounded like a madman, and I looked around as if I had done something wrong, broken some law.

By now I was running so fast it was fatiguing. I saw a log and sat down on it to rest for a few minutes. It was the first chance I'd had that day to look back from where I'd come. Smoke was rising from somewhere in the city, and I knew it must have been an air raid. It puzzled me as to why I hadn't heard it, and then I thought it might have been one of those bombs that don't go off right away. They were the worst, because they exploded with no warning. Digging them up and disposing of them was one of the jobs that my brother Sandor had to do. I thought about him and how odd it was that he survived all that and got killed by a brick that just happened to fall. And I thought about my brother Josef and what might have happened to him. All the thoughts of my family came rushing back to me, and I wondered if I'd ever see my brother or Anci ever again. I even wondered if I'd ever see John again. He was still back in the Red Cross Orphanage. I never said goodbye or let him in on my plan to rob that kid or anything. It was all about survival, and I hoped Joska would go back and pick him up quick. Then I picked myself up and started walking again. Unconsciously I started to sing.

Es geht alles voruber. Es geht alles verbi. "Nothing lasts forever. Everything has an end."

I sang it over and over again in my poor German accent, "Es geht alles voruber. Es geht alles verbi." And before I knew it I was out of the park and that much closer to my parents.

The park had hidden me from more than people. It had hidden me from the ubiquitous stench of the bombed out city. The rubble hid dead bodies, but it didn't hide the smell. Wherever you went it stunk. Dead people. Dead dogs. Dead horses. If you've never smelled a corpse, then suddenly get exposed to it, you think it's sickening and unbearable. Morning, noon, and night it was in the air. It permeated your clothes, and was inescapable. But we actually got used to it. We slept through it, and we even managed to eat through it. It's the ultimate proof that you can get used to anything.

Ahead of me now were huge columns of smoke. It was the railroad yards, one of the main targets of bombing raids. Six years earlier my sister Yolie had boarded the Orient Express here. It had been palatial. Now it was little more than a junk yard that the Nazis had to constantly repair. The closer I got the more I heard these loud wrenching mechanical noises, like gears without oil. When I was only a block or two from the yard I was greeted by wounded people crawling away from the wreckage. They were bleeding and burnt, and most of them were screaming in pain. There had been a raid there the day before and the carnage was tremendous. Worst of all it blocked my path.

As I approached the main rail line a man off to my left tried to stand up. It looked like he had one leg blown off. He froze, gagged and wretched, and fell down. I passed his still body and stood before an entire freight train that looked as if a giant had picked up his toy, twisted it, and thrown it back down. It was one of those endlessly long freight trains, and it was lying on its side. To go around it meant time. But the locomotive that had been tossed up by a bomb was leaning half on another locomotive on the ground. There was just enough space for me to crawl on the ground under it to the other side. I didn't even think about it. I got down on my hands and knees and wriggled through to the other side of the train. Then I stood up and ran. I heard a thundering crash behind me, but I didn't dare look back. A few more blocks and I'd make it to Hungaria Korut.

The highway was littered with burnt out trucks. I crossed it, because I remembered the apartment building was on the far side, the east side. I made it quickly, but I didn't know if I was south or north of the building. I started looking for a building with a number on it. I found a burning factory but it had no address anywhere visible. I went on to the next one, about a block away. It said number 17. I went another block and found another factory. It said 10. I was going the wrong way. I was exhausted, but I knew I wasn't far. Please, let me make it. I had come this far. I sang, "Es geht alles voruber. Es geht alles verbi." One block. Number 33. Another block. Number 42. Another building. Number 48. Only two blocks to go. "Es geht alles voruber." Joska's big beautiful motorcycle was parked outside that building up ahead. I made it! "Es geht alles verbi."

Everyone was shocked but thrilled to see me. Joska was too, if a little surprised. They had just gotten there that very morning, the first day the building was vacant. As soon as I was through the door I collapsed. They brought me some soup to drink and I greedily consumed it. After I ate I washed my face, and told them about Thomas Molnár. Mother looked worried, because she was still unaccustomed to wartime chicanery, but when she saw how impressed everyone else was with my caper, she joined in the congratulations.

"Tommy, old man," effused a jubilant Joska, "You are a helluva guy!"

Rose, my old accomplice in movie smuggling, was equally impressed, and gave me a big hug and kiss on my cheek.

"You rascal. You darling little rascal!" Her reverie suddenly stopped. "John! What about John?"

Now everyone was concerned. But Joska spoke up.

"Don't worry. I know this watchmaker." And that was enough.

Nobody gave John another thought. If Joska said not to worry we didn't.

"This man lives alone, and could use whatever we pay him. He's a kind man, and would gladly hide the boy. I was thinking of him for Tommy, but it's more of an emergency right now for John. I'll go tomorrow and speak to him. If it's okay with him I can get John over there almost at once."

Rose started to thank him, but caught herself. "Good idea," she said, as if it were a strategic decision. Joska couldn't stand any more gratitude. He wanted us to consider him just one of us, and that we were all in this together. And we actually did come to take his benevolence in our stride. Like the smell of death we actually became accustomed to having a savior. As embarrassing as it might have been for Joska, mother couldn't resist sharing with me how he had saved the money back at the restaurant. In recollecting it she even managed to get a dig into Dad. It was reassuring to see some normalcy returning to our lives. Joska had saved us to the point that my parents could argue again like old times. But mother was in earnest about what Joska had done, and adored him all the more.

"He could have gone back for the money and taken off with it. What a mensch!"

Joska did not know how true his words were when he characterized John's situation as an emergency. That column of smoke that I saw rising out of central Budapest while resting on that log in Liget Park, was Gestapo headquarters. The Nazi bureaucrats lost their offices in a bombing raid and they needed to find new ones at once. They had their eyes on the Hungarian Red Cross, and their plan to evacuate the building made getting John out of there a matter of life and death.

They fed me something solid and I lay down to rest. I don't know how long I slept but when I woke up I noticed Joska and Rose were over in a corner talking softly. Once in a while they looked over at me. When I caught them they smiled quickly as if they had been caught doing something wrong, and felt guilty. Joska was doing most of the talking, and Rose nodded a lot, glancing sideways at me from time to time. Several times she nodded begrudgingly. What Joska was explaining to Rose was cold, but realistic and necessary. It would appear to be heartless to explain it to my mother, but Rose understood. Even though we had this apartment, and our family would be occupying over half the building, it was still best if John and I lived somewhere else. We were kids, and we tended to behave unpredictably. Either one of us might do something to give us all away. On the other hand, it was also for the kids' protection. So many fake Christians in one building might attract suspicion and end up getting the children killed along with the adults. In the end it was decided that John and I would be placed with some Christian families. When they told me this they only explained the second part of the equation. They were right on both counts, of course. Sixty three Hungaria Korut was filling up with family, and their lives could be placed in jeopardy by the unpredictable shenanigans of kids like us.

My parents shared a ground floor apartment with Rose, Joska, and my Grandfather. My grandmother had died from natural causes the year before, and my grandfather had to close down his famous café, because it was a Jewish owned business. Leopold Krausz, my grandfather, was an aristocratic man with a huge moustache and a penchant for smoking a pipe. He had been one of the most important impresarios of the night club set prior to the war, and now he was hiding with us.

Others at sixty three Hungaria Korut included my Uncle Sandor Kurti and his wife Adel, along with their grown children Gyuri, Bandi and Andrew. They all lived upstairs. Andrew died from a brain tumor while in hiding with us, so we cannot blame his death directly on the war. He was like so many who died from the horrendous lack of medicine and proper medical attention. Nearly everything that had to do with keeping a person alive was dedicated exclusively to men in uniform.

Kids weren't the only liability. There was Lajos, Uncle Sandor's nephew, who was a part time actor and full time bonvivant. But, unlike my father, who took a prudent hiatus from this avocation, Lajos persisted in socializing. He drank, and we even suspected he did some kind of dope. Against the warnings and exhortations of everybody he selfishly continued to go out as if he were immune to the war. We always feared he'd get caught, not so much for his sake, but for our own. Nobody doubted that he'd fold under interrogation and reveal our hiding place.

Elizabeth, the wife of my brother Josef, was also on the second floor, along with her daughter, Vera. Her own mother, Margit, was there as well. Father's cousin, Camila Kent, was there too.

When we had first arrived in Budapest, years before, we stayed briefly with Uncle Marton. Now, we were glad to be able to repay that debt. He moved in along with his entire family: his wife Szidi, daughter Rose, sister Ilonka, brother Mano and his wife Margit. To distinguish the three Roses they were called Brown Rose and Red Rose, for their hair, and Csipigo Rose, which means talkative Rose. And the in-laws of Rose's missing husband moved in too.

Not everyone was family. Up on the third floor was Zoltan Fischle, my father's best friend. Zoltan brought his wife as well. They were both pleasantly surprised that their old friend Ignatz had come through with anything so clever. Rounding out the population were sixteen other cousins, spread out in apartments on the second and third floors. With forty two Jews hiding in a single building a Nazi raid would certainly earn its leader a big medal.

One final risk was the presence of residents in the building who were supposedly authentic Christians. They could have been phonies like us, but we had to assume they were the real thing. So, nobody spoke Yiddish, or did anything that might conceivably tip our hand. Lajos, with typical theatricality, even suggested that we learn carols in preparation for Christmas. But no matter how much preparation or rehearsal the residents of Hungaria Korut had they lived with unending stress as long as they were there. They slept with one eye open when they slept at all.

CHAPTER FIFTEEN

RUNNING RISKS AND THE TRUTH ABOUT NAZIS

$\mathcal{B}$etween 1944 and 1945 the Weisz family, and all Hungarian Jewry, faced their hardest times.

The Nyilosak, as well as the whole German ge*wermacht,* was out-flanked, outnumbered, and outgunned. It was obvious that the Russians would plow through. Plus the Americans and the Reds both were bombing away. The fascists knew their cause was lost. But nothing dissuaded them from carrying on with the killing. And when the Hungarians didn't display the required resolve to overcome inertia, Third Reich administrators were installed to replace them. The SS took over and packed the Budapest ghetto tighter than ever.

Being placed inside the ghetto was the last step before being shipped off to the camps. In a sense it was a concentration camp in and of itself. You were confined and escape was impossible. There was no food, and people were dying every day. With no place to put the bodies of those who had died from disease and starvation, they were placed in the windows of the closed shops, piled up like cords of wood. The Budapest winter prevented the corpses from rapidly decomposing. At least until the spring thaw.

There was one resident of the ghetto whose presence demonstrated how deeply Nazi racist hatred ran, the *cigane. Cigane* is what they called gypsies in Hungary, a group reviled above all others. It seems hard to believe, but the cigane was perhaps hated even more than Jewry. For example, the Third Reich had to promote anti-Semitism through an intense propaganda campaign, while the sub-human classification of the *cigane* was such a foregone conclusion that no reeducation process was necessary. They had never been accepted in mixed society, and their existence was so much in jeopardy that some gypsies actually tried to pass as Jewish to improve their own pathetic chances of survival.

Being sent to the Budapest ghetto at all was practically a death sentence. Once in nobody could get you out. With excellent contacts and influence perhaps the Gestapo could be convinced that a mistake had been made in one case. But an entire family of forty two people? Thanks to the Cséh family we were spared that.

In Joska's quest to round up papers he found a woman with two very good sets. Her parents had died together in the same car accident just two years earlier. This was a real find. The ages were close enough to an aunt and uncle to match. Although Joska was thrilled to come across the papers, he still bargained the women down, practically getting a twofer. He acted only mildly interested in the papers, and drove the price down as low as he could. The woman was almost in tears over it, but needed the money and accepted Joska's offer.

Joska was indeed treating the whole affair as a business, because he reasoned that he had to stretch the budget. There was no way of knowing if the price would go up suddenly, so he had to make it last. He bargained for the papers of those recently killed, and sometimes even made some people cry over his cold hearted negotiations. He was pragmatic, and made everyone see that what they were doing was all for the best. And what if he did make some survivors cry? She might have been needy for money, but my aunt and uncle were needy for life. So, he had no compulsion over taking advantage of any situation. Being tough was a credo for survival, not just for Jews, but for anyone, in or out of the camps and ghettos. If you were anything but tough how would you get that extra crust of bread before someone else?! And who could blame them? Uniformed armed men come to your door, politely pound on it, and then officially inquire as to the presence of any persons of Jewish persuasion in the building. Unless you're incredibly brave you tell them what they want to know. However, most people were neither courageous nor compensated well enough to lie, so they routinely spilt their guts.

Normalcy was passé, and everyday brought new risks. Even such a simple thing as a taxi ride could be fatal. More than one person on the first leg of an escape attempt had accidentally alerted a taxi driver with their suspicious behavior. You don't earn much money or recognition driving a taxi cab, so if you could report any activity to the Nyilasok or Gestapo that smacked of mistrust you might be rewarded for your patriotic zeal. So, Joska avoided the involvement of strangers whenever possible, such as hiring taxis, and preferred to use his trusty motorcycle. With the sidecar reattached he took me to the apartment of the Christian Debrecens for hiding, then picked up a grateful John from the Red Cross Orphanage and drove him to his new home, stopping only long enough to buy him something to eat. John had long suffered deep depression, and was now nearly catatonic. He had been better, but after being left at the Red Cross center, especially after I had left, his feelings of abandonment were back and redoubled. And now he was to be separated from me, his playmate and only solace. It was unbearable for him. But they had to deal with reality. Joska knelt down and whispered.

"Mr. Hargitay is a nice man. Quiet, old fashioned and conservative, but very nice. He'll protect you. And I'll come and see you often. You stay indoors, because we don't have papers for you. As soon as I do I'll bring them to you and things can be more normal again. Here."

He reached into his overcoat pocket and pulled out a small bag. He opened it and pulled out a crucifix. John was shocked. His emotions were so delicate at that time Joska was worried he might break down.

"Don't worry, Johnny, "Joska consoled, "This will protect you. It's just for now."

As he slid it over John's neck, Joska added his encouragement.

"It'll make Mr. Hargitay feel more comfortable too. And we need to make our protectors feel sure about what they're doing. It's for the best, all the way around."

It was exactly nine o'clock, and just as Joska looked at his watch the apartment door opened as prearranged. This way there would be no alarming knock on anyone's door, making their presence less obtrusive. Our lives were now becoming uncomfortably like spy novels. For Joska it might have seemed adventurous, but for the rest of us it was terrifying. He and John silently entered. Mr. Hargitay quietly closed the door again, and smiled down at John.

"John, say hello to Mr. Hargitay."

John glanced up shyly and managed to mumble, "Hi."

The old gentleman was courteous in an old worldly sort of way, and did his best to make his new room mate feel at home. "Nice to meet you John."

Joska reassured him, 'As I explained to you yesterday, this is all a little tough on him. First his parents go away, then…" But the old man cut him off.

"I understand. This war is hell on all of us. We'll be fine. Would you like a little brandy before you go?"

Joska accepted, and paid Mr. Hargitay a few Napoleons while they exchanged pleasantries. When he got up to go John flung himself at Joska and clung to him. He let John hug his leg for a while, and then knelt down.

"Before you know it this will all be over, and you'll be with your parents in America. They live only to see you again. Don't disappoint them. Stay inside. Stay quiet. Stay safe. Do what Mr. Hargitay says. We're gonna make it, right pal?"

John made a stiff upper lip, and Joska got up and rubbed the top of his head. When he left the apartment he stopped and sighed. With death all around him he still cared for the fragile emotions of a little boy. And under his breath he cursed, "Nazi bastards."

Sixteen hours after John moved in with the old watch maker the Gestapo moved into the Red Cross Orphanage. As it was now headquarters of an important Third Reich facility orphans were hardly desired there. So the ever efficient Nazis took the thousand Christian Hungarian orphans down to the Danube and machine-gunned them into the river. End of story.

While Normandy Beach was being overrun by the allies the Nyilasok and the Nazis were doing their worst to the less attractive tribes of Hungary. The Eastern front edged closer every day, and the Western was growing more threatening to fascist concerns by the minute. With a million of its enemies already on freed French soil, any sane military analyst of the Third Reich should have stridently recommended the commitment of every uniformed German and Hungarian man to fight at either of the two fronts. But the murderous bullies could not relent in their cowardly, pointless war against old men, women and children. My accusation of cowardice is hardly controversial, so I'll dedicate the rest of this brief chapter to the futility of their endeavor.

Basically, the best -or worst- efforts of the Nazis were pointless, because they were absolutely doomed from the very beginning. Contemplating the German character one can only conclude that they knew they didn't have a chance, even from the start. At least Adolph himself. To understand this we must observe the German character, which requires a look at their mythology.

The quintessential Teutonic hero is the legendary knight Siegfried who, despite his prowess and magic accoutrement, is deluded by enchantment, and defeated. Likewise, der fuehrer fights against dragons, though imaginary, aware he'll ultimately be betrayed by the treachery inherent in this world. He sees cosmic conspiracy everywhere, and though he's cognizant of his inability to overcome it, he struggles against it, confidant in the white knight nobility of the gesture. He is doomed before he begins, so he and his delusional cronies play Teutonic knights as if it were a session of Dungeons and Dragons. Hidden behind Siegfried's cloak they are as deluded by the corrupt world as deeply as their revered knight himself, and imagine they are immune to the death they unleash. As certain of eventual failure as a kid playing a tough video game, the Nazis only goal is to rack up the highest possible score, or head count, before the game ends. Like kids gripping a video game control, they're kill crazy.

First, they strike out at their imagined enemies. Then, having generated real ones, they go to the next level and kill as many of them as they can. Besieged on the next level, they begin killing their own kind. Trapped, they kill those closest, including pets and family. Vanquished, with no one else left to kill, they revert to killing the only people they can get their hands on, themselves. The Nazis were kill crazy, and their only regret was not being able to rack up a higher score before the buzzer rang. Deluded by myth they had no tether to reality. They actually preferred fantasy to fact. And nothing, no matter how obvious, could wake them from their dream state. Nothing demonstrates that with greater clarity than the Berlin Olympics.

When the Nazi supermen hosted the 1936 games Jesse Owens, along with nine of his fellow black athletes, repeatedly beat the master race, rubbing their noses in the fallacy of racial superiority. All the little Siegfrieds saw their credo was hogwash, yet they persisted. So, they would waste their lives in a phantasmagorical exercise, and waste as much of the world as possible in the process. But the victims were all too real. And in Budapest everyday that reality was closing in.

Josef Cséh, ca 1939

My immediate family, early 1940. Back: Anci, Rose, Josef, Yolie, Sandor. Front: Grandma, Grandpa, my mother with my nephew John, my father and me.

The Synagogue of Gyongyos. By war's end it was completely destroyed.

Josef Cséh, ca 1939

My immediate family, early 1940. Back: Anci, Rose, Josef, Yolie, Sandor.
Front: Grandma, Grandpa, my mother with my nephew John, my father
and me.

The Synagogue of Gyongyos. By war's end it was completely destroyed.

My grandparents' café in the Buda side of town, before the war

Uncle Imre's jewelry store in Budapest. Pictured leaving the store is the Prince of Wales.

My big sister, Rose, two years before the outbreak of war.

Rose, on the balcony outside our apartment, overlooking the inner courtyard of the building in Budapest.

My sister Yolie, circa 1935, prior to her marriage.

My brother Sandor, shortly before being conscripted into the Work Brigade.

Rose in a rare tranquil moment during the war

Anci was the only member of our family to be deported to a concentration camp. We were close in our childhood, and I've been grateful everyday of my life to have her returned to us.

An adorable Hungarian folk dancer, back in Gyonyos, ca 1937.

A young married woman in Soviet Hungary.

1945: A few months after returning from Aushwitz. Her sores had healed, and her hair was growing out.

Post war: Anci, a friend, rose, and the only picture of a young Joska, our hero.

Eldest son Josef, back from years in Siberia, with his daughter Vera.

My mother and me, around the time of my Bar Mitzvah in liberated Budapest.

My nephew John, recently reunited with his parents in New York.

Me and my dog in Santo Domingo.

I become a true Yankee, an American G.I

Forty years after the war my sisters are happy and healthy in the United
States. Anci, Elizabeth, Yolie, a friend, Rose.

Joska and me in Pecs, Hungary in 2007

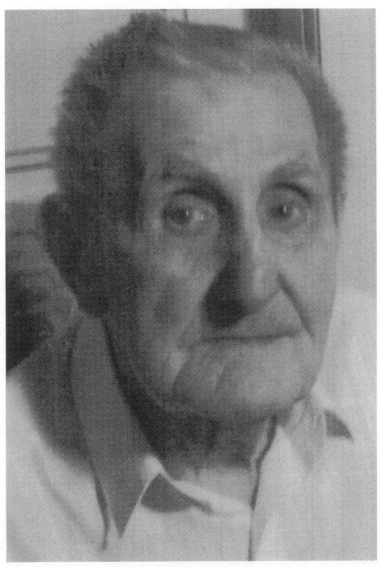

Josef Cséh, our hero!

CHAPTER SIXTEEN

AN AIR RAID PRIMER

With inflation being of more immediate concern to fearless leader Horthy than murdered orphans, he revamped our entire miserable economy. To make that change complete he relegated the pengo to the annals of Hungarian financial history and renamed our monetary unit the forint. Now, in addition to coping with the war, everyone had to learn to deal with a new coin and value. A nearly symbolic gesture at best, it was the last political act of the landlocked exadmiral's quarter century of leading his kingless kingdom nowhere. Soon after, he fell from Adolph's fickle favor and the Nazis had him imprisoned, which was the usual fate for Hitler's underachieving partners in crime.

While authentic gentile children were being blasted to bits this counterfeit Christian waited at sixty-three Hungaria Korut for Joska to take me to my next refuge. It was a military style exercise, and I was ready. Behind my child's exterior was somebody far more grown up than anyone had a right to expect. After all, life was no longer school and play. Thousands of people were out there hunting me, and I knew it. There were uniformed policemen and soldiers of various regimes and status, and plainclothesmen lurked in every shadow. Armed thugs roamed the streets like predators, looking for the day's prey, merrily betting among themselves who could kill more. And our saviors were dropping the same bombs on me as their enemy. To survive I had to know everything any adult knew, and more than most. Plus, I had to learn the lay of the land and how it changed daily. Sometimes it changed by the minute, like during air raids.

You could have papers proclaiming you to be Hitler's own son, but it didn't help during an air raid. Bombs are not selective. To their credit, the Americans did try to be selective and strategic, targeting factories, refineries and rail yards. The Russians, on the other hand, were not overly concerned with pin point accuracy. In reality they didn't feel they had to be. This was total war, not waged politely between armies on the field of battle, but against entire populations. From the Russian point of view, as long as the bomb hit the city it was a bull's eye!

No city on the planet, at that time in history, was adequately prepared to protect its citizenry from bombing raids. How could they? The previous global conflict had no experience with mass bombing from above. The Great War had biplanes and triplanes that occasionally dropped a few small bombs from very low altitudes. Their pilots were dashing cavaliers in the clouds, imbued with an elite ethos that would have made it unthinkable for them to unleash blind death from above on innocent noncombatants. As is always the case with military history, the technological advance of weaponry catches their humans targets by surprise, and defense against it takes longer to develop than the actual weapons do in the first place. So, Budapest, like most other European cities, offered as defense, nothing more than subway stations and basement coal bins, neither of which was originally designed to withstand modern bombers and their payloads.

The subway stations, or metros as they're called in Europe, could hold hundreds of people. Many fled there, finding the comfort of numbers as illusory protection. But when the sirens went off most people ran down to the basements in their apartment buildings and hid in their coal bins. Each apartment had its own coal bin, and it was just large enough to squeeze in the family. But I found coal bins, the metro, or any other indoor facility, to be nothing more than death traps. They gave the appearance of safety, because you couldn't see the destruction just outside. And, on occasion, the metros withstood an indirect hit or two. But a direct hit meant death, and a pretty horrible one at that. Not only do bombs explode, but they bring fire along with them. And if you were indoors you couldn't get outside fast enough

136

to escape the flames. Especially if you were in a basement coal bin. If a bomb fell even near one of those the flames surged in like a cannon shot and you were cooked. So, I had my own ritual when the air raid siren went off. I ran outside.

First I listened to the sound. If it was a low hum it was the Americans, coming from the west. American bombers were only heard, because they were too high to be visible. They were also too high to be hit by anti-aircraft, so I never saw one shot down either. They were also slightly less frightening than the Russians because of their attempts at strategic bombing. I always lived in a residential area, but I was always afraid for my family, because 63 Hungaria Korut was in a factory zone. But there wasn't much in the way of planning I could do if it was an American raid. I just prayed they'd be accurate and not accidentally hit our apartment building. The Russians were a whole other animal. They were louder, because they were lower, and you could see them as well as hear them. Being outside during a Russian bombing raid gave me a few distinct advantages. I could see the pattern of the planes, and in what direction they were heading. I'd run a flanking maneuver, keeping my eyes on the sky as I ran toward them. That is, if they flew west I ran east. This closed the gap between me and the bombers quicker, and accelerated the speed of their passing. There wasn't any point running in the same direction as the planes, because you can't outrun them. Better to close the gap quickly. The most dangerous planes were the ones that got out of formation. They were unpredictable. Another advantage of being outside was better protection from the fires. Inside a building a bomb's flames were trapped by walls in a reduced area, and channeled along a corridor, concentrating their strength until they burst into a small area and turned it into an oven. Outside, explosions and flames spread upward and outward, fanning out. On more than one occasion a bomb fell relatively close to me, and the flames shot just over my head. Also, your ear gets used to the sound of a falling bomb. When you hear its whistle you know it's close, so you change your bearing and run in the opposite direction as fast as you can, and throw yourself down. I was as wise as an adult had to be, but I could run like the kid that I was. I'd run for blocks and blocks, but no matter where you were during an air raid the noise was deafening. And no matter how many times you went through it you didn't get used to it. It was the one thing to which you could not become accustomed. It was too loud, ground shaking, and life threatening to become commonplace. The sky was filled with an ominous drone that started minutes before the explosions, and lasted to just as long afterwards. Anti-aircraft barrages made constant explosions. The screaming lasted from the first detonation till the last. It was a ferocious din. And the danger was incalculable. If just a bullet, tiny by comparison, with a few grains of gun powder to propel it, can cause terrible pain and death, imagine the havoc unleashed by a bomb, which is a hundred times its size. The force of the blast sends countless shards of jagged metal of all sizes ripping through the air at a thousand miles an hour. If whatever it hits is inanimate it crumbles and burns. If whatever it hits is animate it dies and is left unrecognizable. The impact of the explosion alone flattens everything for two hundred feet all around. If you're within a block of one going off the force of the shock wave crushes your organs and you pass your last seconds in excruciating agony. Another block beyond that and it can still fling you against the wall like a rag doll, crushing your bones. Sometimes a plane was shot down or simply crashed on its own. The planes fell, totally out of control at two hundred miles per hour, spinning off pieces of propeller and fuselage. On the way down their seventy caliber machine guns might also be firing, spewing out their giant rounds in all directions. When they crashed it was ten times the explosion of one of their bombs. All the gasoline went up in a fiery ball and rained down liquid death. Worse, it might still have some of its bomb load on board, which could all go off at once on impact. It's chaos. Buildings fall. Bricks and glass become deadly projectiles. People run, scream and die. You see countless pieces of human torsos on the ground. Arms and legs fly by, and blood rains down as if the clouds were wounded. Even after the bombers pass the ensuing firestorm sucks the oxygen out of the atmosphere around you and you choke. It's a nightmarish hell. And though I had my running and dodging, I only survived because I was lucky.

CHAPTER SEVENTEEN

A VOLUNTARY TRIP TO HELL

By now it was clear to most people what awaited Jews in the concentration camps. American planes dropped leaflets over Hungary warning the government not to persist in their foul plan to murder the last intact Jewish community in Europe, threatening them with post war reprisals. But despite their certain doom, being trapped between the Russians and the Americans, they were so full of themselves they couldn't see the handwriting on the wall. Mad with blood lust they would play the game out with no thought of consequences.

Ever since Joska had heard of the plight of Rose's baby sister he wanted to try and help her. With the family now hidden as well as any mortal could be in 1944 Hungary, Joska sat Rose down for another short chat. But this didn't make Rose nervous, because there was nothing he could say to damage his reputation with her. He'd already done so much for her and her family that he could tell her anything and he'd still retain his saint status. He could tell her that he was going off and help somebody else. He could tell her he was in love with another girl. He could tell her absolutely anything, without blemishing his name with them.

"Rose, I have a friend. He's my contact in Vienna to get things for my black market business here. Well, he has a friend, and this guy was appointed to an important office with the Nazis."

Rose looked at him as wide eyed as when he first declared his intentions to her. But, for all her experience with him and his good deeds, she was still unprepared for what he now proposed.

"So, I paid him and he did some research and learned that there's every probability that your little sister Anci is in a concentration camp at a place called Auschwitz-Birkenau in Poland."

There were rumors about such places, but just knowing where Anci was, even if it was in the worst place in creation, brought her little sister back to life, and she was grateful for that.

"They have this document," continued Joska. "An exemption paper. I'm going to get one and try and get her out."

As joyous as those words sounded, Rose knew it was probably even more than Joska the miracle man could handle. It was unacceptably risky, and she had to try and stop him.

"No, my dear, it's too dangerous. You'll get killed. We've all heard things about places like that. Many people go there, but nobody ever comes back. You've already done so much. We all owe you our lives. But this is insane. Stop thinking about it. I've never heard such madness! You can't go and that's final!"

But trying to tell Joska Cséh he couldn't do something only fueled his determination.

"Everyone here is safe. It's not fair to little Anci. I'm leaving at once. Make sure everyone stays inside. You go out for food. I'll pray the allied bombs don't fall here, and I'll see you when I get back.

There was no point in arguing with him.

"Alright, Joska. But we're not telling my parents or anyone else. They'll be too frightened for you, as I am. Besides, they might get their hopes up, and be too disappointed if you don't make it back with her."

She took Joska in her arms, "Oh, how could people like the Nazis exist in the same world with someone so good as you?"

She kissed him, then pulled back and looked at him.

"If you get there and it looks too dangerous, just stop. At least promise me that!"

Joska looked at her, but said nothing. But Rose insisted.

"Please, I beg you. If you get there and it looks too dangerous, just stop. No one will think the lesser of you for that. If it looks too dangerous, stop and turn around. Return safe to me. Do you hear me, Josef Cséh?! Swear it!"

Finally he nodded, "Alright, alright! You Jewish girls are such a pain in the neck. I swear it!" This made Rose release a little laugh of relief.

To imagine somebody voluntarily going to Auschwitz so staggers the imagination that any attempt at comprehending it is futile. And, as if this weren't daunting enough, unbeknownst to Rose, Joska actually had two stops on his valiant itinerary. Rachel Giller, the girlfriend of Joska's friend, Stephen Seredy, who had driven Joska over with the ladders for my family's exit from Harsfa Street, was prisoner in the Vienna ghetto, and he begged Joska to try and get her out. While Stephen sympathized, and even leant his auto to help us, physical involvement on his behalf was beyond the parameters of his commitment. Not everybody was as brave as Joska. Anyway, it was certainly easy for Joska to relate to his Christian friend having a Jewish sweetheart, so naturally, he promised to try.

Not if he were literally dressed in shining armor, seated on a dazzling white steed, lance in hand, could Joska possibly conjure up a greater image of a hero. He was a disabled man, unarmed, and utterly alone, and he dared venture forth in defense of the weak. If there were no God you'd have to invent one just to pray to Him to protect Joska Cséh.

Under normal circumstances a trip from northern Hungary, where Budapest is, to southern Poland, where Auschwitz-Birkenau was, wouldn't have taken very long at all. But in 1944 Europe there was very little of anything called normal circumstances. So a brief train ride through Czechoslovakia, the geographic entity separating the lands of the Magyars and Poles, was out of the question. The train yards were under constant bombardment so Joska hardly considered the Budapest train station to be a good starting point. A taxi might offer a safer alternative for starters, so Joska, considered the cost. He had most of the tobacco he had saved from his black market activities, and Stephen Seredy had given him all he had, so at least he felt decently financed.

Europeans were such resolute smokers that tobacco was nearly as precious as gold. Decades before it was to become a popular opinion, endorsed by learned men of medicine, I already observed the addictive sway of that plant. I'm ashamed to say it, but I actually saw my own father trade food for tobacco on occasion. Later, in anticipation of the occasion of my father's visit to me at my hiding place in central Budapest, I went on the street to collect discarded butts and merge the used tobacco into a pouch for the old man. To leave his refuge in Hungaria Korut to check up on his sole surviving son was actually the bravest thing he did in the war. It truly was a risk, as my father did have what the fascist would have characterized as a typical Jewish look. But he had papers that said the contrary, so he accepted a lift from Joska in the side car of his motorcycle and came to see me and meet my protectors. They rewarded his bravery with a hardy lunch which he later declared to be the best meal he'd ever had. In any case, I agreed that he was brave for coming, and he deserved his hard earned sack of tobacco. Truth be told, the old man was far from alone in his fondness for this shredded brown leaf, so I could have sold it for a tidy sum. It was the popular lust for tobacco, even among war impoverished countrymen, that helped finance Joska's trip to Auschwitz, and a chance to win my sister's life.

As popular as smoking was no government had yet to declare tobacco legal tender, so you still needed money. But of course, if something's not for sale, all the cash and tobacco in Europe are useless. And gas was at a real premium, making automobile transportation unpredictable at best. Joska couldn't rely on any one mode of transportation, but with only a small shoulder bag to carry, he felt flexible enough to try anything. Plus, he was an experienced traveler through these lands, and felt confident. But then again, Joska Cséh always felt that way. So, armed with that confidence, some black market goods, and a respectable sum of gold, he set out bright and early to save Anci. Step one, hunt up a cab.

If, on the streets of late 1944 Budapest, you waited for a clearly marked and identified cab to drive by, you would be wasting your time. You simply flagged down any car you saw. And, almost at once, Joska saw what looked to him like man and machine on the prowl for commerce.

"Where to, sir," inquired a chubby man with an enormous moustache that didn't really hide his poorly kept teeth.

"Well," began Joska, "I have to make a little trip. Could you please pull over, and we'll discuss the fare?"

The cabbie enthusiastically did as Joska asked. A long trip meant a good fare to this simple man, and he was all ears. He noted Joska's limp and courteously spoke up.

"Oh, please sir. Sit down. Sit down at once."

"You are most kind," Joska smiled. "Tell me, isn't it difficult to get gas?"

This made the man a little nervous. Of all the scarce and rationed commodities, gas was the most coveted. It was also a touchy subject. What with new laws and social regulations popping up every other day, you never knew what the rules were. For all that this poor fellow knew he wasn't even supposed to be driving a civilian vehicle. Who could keep up? Joska observed his uneasiness and immediately set about to calm him.

"I mean, I need to make a long trip, and I would hate to get stranded. I'm sure you wouldn't like it either."

As always, Joska seemed reasonable and most unNazilike, and the man dropped his defenses.

"Where are we off to, sir?"

Joska was all business now, "I need to get to *Esztergom.*"

He didn't want to revive the cabby's paranoia by mentioning a foreign land, so he named a northern town on the Danube. The fabled waterway flows north through Budapest, but meanders west about thirty miles north of the capital, forming a border between Hungary's northwestern half and southwest Czechoslovakia. There he might be able to pick up a train. The cabbie was glad to hear they'd be going west, as opposed to heading straight into a possible Russian invasion.

"I can get gas enough if you can pay, sir." Now, the cabbie was all business, and it amused Joska, always appreciative of vital humanity.

"How about twenty five gold Napoleons?"

"Well, sir," the astute transportation professional countered, "That's fine for getting there, but how will I buy gas to get back, as well as justify returning empty, which will almost certainly be the case? I'll need another twenty five to justify the return, plus wear and tear."

"Fifty?" gasped Joska, feigning shock. He was enjoying the bargaining, but knew it'd all be over as soon as he said, "I'll give you Forty Napoleons and some coffee."

Happily defeated, the cabbie announced departure, "Climb aboard, your honor. It's a lovely day for a drive through the countryside. I'll just have to stop and tell the wife. Name's Ernst!" And they were off.

They would take the perimeter road that hugged the Danube's eastern bank until they were thirty miles north of the capital. There, in the town of *Vác*, the mighty river swooped west. Crossing it by bridge they'd continue west along the southern bank until *Esztergom*. Six years earlier it would have been a leisurely scenic drive. Now, like all other activities, it was a crap shoot, fraught with detours not even imagined back then. They could be blown up by any of several agents of destruction, have the car commandeered by partisans, be stopped by authorities and shot for carrying contraband, or just find the roads impassable or a bridge wiped out. The one reality of which they were sure was that the entire itinerary was in territory still held tightly by the Third Reich.

Despite potential for catastrophe the Cséh luck held. First, Joska guided Ernst to the clandestine station he always used to fill his motorcycle. The trip didn't require a full tank, but it was prudent to bring an extra can or two along in case soldiers stopped them in search of the precious petrol. After a routine roadblock at the northern city limits they traveled unencumbered along the eastern bank of the mighty Danube, constantly observing and discussing its magnificence. Three hours at a cautious gas conserving pace and they rolled into Esztergom. Joska thanked and paid a relieved Ernst, and they parted company. Then, Joska walked over the narrow foot bridge.

At this point in time crossing borders in central Europe was unlike Yolie's earlier Orient Express experience. Now, Nazis held all sides of all borders, and a single encounter with authority was adequate. Not having as yet suffered the affects of an arduous journey, his still pristine and relaxed Teutonic countenance made the border guards snap to attention with their rifles held in salute.

"Willkommen mein herr, papieren bitte!"

Joska's papers were like chain mail and his flawless German his armor. They barely regarded his papers. This man was obviously one of them.

"What is the reason for your trip, please sir."

If his papers were his chain mail, and his looks his armor, Sir Joska's tongue was surely his lance. If Hollywood executives would have known of Joska's talent for storyline and plot construction they would have cursed this war more than they already did for taking Clark Gable away, for preventing this Hungarian genius from joining them in inventing situations for Errol Flynn to get out of. The white knight, in high spirits, did not hesitate in confiding his mission to the guards.

"Well gentlemen, it's like this. A Gestapo Captain in Budapest has this mistress. One night, after a particularly energetic tryst, bolstered by one too may bottles of fine Hungarian wine —we must allow them that, anyway- she wanders into a building designated for Jews. Stinking drunk, she collapses in the hallway. During the night some sly Jew witch switches papers with her. Wouldn't you know it? At the crack of dawn the whole building gets rounded up for transport to Poland, and the captain's mistress is mixed in with the swine. So, now I have to go and bring the bitch back. Apparently she can suck cock like nobody's business, and the captain can't live without her."

Hanging on his every word the guards were convinced, and allowed him entry into the second leg of his journey, southern Czechoslovakia, even going so far as to wish him good luck.

He was in, but literally on foot. *"Danke schoen, comraden,"* waved Joska as he headed north.

After walking for about an hour through the hilly terrain, thinking of Rose and rehearsing his next encounter with the Nazis, he heard an automobile behind him, coming around a bend in the road. He turned around to see a military ambulance rapidly approaching, and immediately stuck out his thumb and smiled. The ambulance roared up to him, slamming on its brakes and sliding half off the road before skidding sideways and stopping. Even before it completely stopped two armed men in unbuttoned German military blouses jumped out and menaced Joska in a Slavic tongue.

"Nazi scum!"

In a second Joska knew these were Czech partisans, and that his Prussian appearance would do him in, instead of do him good. So, he threw up his hands and spoke as quickly as he could so they'd know he was Hungarian instead of German. If he'd hesitated two seconds they would have killed him, believing him to be what the Nazis themselves believed him to be. Being from a region that bordered their southern neighbor the partisans recognized Joska's speech, and made a few clumsy inquiries in broken *Ungaro*. Joska replied in a Slavic no less fragmented, and the atmosphere relaxed a bit. The men bragged that they had ambushed a small German unit, killing everyone, stealing the ambulance, and killing its occupants as well. Now they had the means at their disposal to sneak up and ambush even more Nazi scum, and make a motorized getaway to boot. Joska congratulated the men, and they jumped back in their stolen vehicle. As they revved their engine Joska was hit by an idea, and he called out to them to stop. They jerked to a standstill and Joska hobbled over and asked if they had an extra German tunic. One of them thought for a second, and turned to his comrades to get their opinions. The driver shrugged, and one of them in the back reached down and grabbed a bloody uniform top and tossed it to Joska. As they roared off Joska shouted an unintelligible word of Slavic gratitude. They disappeared around the next hill as quickly as they had appeared. That he was not offered a lift didn't concern Joska, as he was not eager to ally himself with any overtly military cell. His combat was not one of resistance, but of passive-resistance. He admired these partisans, and truly wished that they would kill every German they could find. But he was disabled and probably would have proved a liability to any group of soldiers willing to take him on. His leg left him on the sidelines. It was the one thing that made him less of a man than the combatants. He limped and was slow. But he was lucky to have survived the polio of his youth. It killed thousands of Hungarian children, and he himself spent a month and a half in an iron lung when he was nine. But he survived. The result however was a man who was not physically the match of most men. So, he had long since developed a talent for self defense that did not rely exclusively on brute strength and quickness of movement. As he continued to walk along he thought about the Czech partisan cell and was impressed by their daring. Like him they were imposters. They pretended to be

146

Germans just as he did. But they did him one better. Instead of trying to convince Germans they just killed them. Much more efficient. But Joska knew his talent rested in persuasion, and ultimately denying the Germans their victims. That was his battlefield, and he felt proud of it. But now more fear than pride was entering into his life. He was not a day into his trek to Poland, and already he was in a strange and foreign landscape. He had choked back fear before, but now he was truly on edge. He'd committed himself to this course of action however, and would not go back. The partisans brought to light the battle at hand, and he could not shrink from it. Almost subconsciously he began singing, "Es geht alles voruber. Es geht alles verbi." He had never considered the words so clearly before. The song itself, like him, was an imposter. It could masquerade itself as a romantic ballad about love's waning and ebbing, but everyone knew what it really was that couldn't last forever. And like me and Rose, and the rest of Europe, he took heart from it.

As he courageously limped on he toyed more with the plan that was born in his head when he saw the partisans and their stolen uniforms. If he came across a real German ambulance he would play a wounded soldier, and hitch a ride. He wanted to try and get to Anci as soon as possible. That was his mission, and like all military exercises, the objective comes first. That's why he asked the Czech partisans for the uniform. While the Czechs were bragging of their exploits he was thinking that one German ambulance represented the need for more. Europe was one big combat zone, and at any moment soldiers of one army could come upon him and kill him for being on the side of the other. This was much more dangerous than Budapest. He was out in the open, could barely communicate in a Slavic tongue, and didn't know who he might meet next. At least in Budapest he knew who the enemy was. Then he heard a motor.

Was it a German, Czech, Russian, a partisan? Anything was possible. He turned, but couldn't see it. His only protection at that moment was the fact that, if he couldn't see it then it couldn't see him. The dense forest impartially provided refuge for everyone, regardless of uniform, and he was even at a momentary advantage, not having made any warning noise like this approaching intruder. So, he hid in the bushes near the path and waited. The sound of the motor was very familiar to him. It was a motorcycle. After about a minute of engine noise a BMW with sidecar drove by. An aficionado, he was momentarily distracted by the beauty of the machine. He also observed that it wasn't in any hurry. He tried to think what that could mean. The driver wasn't bloodied or desperate looking either. Another riddle. The man was alone, so it probably wasn't an organized retreat. He didn't have any major weapons so maybe he was going to retrieve someone. If that was so, Joska would have to be careful of his return. Why was he going slowly? Were the Germans so well entrenched that this cyclist had no worries? Or was he just conserving fuel? Maybe the fuel would have to last a long time, because he was heading back to his own lines far away. There were so many possibilities. Finally, he factored in the tranquility of the cycle driver with the plans of the partisans, and he came up with a scenario that had the Germans well entrenched in the area. Based on that he donned the bloodied uniform and determined to hitch a ride with the first Nazi heading north. If he found partisans he'd speak Hungarian and hope for the best. In any case he'd hide until he could get a good look at whoever was coming next. If they weren't German he might have time to strip off the uniform. He squatted and waited, thinking about Rose. What was she doing now? Were the Russians bombing the neighborhood? How was Tommy? Thinking of me and the stolen birth certificate made him laugh. He looked up at the sky. The sun was starting to sink, and soon it would be dark and cold. He wasn't looking forward to that. The cold always made his leg hurt more. What's more, he was hungry. He had counted on staying within urban areas where he could buy food. None of this was expected. But, even with the cold, hunger, darkness, and fear of approaching armies, he took momentary pleasure in the tranquility of the countryside. It was a stillness that reminded him of his youth in Pécs, the college town he grew up in. He often went outside the city for picnics, and he loved every chance to commune with nature. He even thought of one picnic he and Rose enjoyed in the Liget Park before it became too dangerous. He was lost in thought when he heard a car in the distance. He slowly peered up from behind his hiding place, and saw a German ambulance. This time though it was not driven erratically, like the partisans. He reasoned the driver was a disciplined German or Austrian. He hoped he was right, and went into his act. If they didn't see him he might be trapped out here all night and freeze. Of course, he might be wrong about the allegiance of the driver and be shot dead at once. But it was too late to reconsider. The vehicle saw him and was slowing down. The orderliness of the maneuver assured him he'd made the right decision. He staggered to the vehicle, groaning. A German soldier was at the wheel.

"*Vas macht du heir?*"

Joska chose to ignore the interrogation and, panting, thanked the driver for stopping, invoking *Gott* in the process.

"I was afraid you might be a partisan. Those weasels are all over here. They got the drop on us about a mile east of here. We got 'em all, but I'm all that's left of my squad."

The driver bought every panting syllable Joska manufactured, and helped him into the back of the ambulance. It was already filled with wounded German boys, none of which looked more than sixteen. He took note of the arm patches, preparing himself for a debriefing. He could bluff that much now, but if they asked him who the commandant was he'd be lost. Unprepared to fully explain himself he took the offensive.

"The old man sends us out without any good intelligence and those subhuman Slavs are all over us like insects. *Gottinhimmel!*"

There were no arguments.

To further distract the soldier Joska asked, "Have you got any water or rations?"

The driver finally replied, "You'll have to hang in there soldier, until we get back to base."

"Then let's get going," demanded Joska, and he banged on the side of the vehicle like a typical German *soldat.*

The drive back to German lines was mostly quiet, and it struck Joska as odd. Most of the German soldiers he had dealt with were a chatty group, boisterous and high spirited. This low morale meant that the war was not going as well as the ministry of propaganda would have the masses believe. Of course, the utter destruction of radio and newspapers silenced the government sanctioned lies, and had already told us the subhumans were doing far better than we were ever supposed to think. But now Joska was seeing it from the inside, instead of his usual brushes with authority. He'd made trips to Vienna, to keep up appearances for the shoe trade, as well as stock up on black market merchandise, but it had been quite a while, and now it was obvious that things had gone downhill for the Third Reich. He was glad for that, because he craved their defeat. But having them in a bad mood wasn't going to help his mission.

Political analysis aside, he was going to have to come up with a scheme to get away from these soldiers and continue on his journey to Poland. His ruse had won him a ride, but upon arriving they'd discover that he wasn't wounded at all, and guilty of impersonating a German soldier on top of that. Maybe this time he had bit off more than he could chew.

At least it was night. The darkness would be Joska's willing accomplice in whatever plot he hatched. What he had to do was disembark before they arrived. And not knowing when that would be he decided it had to be now. Earlier he speculated on why the ambulance went slow. Now, he was just glad it did. He clutched his little shoulder bag and lifted up a corner of the canvas flap behind him. It was a lucky break that he was in the rear. He gave a look around to make sure that no one was alert enough to catch him. No chance. These boys were seriously wounded, with half of them probably dead by now. Maybe they all were. The ambulance slowed even more on a turn, and Joska rolled out the back. Whatever thud he made was drowned out by the loud motor, and the vehicle drove on. He rolled for a few feet, and then darted to a bush for cover. He tried to calculate how much progress he'd made. Although he didn't know how to read the stars he just figured the krauts weren't doing well enough to head back east. So, they had to have gone either north or northwest. In the morning the rising sun would tell him. For now, he walked.

His uniform was more of a liability than an asset, so he shed it. It was nearly pitch black out in the countryside, and it seemed to make time stand still. Alone with his thoughts he marveled at the starry sky. There was no moon so the stars had nothing to dim their magnificence. He imagined that the Nazis would probably like to conquer them as well, eliminating the ones that were too small, and putting the undisciplined comets in cosmic concentration camps. Most of all he wondered if Rose was looking up too. With no electricity in Budapest she could probably see them as clearly arrayed as he did now, and the thought that they could share this moment gave him solace and resolve. It even quelled his hunger. He craned his neck upward for so long it hurt. And when he lowered it again he noticed he was coming upon a large sign on the side of the road. He lit a match and read it, *Nové Zámky 2 Miles*. He strained his eyes, but couldn't make out any light in the distance. Bombing raids must have knocked out their electricity too. He didn't carry a map, because a soldier once told him that any civilian who carried one was labeled a spy. But the name of the town was familiar to him, and he tried to remember how far north it was. After walking just a few more minutes it came to him. On routine trips to Vienna he had always passed through it. As he didn't recall stopping or dining there it meant that it was not far along the route north. That meant that he couldn't have traveled more than thirty or thirty five miles! He still had most of the country before him! But what could he expect? He walked with a limp, and the ambulance moved like a tortoise, as well as taking him northwest, instead of due north, as he required. Just thirty five miles. Would he ever make it at all? But his disappointment dissipated as he came to the realization that his fatigue had betrayed his powers of observation. His familiarity with the name of the town was, after all, the result of numerous train trips through it. It might have been an insignificant stop, but at least it was on the rail line!

A train would reduce his trip to mere hours. But would there even be a train? He hadn't dared go near the Budapest station, because the air raids constantly targeted them, but now he was out in the countryside, far from anything of strategic importance. It was little Nové Zámky, not the capital, so the allies probably ignored it. Of course! They wouldn't waste bombs out in the middle of nowhere! His hope was reborn and he quickened his step.

No sooner had hope risen on the horizon when the sun did too. Its warmth hit Joska's back, so he knew he was headed west. But the rail line that ran through Nové Zámky headed due north, so he eagerly strode toward this southern Czech town.

The sun rose higher, and he could now make out the diminutive burg. For the first time he could see it in its totality and it was even more unimpressive to his eyes than the narrow view of it that the train station had afforded him on his previous brief stops. His condemning assessment of the tiny town evaporated as a train whistle heralded both a train's arrival and his. Joska practically ran the rest of the way, and got to the station just as the train did. Miraculously, everything seemed normal.

As he entered the station proper he encountered a cadre of German soldiers. He hadn't spoken to anybody in an entire day so it took him a moment to reclaim his glib self. As his life depended on a clear head he snapped out of it, and spun his Gestapo mistress tale. He had to add on a broken down car twenty miles back, but his persona basically held up well enough to get him on the train to *Ostrava*, two hundred miles north, on the Polish border. Just before boarding he found some biscuits and coffee for sale, and ate breakfast standing up. He stuffed some more biscuits into his pockets for the trip, and boarded.

Whatever relief he had discovered at finding a functioning northbound train evaporated upon entering the train car, and faced wall to wall uniforms. There was martial dress of every axis nationality: German, Hungarian, Czechoslovakian, Austrian, Romanian, Italian, even Bulgarian. He didn't allow it to break his well rehearsed veneer however, and he gave a curt half bow. Not from a single one of these nations came a friendly response, but he didn't let it faze him. He sat down on the only empty seat, and contemplated just how bad the war must be going for them. Their unfriendly demeanor told him it was probably going even worse than he imagined. Inside he was jubilant, but externally revealed nothing. Not that he invested much time in it. He hadn't slept in over 24 exhausting hours, so he dozed off at once.

An unconscious and mildly snoring Aryan was practically invisible to these troops, who all had greater things on their minds. So, inconsequential Joska was blissfully unmolested until *Vsetin*, when most of the soldiers changed for a west bound line. Now, Poland lay only fifty or sixty miles away. Joska fell back asleep, and stayed so until the train rumbled to a stop on the Polish border. Joska alit and found bustling activity. There were several other trains he could barely make out through the steam from his train's locomotive. When he tried to get a better look, an armed guard yelled at him to go the other way. Obviously, Joska was not supposed to see this other train, and he obeyed his orders and walked in the opposite direction. It was only early afternoon, so he hoped he could continue his journey, and he inquired at the ticket office if he could pick up another train across the border. He was told it was impossible, so he decided to try his old reliable naiveté.

"But I only need to go another thirty miles or so."

"Oh really," mocked the ticket seller, "And where is it you want to go?"

"Well, I'm on a mission to go somewhere called Berkinau. Do you know it?"

At this the ticket seller's face fell. His gravity spread a pall over Joska, and as uncertain as he might have felt the day before, he now felt like he was in completely foreign territory.

"Sir, as I said, it is impossible. Now, please step away from the booth. Thank you."

Joska had rarely encountered such a flat refusal. He reflected on all of the run-ins he'd had with Nazis and Nyilasok, and determined that the situation here was on a level never previously encountered. He was going to have to be sharper than ever. He nodded in assent and walked away from the booth. As he did the man in the ticket booth called over a Gestapo agent, and pointed out Joska.

Just as Joska was exiting the station he was tapped on the shoulder, and a man's voice intoned, *"Bitte."*

He anticipated a harsh interview with a stern representative of the Third Reich, and in the split second before he turned around he reminded himself that people's lives were in his hands, and not to be intimidated by these bastards.

Joska spun and said, "Yes," as if he were annoyed.

Everyone was afraid of Nazis, and when they failed to elicit the usual frightened reaction the fascist goons were either taken aback or angered at the effrontery. This one was unfortunately a member of the latter school.

"Papieren bitte," he snapped.

Long before political scientists awarded bullies their own unique political category, fascism, authoritarians had already existed. What we don't know is exactly when they adopted mock politeness as their standard mode of expression. Maybe the Nazis themselves can take the credit for inventing it. If they didn't they certainly honed it to a fine edge. Whoever developed it also deserves the nod for most ironic. Because the Nazis employed all the courteous phrases we learn at our mother's knee, while exhibiting the most brutal behavior in Christendom. They always said please and thank you and excuse me. It was uncanny. They'd arrest you by saying something like, *'I beg your pardon, but you are under arrest,'* or *'I regret to inform you that these papers are not in order.'* Just as they made all their murderous activities legal they made their perpetrators perfect gentlemen.

"Certainly," replied Joska, "Now, can someone tell me why I can't get some transportation to Berkinau? I have some pressing matters to attend to there."

The Nazi demanded, "And what exactly are those pressing matters."

Joska told his Gestapo mistress story, but he read this man, and kept the comedy out of it. Then he took the offensive.

"So, what is the problem in getting some transport there?"

But this Nazi was not so easily dissuaded from his duty. "What is the name of this Gestapo Captain in Budapest, and what is the name of his mistress?"

"*Anfuhrer* Steiner, and the foolish girl's name is Maria Willem."

The Nazi pressed on, "Then you won't mind if we call Budapest and speak to this Anfuhrer Steiner?"

"I was just going to suggest it myself," bluffed Joska. "I don't mind telling you I'm not accustomed to such treatment. In Budapest I am regarded with the greatest deference."

Joska counted on it being impossible to call, but his dueling partner thrusted again.

"You are not in Budapest, Lieutenant Cséh. I might add, you are quite a long way from there. And you are requesting transport to a very sensitive facility. Let me see this exemption paper for this woman."

Joska took it out and handed it over to the Nazi, who read it carefully, turning it over and inspecting it thoroughly. All at once he became aggressive.

"Weisz is a Jewish name. What do you think you are trying?"

154

Without batting an eye Joska fired back, "That's the whole point *mein Kapitan*. She's probably not known by any other name. Now please return my paper and let me get on with my official business."

At this the Nazi hesitated. Joska read this hesitation like the experienced Nazi taunter he was.

"I must insist, *Hauptmann*. I want to finish my business today and catch the train back with her tomorrow." Now he dared to lighten the mood, "Maybe I'll get a blow job myself, if she's not an ingrate."

The Nazi gave Joska the once over, recognized defeat, and exhibiting a hint of a reptilian grin, handed everything back. Obsessed with having the last word however, he dismissed Joska with, "You may go!"

Joska gave a curt, "*Danke,*" and strode to what he hoped was a taxi.

"Have you the gas to drive me about thirty miles into Poland?"

The Czech civilian gave Joska no less a once over than the German, "You're still in Czechoslovakia. I can take you to *Orlová*. Once there you can try and get a Polish taxi."

Joska tried to engage the taxi driver in pleasant conversation, but found the man reticent. Clearly, Joska was in territory stranger than any he'd know before. Every step in this journey was becoming increasingly more nerve-racking.

When they arrived in Orlová he paid the man, who wasted no time in turning around and speeding off. Joska walked across the border and presented his papers. He behaved as he did with the official in Ostrava, but got nowhere.

"But I must follow Captain Steiner's orders and retrieve this girl. Get me a car, please."

These Nazis were even more officious than his previous encounter.

"*Mein herr*, you cannot go to Auschwitz or Birkenau. We cannot get a car for you, and it's a bit cold to walk so far. It would take you days. If I were you I'd just forget it."

Though he felt truly anxious Joska remained impassive.

"Very well, gentlemen," he said in perfect phony fascist gentility, "Then I must try and perform my duty. I shall walk. Good day. Heil Hitler."

They returned his Nazi slogan and talked amongst themselves. Joska smartly spun around and walked away. His deliberate stride was meant to impress upon the guards that he was a man on a mission. Also, the energy put into his gait would call extra attention to his limp, with the intention of eliciting sympathy and perhaps even some begrudged assistance from the guards. But his theatrics failed to jar them.

That his performance fell on deaf ears was something that Joska took as an omen. There was something ominous about this place, something that should have warned anyone not to continue. He should count himself lucky to be free and retreat. If ever there was truth in discretion being the better part of valor it was now. But he thought about Mrs. Weisz, and how happy she'd be to have her little Anci back. He thought of all of the Nazis' victims, and the injustice, and walked on. He blotted out of his mind any consideration of turning back. Rose had assured him that he'd already done enough, that he didn't owe so much to anyone, and that this was far too dangerous. Then he thought of something that made him ashamed for not having thought of it earlier. Rose's own husband had vanished after being conscripted into the Jewish Work Brigade. These armies of slaves were now being sent to battle zones, so there was no way of knowing where he was now. He could very well be here in this camp. The man was simply never mentioned any more, and Joska felt terrible for neglecting this reality. But even if he knew he was here Joska was ill equipped to do anything for him. Be that as it may, he was at least prepared to help Anci, so he would not turn back. Besides, he'd come so far. He'd already risked his life impersonating a German soldier. Did he do that for nothing? No! He must go on. He was so close. He was already on Polish soil. If only he could find transportation he'd succeed. He must not be afraid. He could still do this.

After he walked about two miles the cold made his bad leg throb, and he had to rest. But the terrain was now barren, a rare patch of treeless land with not so much as a trunk or log to sit on. What a hostile uninviting place. Gray rolling mud and rocks. He just stood there, leaning on his good leg, the only available rest, and surveyed the barren landscape. It had probably once been fertile farmland, but now the soil was leeched of its richness, and no one dared to till the fallow dirt. He squinted into the horizon, desperate for some relief. All he saw was more grayness. The sky was full of clouds, and they obliterated any hint of sunshine. And it was deathly still. With no branch to perch upon there was not the sound of a bird. No planes in the sky. No vehicles. No buildings. Not so much as an insect. Just the wind. There was nothing to engage his senses in this lifeless vacuum, made even more inhospitable by the cold. He had no choice but to go on.

After another aching hour he saw a dot on the horizon, and it actually startled him. He couldn't imagine that anything in this hostile environment could be of any use to him, and he was now stuck with a situation in which he saw something that must have likewise seen him. So, he had no choice but to keep walking toward it. But he couldn't avoid feeling threatened. What was he walking toward? If they were military men maybe they had binoculars and could observe his trepidation. Maybe they already had. He must snap out of it. He was sent by Unfuhrer Steiner in Budapest, and he must not forget it. On he limped.

It was a car. A private car. He tried to remain passive, disclosing neither relief nor fear. The man was working on the motor. He heard a stubborn whining, growing fainter with each attempt, and he recognized the sound of a dying car battery. The lifeless auto seemed right in tune with this place. The man, blessedly free of any military uniform or insignia, was himself jarred by Joska's usual quasimilitary presence. But Joska's smile allayed his anxiety. With his minimalist vocabulary of myriad European languages Joska recognized the man's Polish greeting, and returned it, if in somewhat broken fashion. They were off to a good start, but they'd have to depend on the expressions of various idioms in order to successfully communicate. Joska looked at the motor, drew a finger across his throat, and said to the man, "*Kaput?*" He nodded, but agreed in his own language. Joska held up his hand as if to call a temporary stop to the proceedings. With sign language he indicted that they should push the car. Popping the clutch was the only option and the man begrudgingly agreed, tossing in a variety of foreign *yes*es. As embarrassing as it was, the reality of Joska's bad leg made it necessary for him to sit while the other man pushed. Actually, the stocky fellow looked muscular enough to push the car halfway to Krakow. So, after some exaggerated gestures and mime the burly fellow shrugged and walked to the rear of the auto. Joska slipped into the driver's seat, turned the ignition to the start position, shifted to second gear, depressed the clutch, and waved for the man to start pushing. The car was already on the road so it seemed sensible to keep straight. Unfortunately, they'd first have to overcome a small upward incline of about ten feet. But once they got to the crest it was a friendlier down-hill trajectory, and then flat ground. Joska didn't want the poor man to have to get the car going from a stand still again, so he wanted to wait until they were going at a decent clip. Of course, the man had already decided that they were going fast enough for the trick to work, and was by now shouting Polish obscenities at Joska. Just when he shouted the loudest Joska popped the clutch and the motor jumped to life. It sputtered, but Joska revved it and it continued to run. The man was jubilant and he ran to the driver's door, using up his entire vocabulary of foreign *thank yous*. All smiles, he shook Joska's hand as if he expected water to eventually come out of his mouth. Then he introduced himself.

"I am Wladislaw."

Joska smiled back, gave his name in return, and when his hand was finally released slid over to the passenger's seat. Wladislaw sat down, still breathing hard, and Joska patiently waited for him to catch his breath. When he did so he looked at Joska wide eyed and pantomimed a 'So?' Joska didn't waste any time, and proposed a trip to Auschwitz. As anticipated, the burly Wladislaw fell grave. Shaking both his head and one index finger from side to side for emphasis, he refused. With-out hesitation Joska reached into his pocket and pulled out some of his coveted tobacco, and offered it to the reticent Pole. As ubiquitous as jokes that denigrate the intelligence of Poles might be, the cagey Wladis-law contradicted them all. He knew perfectly well why this stranger had helped him with the car, and why he was now proffering this pre-cious gift. This disheveled foreigner wanted something. He'd probably traveled a long way with the insane idea of going to Auschwitz, a mis-sion too eerie and perilous to involve a simple Polish farmer. But, in spite of his astute analysis of Joska's intentions, there was still tobacco involved. If Joska had never learned of the overwhelming human lust for sense gratification, regardless of the risk, he had it hammered home now. Wladislaw looked at Joska, at the tobacco, then Joska again. To push his new friend over the edge, he pulled twenty gold Napoleons out and held it in the palm of his hand, saying, "Auschwitz," adding hand gestures to indicate 'there and back.' Wladislaw thought for another moment, then made a 'maybe' face. He added on 'wash-up' and 'come-on' gestures, and they were off.

They soon arrived at Wladislaw's farm house. If the man's eyes had grown wide at the sight of tobacco his wife's nearly left their sockets. She looked like she'd sleep with Joska just to get a smoke. But when she heard the name of their considered destination, she went ashen. She spoke to her husband in a hushed sidebar, and though Joska didn't understand the words he knew exactly what she must be telling him. Joska just hoped that his host was not hopelessly henpecked. But it never got that far. The gold closed the deal. The woman crossed herself and kissed her fingers, then offered Joska some soup. Relieved, Joska gratefully consumed two bowls of tasty broth with vegetables. Wladislaw showed Joska to a crude bathroom, which was clearly the pride of his humble estate, and Joska reclaimed the appearance of the dapper, clean shaven gentleman he needed to be. The couple was impressed with Joska's transformation, and the little cabin was all warmth and smiles. But the sun was still high enough in the sky for Joska to consider forging ahead, and he made a show of consulting his watch, and opening his eyes wide for the clever Pole to read him. 'Now?' The incredulous syllable reflected his desire to procrastinate as much as possible, but Joska knew there was no time to waste. Already regretting his commitment, and cursing his cigarette lust, Wladislaw reluctantly dragged himself toward the waiting automobile.

The drive to the farmhouse had charged the car's battery just enough for it to barely start, and Wladislaw looked a little disappointed that it did. The man's wife gave Joska and her husband a religious send-off, crossing herself repeatedly.

Setting sail so inauspiciously did not bode well for Joska, and he was feeling contaminated by such negativity. The woman's Catholicism led Joska to believe her trepidation was based on superstition, and he was not given to falling victim to hysteria. After all, it was this blessed characteristic of his that allowed him to escape the mass psychosis of fascism. Wladislaw, on the other hand, had already demonstrated enough sense for Joska to allow him a more reasonable influence. And the lack of language common to the two travelers, along with their languid pace under a bleak sky, contributed to the morose mood that had infected Joska since arriving in *Orlová* that frigid morning.

The gray featureless landscape was now invaded by a few scraggly stands of leafless trees. Their naked branches stretched heavenward like bony supplicating fingers and completed the ominous pall that dominated the region. Joska felt no sign of welcome. He had traveled all over central Europe for a decade, in all seasons, yet he'd never felt such an unearthly atmosphere. Maybe the woman was right. It couldn't be for nothing that everyone he met on this trip warned him not to continue. But he was used to going against the current. He thrived on it! He did not allow himself to be swept up in Hitler's tide of hysteria, and he never let a Nazi back him down. Why change now? True, he was far from home, and without as much access to resources as he would have liked, but he could still hold his own with these bullies. He must be more resolute than ever. Despite common sense Joska convinced himself to go through with it.

The road cut into a forest as equally lifeless as the few trees that heralded its appearance. Devoid of color they seemed as awful silent sentries to some terrible secret, hidden deep in the woods, and not meant for any human intrusion. The car now crept along, its driver reluctant to make their presence known. The two men occasionally glanced at each in disbelief. Joska tried to remain serious, but Wladislaw was blatantly afraid. And when they came to the *verboten* sign he was relieved to be forced to stop. He made his fingers walk in the air, and Joska understood that he'd have to go on foot, alone, from that point on. Joska made signs indicating that his companion should wait for him, and he agreed. As much discouragement as Joska had received these last few days he still managed to draw himself up as tall as he could, the better to convince himself of his ability to prevail, and continued down the black dirt road.

As visually oppressive as their journey had been so far his other senses now became engaged by all manner of negative stimuli. He was supposedly approaching a work camp, yet he heard no signs of industry. He heard nothing, and it was the loudest silence he'd ever encountered. There was no animal scurrying through the undergrowth or bird on a branch or in flight. Not even the wind dared to enter this gloomy place and be accomplice to spreading such a stench as offended Joska' nostrils. It was not a musty aroma that nature had designed, but an odor only man would dare devise. There was no fire, but Joska felt he had come to hell. And the road now widened to prove him right. He followed a sharp turn and saw in the distance a wall of barbed wire a hundred yards wide, studded with towers. In the middle was a crude log archway with smaller branches cut to form the words '*Arbeite Macht Frei,*' Work makes you free. This is it, the work camp! This must be where they have Anci. Farther yet he saw smoke stacks spewing black clouds. Again, that ironic presence of silent industry! If it was a labor camp, with the smoke testifying to some form of mechanization, where was the whirr and hum of machinery? Why was it so deadly still? He lowered his gaze and made out some low long black buildings.

"*Halt!*"

There was no time to wonder about the grim panorama. He was just a few paces from a road block and guard house. The 'Halt' snapped him out of his focus on the miasma around him to the more immediate menace before him. It was time for the performance of his life.

Joska's audience consisted on a pair of immaculate SS troops. Their thick, gray, woolen uniforms were in perfect repair, and every metal buckle, button, and gun barrel gleamed. They stood in knee length leather boots with mirror finishes, and their helmet chin straps framed faces devoid of humor. By comparison Joska's full length trench coat seemed like leisure wear, and he was as civilian in their eyes as a woman. Before Joska could draw first blood one of the guards made a peculiar comment.

He said, "The Fuhrer is in good spirits."

All Joska could think of by way of a sensible response was, "He's conquered Europe. Why should he not be."

The guard knitted his brow and repeated, "The Fuhrer is in good spirits," pronouncing each word as if he were addressing a child.

At sea, Joska tried, "I'm delighted to hear it."

Now, both guards lowered their guns at Joska. They demanded, "What are you doing here? And why don't you know the password?"

And without waiting for a response they pressed their advantage with "Why are you on foot?" and "Your papers!"

Joska answered their barrage with one of his own, but they were incredulous of every word he uttered. Nonplussed, the guards continued their impromptu interrogation.

"But why didn't you contact the military office in Birkenau? Why do you just show up here? Didn't you see the sign that says Verboten?"

Joska maintained what had always been his best military demeanor.

"I ask you, *mein gut Sergeant*, what was I to do? The craven Pollack cabbie dumped me off at that sign and fled the place without a word. I couldn't walk back from where we'd come. It was miles! I figured this was closer and made more sense. And as for the password, *Anfuhrer Steiner* made no mention of it. And allow me to inquire as to how it is that noncommissioned officers such as you dare to address a veteran officer such as myself with such insubordination?"

Joska hadn't made a dent, but neither had their suspicions grown any worse.

"This post is classified, and we have the authority to detain anyone who approaches. Now, you're not making much sense to us at all. So please, succinctly state your business."

The whole reason Joska had come here was at hand. "I am adjutant for Anfuhrer Steiner of the Budapest Gestapo. I am here on a personal mission on his behalf. He was to call ahead to facilitate my mission...."

They cut him off, "And what is this personal mission, Lieutenant Cséh?"

They were impatient with Joska's tale, and demanded to see his document.

"Let me see this exemption order."

Joska produced it, and they glanced at it.

"You will have to show this paper to the proper official in the camp. But be prepared for a good long wait. Do you know how many prisoners there are named Weisz here?"

"I cannot imagine," admitted Joska.

"You are right, lieutenant. You cannot!"

Joska attempted to steer things his way, "But I must comply with *Anfuhrer* Steiner's orders. He is most insis..."

"Save your breath. I must contact my immediate superior, but regrettably the fucking phone line is out. So I must walk there and back. Wait here."

Joska made one last attempt at imposing his will, "May I sit, please." But he was quickly taught a lesson.

"This is an SS military installation of a most sensitive nature, and not a social welcome center. I'm sure your good Anfuhrer will appreciate that. Stay here!"

The soldier walked away, his rifle slung over his soldier.

The other soldier asked Joska, "You're not going to give me a hard time, are you?"

Joska was about to answer when the soldier provided the proper response.

"Good, I thought not. I have to study for my next rank exam. So, just wait there like a good little Hungarian adjutant, and don't ask any stupid questions or make any noise. *Zehr gut?*"

All Joska could say was, "*Ja Wohl.*"

He took it all in. He was outgunned, and there was no doubt about it. He was so deep into the Nazi machine he could feel and smell the grease. He wasn't very religious, but he felt as if God was telling him to get lost. And as one last act of mercy, God had even arranged for him to get his papers back. He was probably luckier than any civilian that had ever come here, and he didn't think it wise to strain that luck any more. And finally, he remembered the vow that Rose had exacted from him, to leave if it looked too dangerous. She made him swear it.

He took one step backward. Then another. And another. The guard was engrossed in his military manual. Joska wanted to stop walking backwards and attempt a full retreat. He thought up a credible excuse as to why he moved from that spot, in case they caught him. He wanted to take a piss, so he took a little stroll into the wood. He even directed his consciousness to his groin to see if he had a little urine to give in case he had to make it look real. A few more steps and he'd be back at the turn in the road. His heart was pounding like it never had in his life. Still no angry guards. On he walked, almost running. No shouting SS troopers. He was almost there. No shots. He saw the *verboten* sign, but where was Wladislaw?

He was doomed! The cowardly Polack had stranded him there! For the first time in his life Joska was overtaken by panic. He couldn't walk out of there. He couldn't hide. He didn't know anyone, and they'd be coming after him with dogs and troops. Yes, he might see Anci soon, but as another prisoner.

"Psst"

Wladislaw was hiding behind some trees.

The chubby Pole was a vision of beauty. He'd hidden the car from sight of the road and even turned it around. Joska was ready to kiss him, and felt guilty for having just condemned him. He made a sign that they should depart and both got in the car quickly.

Wladislaw turned the key, but no sound. The silence of this place had engulfed the car. Now, they were both trapped. The two men looked at each other. Wladislaw turned the key again. Still nothing. Wladislaw recognized the panic in Joska's eyes, but he held up his hand to calm him. After all, who knew this car better than him? The third attempt produced a faint electrical whirr. The fourth turn of the key produced the same sound, but more chronic and insistent until the engine jumped to life, and Wladislaw pumped the accelerator to encourage it. One last gift from God to get them on their way, and Joska was grateful. Wladislaw put the car in gear and off they sped. The lethargic pace that brought them in was now retraced at triple the speed. But there were no smiles. They were still within range of the camp, and swastika clad troopers could leave in hot pursuit at any moment. Plus, Joska was thinking about Anci and Rose, and how he had failed.

The greatest irony is that even if Joska had persisted and won SS cooperation, they would have found that just the day before Joska's arrival Anci was shipped from Auschwitz to the munitions plant at Bremen. She had spent three months waiting to be gassed and burnt, but had been spared in order to be used as slave labor.

When transports arrived at Auschwitz the people were divided into two lines. One line was for old people and those too sick or young to work. They were gassed immediately. Mothers with babies in their arms were automatically part of that group. Often, an old person relieved a young mother of her infant and spared her life. Over a million children died like this. The other line was for those considered strong enough to provide free labor to the Third Reich, and they were sent to the other half of the camp, Birkenau. Once there the Nazis would do their best to work you to death. But basically, if you survived the first night's selection you had a slim chance at life. Of course, recently arrived inmates could not know that, so they were fed no hope from the process. Only false hope was held out that first night. The cynical and pragmatic Nazis put up a sign over the entrance that read 'Work Makes You Free.' The newly arrived, fearful of imminent death, were relieved to learn that they'd be put to work, and reasoned that any activity signified life. In this state of relief they were unlikely to protest, and it was easier to send them to their death. For those that survived the first few days a pecking order was quickly established. If you were a healthy Jewish man, or a Pole, for example, you were a likely candidate for work detail. It was a rare woman that was chosen for work detail. They were either killed outright, or used for experiments. Sometimes, officers picked attractive Jewish girls for sex. For whatever reasons Anci was chosen for experiments by Auschwitz's infamous angel of death, Dr. Joseph Mengele. And once those experiments were over, if the inmate survived at all, they were usually gassed. But Anci was sixteen and resilient, and she went back to work detail. Every day though, she expected to be selected for death.

After three months on death row, and the day before Joska Cséh arrived with her exemption paper in hand, Anci was shipped off to become a human cog on an assembly line, helping to make bombs and bullets for Hitler. She got to Bremen on the same kind of transport that had originally taken her to Auschwitz-Birkenau, a cattle train. Each car was crammed so tight with its human cargo there was no room to sit down. She arrived in Bremen in the middle of the night, and was taken immediately to the factory to start working. She had been on the train for a day and a half without food or water, and was taken directly to work. After her shift they finally fed her the usual diet for camp inmates, one small slice of bread and a small cup of watery soup. But now she had to work on this regimen, on her feet for sixteen hours. Plus, they put her on the night shift, but permitted her to sleep even less than at Auschwitz. If you passed out you were taken away and killed. If they were in a particularly impatient mood they shot you where you fell. But Anci knew she was one of the lucky ones. If you could work you stood a chance. They might try to work you death, but it was preferable to being selected for immediate extermination. It was torture, but she knew the Nazis were besieged from all sides. If only she could hold out a while longer. Surely the Russians or Americans or British would free them. And if only she could manage to steal an extra little morsel of food now and again, she felt as if she'd surely survive. Soon enough that opportunity came.

A camp inmate's entire life revolved around food. They were only fed once a day. And if they couldn't find some way to get a little extra they perished. Women had a chance of being able to offer sex to a sympathetic guard for an extra piece of bread. And the luckiest inmates of all worked in the crude kitchen. There they had opportunities to filch extra portions. They were watched by guards who shot them if they caught them, but it was worth it. When Anci was told to report to the kitchen she thought she was one of the lucky few. But it turned out that she was not going to work there after all. Instead she was selected to carry the bread over for distribution to the inmates. She was ordered to hold her arms straight out in front of her. Then they loaded her frail arms with a stack of loaves, and commanded her to carry it back to the prisoners. If she dropped it she would be shot. And she was warned not to dare to steal any. And they had intentionally loaded her arms in such a way as to make it impossible for her to use her hands to grab any part of it. Her arms were loaded, and it all leaned against her frail chest. But when the guards turned away for even a second she craned her neck forward just enough to take a nibble of the bread. She dare not take more than a nibble, as more might be visible in her mouth. It was all the difference she needed. If she could keep this job and not fall at her place, she might make it.

As she walked along with the loaves she was encouraged to think of the same song that her kid brother hummed on his way through the rubble back home. As inconceivable as it might sound, there were dozens of songs that camp and ghetto inmates kept alive. How could they nurture the muse of music in such dire conditions? How could such a luxury exist among people deprived of beauty? How dare they sing?! As long as they kept the songs alive, these anthems in turn gave them the hope to live another day. There was hope, and always the certainty in their minds that Hitler and his henchmen would be defeated. The songs were their secret weapon, nurturing their will to survive. Survival would be their victory over their brutal tormentors. And these songs of hope were the ammunition in that struggle. It was all they had. How dare they sing? How dare they not?

CHAPTER EIGHTEEN

DETOUR TO VIENNA

Joska Cséh went to the Auschwitz-Birkenau concentration camp and lived to tell the tale. That, in itself, is an astounding accomplishment. Of course, gallivanting around Europe in the hottest days of World War II, trying to help Jews, was utterly insane to begin with. In spite of that however, he felt nothing but disappointment over having failed in his mission. Of course, he was sensible and pragmatic, and understood that there was still more to be done. So, he focused on Rachel Giller, someone in an Austrian ghetto he had never met, the girlfriend of his old pal, Stephen Seredy.

As he'd already established a close working relationship with Wladislaw he offered him the job of driving him to the Czech border. And, as this was a mere picnic compared to what they'd already been through, and as he and his wife still liked to smoke, and gold was still gold, he was delighted to accept the job. Nazis from Auschwitz could have been hunting for them, but the further south they drove the more secure they felt. To be sure, any long auto trip at that time was a risk, because you always had to carry about five spare cans of gas in the back seat in case you ran out and couldn't find any for sale anywhere. One stray bullet into your car, and you could turn into a ball of flames. But the afternoon drive was uneventful, and Wladislaw left Joska off at the border town train station of Orlová.

Joska's luck seemed to be back. He caught two more trains through Czechoslovakia, including a well timed transfer to a west bound coach train to Austria. In just one day he managed to make it to Vienna. Once there he was on his home turf. Everybody knew him, and he had no end of contacts. Plus the friend on whose behalf he was here had provided him with sufficient funds to finance the new caper. He was even able to pick up some more tobacco. So, after a relaxing bath in one of the few remaining hotels unintentionally spared by allied bombing, he looked up his friend in the German captaincy, Corporal Rolf Holstein.

Rolf had expected him, and was happy to help. After a show of *Heil Hitlers* in front of the other office staff they repaired to a small park where they could discuss their plans more openly. They found a vacant bench and sat down. Before starting Rolf made his usual opening statement. He always liked to remind Joska that Austrians were less enthusiastic Nazis than the Germans. Of course, there were even Germans that tried to help victims of the Nazis, and they too were quick to point out that, 'Not all Germans are bad.' Despite the great shame over what their countrymen did, their feelings of patriotism were undiminished, and they assumed the burden of toting around the whole moral weight of their country on their slender shoulders. Whenever Joska heard one of those good Germans brag about not being all bad, he felt like saying, "No, only ninety nine percent of you are vicious bastards." But he kept his sarcasm to himself. And, despite living in a country that surrendered to Adolph Hitler with open arms, Rolf was still proud of being Austrian, and he never missed a chance to point out that many of them were good. With his national shame exorcised Rolf got down to brass tacks.

"These girls are kept in one of the ghetto buildings. I'll show you where. It's a circular building with an interior garden. Naturally, they don't get to enjoy that garden. But, if they volunteer for a work detail they get to go outside. They're transported in trucks to the work sites. Once they're in the trucks they leave the compound. Whatever you do will have to be during one of those trips. We'll take a cab and drive by the building now, so you can know it, and the neighborhood as well. I'll make some insulting comment when we're in front, and leave you off nearby. I have to return to my office as soon as possible. I'll say goodbye for real now."

He shook Joska's hand and sincerely intoned the most oft repeated parting phrase in Europe, "We'll meet again, in better times."

They hailed a taxi and rode through Vienna. To Joska's eyes allied bombing did not appear to have pummeled Vienna as badly as it had Budapest, and at least for the time being, more of the old Europe seemed to be left standing. For the benefit of the taxi driver Rolf blasted the weasel Viennese Jews who directed allied bombing. Oddly, it was a credible ruse. Citizens of the Third Reich were brainwashed to blame everything on the Jews. Even though the citizenry had already observed that the Jews were denied pets, homes, businesses, jobs, and finally freedom, they still imagined that they somehow, even mystically, wielded great power. So, Jew bashing was always a good way to dispel any suspicion that you were less than sympathetic to Nazi values.

Finally they drove by the ghetto building, and Rolf identified it by delivering a performance that was so overboard Joska could hardly resist rolling his eyes heavenward.

"Hold your nose, Herr Reinhardt. They house Jew vermin in there. How, in 1944, they can still allow any of those rats to contaminate the air of Vienna is a mystery to me. I should have warned the cabbie not to drive by. I apologize."

Shortly thereafter Rolf got out. And after another few blocks so did Joska. He was more confident now of success than he had been in Poland, and was determined not to fail again. But he was back to square one in this case and would take a few days to work everything out.

The next day Joska rose early and strolled by the ghetto building. He took note of the position of the main gate, and the security. Then he went up the block to one of the few outdoor cafés still operating, despite the cold weather and proximity to a sensitive facility. After a half hour, and three coffees and strudels, a truck emerged. The back was open, and he could see the disheveled inmates in their stripped uniforms, sitting with shovels and picks. He took note of the time, then went out in search of another Wladislaw, a taxi driver he could trust. He did this by testing their eagerness, or lack thereof, to respond to Nazi stimuli. He'd say, "*Heil Hitler*," and assess their reply. Was it sincere, or just polite? Then he'd talk about the allies and their advance. He'd bring up every war topic he could and watch their faces. He felt it best not to use his officer persona, but rather depend on bribery and a volunteer spirit. Anyway, a civilian cab driver might feel exempt from the usual military protocol. After four secret interviews he opened up to a friendly man about sixty.

"So, who do you hope gets here first, the Russians or the Americans?"

Unprepared for such frank and blatant conversation of capitulation the man was speechless. When he recovered from the shock he managed a well rehearsed declaration.

"I'm just a simple cabbie. What do I know of such things?"

Joska offered him a cigarette, which the man accepted without a hint of the indifference that had characterized his previous response. When he had luxuriated in the first puff he was probably as relaxed as he had been anytime since before D-Day, so Joska forged ahead.

"You know, what with the Americans crossing the Rhine and all, I heard they're thinking of releasing the Jews. What do you think about that?"

The cabbie had no specific reply to this new challenge, so he repeated his previous dodge.

"Like I said, I don't know anything about those things."

Joska looked at the man calmly though quizzically through the rear view mirror, but the man avoided his gaze. Finally, the driver brightened up as if he had finally devised a plan to take the pressure off him.

"What do *you* think?"

Joska liked this answer, and was encouraged to dig deeper.

"Would you still live in Vienna if the Jews were allowed to move back?"

Curious, but cautious, the old fellow said, "If our leaders think it wise who am I to argue? Hell, I did before. I mean, we all did!"

That's all Joska needed to hear.

"You're a decent chap. It'll be good when the war's over, eh?"

Without hesitation came the reply, "You can say that again!"

Joska went for broke.

"Regretfully the war's on, and they're still arresting people just for being born. I'm going to help someone who's being held against her will, and I need transportation. It pays well. Interested?"

The man now erupted into uncontrolled coughing. While he coughed Joska pressed on.

"I pay in gold. And I'll get coffee and sugar for your family. And tobacco."

Once the hack stopped hacking he asked, "What would I have to do?"

"Just drive," assured Joska. You're doing that already."

"Yeah, but this wouldn't be a usual fare. Tell me everything, and how much you can pay. Then we'll see."

Joska appreciated this prospective resistance fighter's candor and opened up to him.

"My name's Joska Cséh, and I'm from Hungary. I've been helping people like this for a while. And I tell you, it's more than just money. This war is going to be over soon my friend, and that's a fact. And when it is you're going to ask yourself if there was anything you could have done to do any good at all. Don't worry, I'll pay you. And yes, you're going to be taking a risk. But a bomb could fall on you tomorrow anyway. This is a chance for you to help an innocent victim of this war. You'll be a better man for it."

The cabbie looked down. Then he looked at the sky, perhaps considering an allied bombing raid. Seeing this Joska pressed on.

"You're thinking about the American bombing raids. Pretty terrible, huh? Their planes are enormous, and there's no end to them. We get creamed in Budapest too. I tell you, they're unstoppable. They're going to win, and I'm glad. The Americans are good people. But meanwhile, there's still suffering going on here. Let's join the good guys and help one victim. One victim! You'll be glad you did! Proud you did!"

"And what exactly am I supposed to do."

The man was all common sense now, and Joska was impressed that he was not too overwhelmed by it all. He deserved to know the full truth.

"I need to be constantly mobile, speaking to people face to face, so I'll need you every step of the way. We're gonna contact a man I know from Hungary who oversees the workers who leave the ghetto to clean up bombing rubble. He'll get word to the girl to volunteer. I'll also bribe the driver of the truck to slow down at a certain point where we'll be waiting. When she gets to that point she'll jump off and run to us. She'll change to civilian clothes in your taxi, and we'll drive to a safe house I'm going to rent in the suburbs. She'll eat, bath, dye her hair blond, and rest for the night. I have Christian papers for her. In the morning we head southeast to *Eisenstadt*, then to the Hungarian border. Once there you drop us off. You get 400 gold Napoleons, and my Viennese contact for black market goods. Drive us thirty more miles into Hungary, to the town of *Sopron* and get an extra hundred. Then you go home. And for the rest of your life you'll be able to look at yourself in the mirror with pride."

The fellow looked at Joska then down in deep thought. Then finally he asked, "So, it's a Jewish girl we're rescuing from the ghetto?"

Joska nodded gravely. This detail made the situation even riskier. The cabbie drummed his fingers on the steering wheel, and looked at Joe in the mirror. He nodded almost imperceptively, and asked, "And when are we supposed to do all this?"

Without hesitating Joska said, "We need to start at once. This afternoon. The girl could be shipped off to a concentration camp at any moment."

The taxi driver had survived the entire war, and now some stranger wanted him to take risks. Joska didn't want to let him face too many interior devils, so he interrupted his meditation.

"Look, the quicker we start the quicker it'll be over. I'll even give you a deposit, so your family can benefit immediately."

Every Viennese sound seemed to evaporate as the cabbie mulled over his existence. There was no bustling traffic or crowded sidewalks. No flocks of pigeons looking for a handout. No distant rumbling of approaching bombers or artillery. Just the man and his screamingly loud thoughts, "Why did he pick me? What should I do? Is this guy for real? Four hundred lovely little gold coins. I could get killed or tortured. What'll my wife think? She'd finally have some coffee and sugar. Is it worth it? Have the Americans really crossed the Rhine? Maybe it's time to choose sides. They shoot traitors. What should I do?"

Finally, he broke the silence with a purely practical concern, "Four hundred?"

"And other perks," Joska reminded him.

For the first time he looked Joska in the eye. "Okay."

They shook. "I'll have to stop by the wife and let her know."

Relieved, Joska asked his name.

"Günter. And let me tell you, it's a good thing you asked me. A lot of cabbies are stubbornly loyal to this whole Nazi idea."

"I know," said Joska. "You're the fifth candidate today."

This obviously shocked Günter, so Joska calmed him again.

"Don't worry, Günter. After you give your wife some sugar and coffee, and a smoke, you'll feel a whole lot better about this whole affair." "Actually," said Gunter, "She doesn't smoke."

Joska said, "More for you then," and made Gunter laugh.

"Just drive where I say my friend, and we'll get this over quickly."

After stopping by Joska's black market connection for coffee and sugar, and dropping it off with Günter's wife, they secured gasoline for the whole operation. With five large cans in the back seat they bought some food for the trip, and drove out to the suburbs to a house Joska knew. He spoke to the owner, and paid him to move out for two days. Here he would bring the girl and prepare her for the return trip to Hungary. They stashed the cans of fuel as well.

Joska felt much better than he had in Poland. He felt like his old self. But he knew this operation was more dangerous than his usual con jobs in Hungary. There was one especially weak point he could not control. When the girl jumped off the back of the truck she might be seen by bystanders who are not bribed to turn a blind eye. If they called out then the driver would be forced to do something, lest he be liquidated himself. But it was something beyond anyone's control. They would just have to be lucky. Maybe, Joska admitted to himself, he'd done nothing but rely on luck from the beginning. After all, he wasn't the only potential victim with a handy story for the Gestapo. And so many members of the Weisz family had their own brand of good fortune that had nothing to do with the glib Mr. Cséh. That little scamp Tommy ran through bombing raids without a scratch. His sister made it to Paris and back, then to New York. And Rose seemed blessed in so many ways. Maybe it was all their entwined destiny to survive this war. But why would their fate differ from that of the other victims in the war? In general, luck had run out for the Jews of Hungary. Of all the Nazi occupied territories none lost a higher percentage of them. No other Jewish community had to contend with two separate fascist regimes, the Nazis and the Nyilasok. Perhaps luck was not a thing to be considered after all. Yet there was no other alternative for saving this girl. When she jumps off that truck her only protection will be a mysterious unknown quantity, and for lack of a more precise definition, Joska called it luck.

As helpful as luck may be, it's not how you plan an escape from the Nazis. So, early the next morning Joska and Günter waited near the Ghetto gate for the trucks of volunteers to come out. When they did they followed them at a respectable distance. There were five trucks, so they'd have to make sure she was in the last one. That detail definitely could not be left to chance.

The trucks soon reached a neighborhood that had suffered massive allied bombing raids. They parked and the inmates were directed to get down and get to work. Joska and Günter were about a hundred yards away, and Joska scanned the area for his contact, Wilhelm Kiraly.

Wilhelm was a Hungarian who happened to have one Jewish grandparent, which was enough to get him arrested. But he was a Christian with some good contacts and ended up in Vienna with the job of overseeing the Jewish slave labor crews from the ghetto. He was also sympathetic to anything he could do to help the victims. After a half hour of watching the labor Joska got out of the cab and walked toward the work site. He slowed his pace to give time for Wilhelm to notice him. He stopped and tied one shoe, and took a stone out of the other one. Finally Wilhelm saw him, though you'd have to be closely observant to discern it. As soon as Joska knew they had made eye contact he walked off to one side where the remains of a building might hide their clandestine meeting. For his part, Wilhelm waited a few minutes, so as not be overly obvious, and announced he needed to take a piss. Normally, Nazis didn't afford their prisoners the luxury of privacy, but Wilhelm had long since established himself as a reliable old trustee, and the guards had grown accustomed to allowing him brief excursions into normalcy.

Just as brief were these meetings. Though Joska and Wilhelm were friends, and had not seen each other for six months, there precious few seconds together could not be wasted on platitudes about health, wealth, family or happiness. Devoid of sentimentality their entire exchange took place while the old gent pissed. Economy of word and gesture was a life and death consideration, and as Wilhelm relieved himself Joska slipped a handful of coins into his pocket.

"Share some of this with the driver of the last truck. Rachel Giller needs to volunteer for the work detail day after tomorrow, and jump out at Haydn Strasse, where the driver will slow down, and run down to her left to a waiting taxi. For confirmation I'll stand in the same place tomorrow. If it's okay scratch your head. If not, take another leak."

With that he left. Wilhelm never said a word. Joska got back to the car, and a heavily perspiring Günter was eager to hear a positive progress report. But his face fell when he heard they'd have to return the next day for confirmation.

With time to kill that day Joska went and bought a crucifix for Rachel Giller, or Gilda Gorbetsten, as her new papers identified her. He wanted to buy her shoes, but had no idea of her size. So, for the rest of the day they engaged in the number one favorite pastime of Europeans, discussing what they would do after the war. With no radio, magazines or cinemas, it was the hot topic. Even so-called loyal never-say-die Nazis did it when the more fanatical of their number were away. Joska confessed that he hadn't any plans beyond marrying Rose. But Günter was full of ideas and capitalistic schemes, especially now that his estate had increased by four hundred gold Napoleons.

He'd sell the taxi and get an ambulance, coldly calculating how the war's aftermath would have sick people for years. And peace would bring tourism again, so he'd transport the health conscious to the many spas in the area. Or he'd open a little bakery, because his wife was such a wizard with pastry. He chatted blissfully, enjoying a cigarette rolled in old newspaper, until the drone of American bombers, the masters of the skies, crept into the conversation.

He fell silent all at once, as was obviously his ritual, and closed his eyes in concentration, the better to divine from which direction came the unstoppable Americans. After a few seconds the wily Austrian's senses told him what to do and where to go. He ordered Joska into the car and they took off at a perpendicular direction from the flight path of the conquerors. After all, if a ten year old child could calculate an air force flight plan why not a sixty year old cabbie?

Günter drove with alacrity. He was focused, and did it with a sure hand that hinted he'd done it often, which was no doubt the fact. Joska also observed that there was no concern for the pastry wizard, but felt it wiser not to ask. He briefly reflected that this Austrian couple's relationship was a pragmatic one, recognizing that romance afforded little defense against the visits from the Americans.

As they cruised through old Vienna Joska had an opportunity to observe the remnants of various Baroque and Rococo façades, just barely held up by some ancient concrete. It was even sadder than Budapest. For, as lovely as that capital was, Vienna was nothing short of resplendent. But everyday the Nazis persisted so did the Americans. Buildings, bridges and statues that had witnessed a Roman presence, the Middle Ages, The Renaissance, and the advent of talkies, fell before Liberators and Flying Fortresses. Taking off from England, France and Italy, these latest developments of the Allied war machine blanketed the skies like locusts. Their mission was nothing less terrible than to smash the axis into submission. But the axis would not surrender. On the contrary, its scientists were developing new super weapons that Hitler was certain would wreak havoc on the allies, and allow them to snatch victory from the jaws of defeat. Hitler wouldn't throw in the towel, and everyday more Viennese masterpieces of art and architecture were surrendered to his hubris, and blown to smithereens. The raids lasted all of five minutes, but cleaning up and replacing the infrastructure would take decades. And, while Joska lamented the loss of human life, he felt no less pain for the loss of so much of their best artistic endeavors.

After the raid this liberation army of two went through a rehearsal. They parked on Haydn Strasse, and waited until the afternoon return trip of the ghetto trucks passed by. Satisfied that it was as well planned as could be they repaired to a pricey restaurant for a formal Viennese dinner. Joska splurged on the meal not so much because it was courtesy of another, but because he figured that tomorrow could be their last day of either freedom or life, and there was no good reason why it shouldn't be bolstered by a good meal. In any case, Joska didn't consider it a good idea to share such thinking with Günter who was finally starting to act like a friend.

While really not properly dressed for it, the establishment waved their dress code upon Joska's request, and the pair of men sat and let themselves be pampered. It was practically the last such establishment in Vienna that functioned at even half its old level. Nazi officers frequented the place, but the two would be liberators had nothing to fear. They were legal and had money.

While they ate Joska regaled Günter with stories about the whole Weisz family, and the time went by pleasantly. Günter was by now feeling completely comfortable with this crazy Hungarian. He loved to hear about the brave Ingrid Bergman look-alike and her rascal kid brother. He sympathized over the ordeal of confronting the Nyilasok in addition to the Nazis, and by the time their *Zacher* torte and brandy came they were comrades in arms.

The next day they followed the slave caravan again out to the site that they'd seen bombed the day before, and were relieved that it followed the same route past Haydn *Strasse*. So far, so good. But when they got to the site Wilhelm did not scratch his head. This time it was the old man's turn to talk.

While the old man was forcing himself to pee he said, "She has two cousins in there with her and won't leave without them. All three volunteered for work tomorrow. I need two hundred more."

Joska was caught off guard for about a half second, then reached into his pocket for the gold. He paid the old man, then turned and walked away as briskly as he could. He didn't want either of them to be caught talking. Wilhelm was important. Besides being as worthy of life as any other human being, he was an important link in getting people out.

Wilhelm had spent two years in the Viennese ghetto, but was always passed over for transport to the rail yards. The guards knew he was mostly Christian, and found his multilingual talents helpful. They'd made him a trustee early on, and even developed a fondness for him. Of course there were a few guards that had an even greater fondness for him, because he knew people like Joska Cséh paid to make a few Jews here and there disappear before the trains did. None of that made it any easier to tell Günter.

As he approached the cab he seriously considered not telling Günter, and relying on things taking their natural course during the escape. His mind really wasn't made up when an edgy Günter asked, "Well, is everything okay?"

Joska decided to be selective in his telling of the truth and replied, "It's on for tomorrow."

Knowing the whole truth wouldn't have made Günter feel any more nervous, as he was probably at his stress threshold already. So, Joska thought it best to wait for an opportune time to tell all.

"We need to do a little shopping. Come on."

But when Joska bought two more dresses and crucifixes Günter's curiosity and suspicion had built another wall between the two men.

"Gee, you're buying a whole trousseau for this Giller girl. And I guess it's important to have extra crosses in case she loses hers, huh?"

Clearly the wall needed tearing down. "Günter, if the Nazis catch us you know we'll be in the same boat as Rachel, right?"

"Maybe worse," affirmed the cabby.

"I mean," continued Joska, "If we tried to liberate the whole ghetto our punishment wouldn't be any worse than trying to free just one girl."

"Are you saying we're gonna try and free the whole place? Because if that's your plan I'm out! You may not have counted, but there are probably a thousand people in there, and my taxi only holds..."

"Five," inserted Joska. He had found the perfect place to interrupt Günter.

"What are you talking about, Cséh?"

Günter's reaction triggered Joska's confession, "We're not trying to liberate a thousand people, just three. Plus the two of us makes five. No problem."

Günter practically screamed, "What?!"

Joska took him by the shoulders and looked him in the eye, "Rachel's in there with her two cousins and she won't leave without them. Everything's set up for tomorrow morning. There's no turning back."

Günter was bug eyed, "Maybe not for you, but I agreed to one girl, not half the ghetto. Get yourself another taxi! Now, get out!"

Joska lowered his voice, "Calm down, Günter."

But Günter and calm were separated by a huge gulf of mistrust. "You lied to me. You said one girl, not three!"

"But until this morning it was just one girl," answered Joska. "Rachel sprang it on my contact and he just sprang it on me. I swear. I came from Hungary with the sole purpose of getting this one girl out. That's all! I never lied to you."

Günter would not back down, "Why didn't you tell me straight away as soon as the old man told you?"

"Alright," confessed Joska, "I should have. I was just waiting for the right moment. I mean, I was kinda shocked myself, you know? It's a bigger shock to me than you!"

"How do you figure?"

"Well, all along I had this plan to liberate one girl. I made preparations even before I met you. Now this! Look, Günter, I gave you my black market contact. I gotta see this through. After this I'm gonna lie low in Hungary till the war's over. Nothing's changed. It's more girls, but I gave more money. It's still the same setup!"

"More money, huh?"

Joska didn't like the sound of that, but at least Günter was still there. So, he stuck to the topic at hand. "Look, Günter. If that's what's eating you we can make another arrangement."

The silence that followed nurtured Joska's confidence that everything would be alright. It didn't take an immigrated Austrian Jewish rocket scientist to see the wheels in Günter's head going around. Joska did the math for him.

"Günter, you deserve another thousand, there's no doubt. And I'll get it from my friend when we get back."

But the future tourist and bakery entrepreneur stuck to his guns, "I gotta have it now. Sorry, Joska."

The fact that Günter apologized showed weakness, and Joska exploited it to the max. These three girls' lives depended on him, and he plumbed the reserves of whatever brashness remained in him to get this Viennese cabbie to stay on board. Joska played the shame card.

"You know, Günter, the old man lives in the ghetto just so he can help these people. He risks his life, and surrenders a freedom he could buy at any time, including today, just to do his bit. And all he's getting out of helping two more girls is an extra fifty. I need to hold onto whatever I have left to get us across the border. Once back in Hungary my friend will give me the other grand and I'll get it to you."

"How?" demanded Günter. Joska just had to push him over the edge.

"Günter, if I can figure a way to pull off all this don't you think I can get a measly little package to you?"

The Austrian was still indecisive, so Joska went for broke with the one tool he rarely liked to use, the truth.

"Günter, what are we talking about? We know each other. We're alike. We both want to do some good in this crazy war. If we were happy to help one girl we should be ecstatic to help three."

Now the cabbie entrepreneur was all logic.

"It's just that it attracts so much more attention to have a whole group of girls dressed in prisoners uniforms running through the streets than just one."

Joska's gravity matched Günter's.

"But the equivalent bribes are in. I have all the same concerns as you. The odds are still the same."

"I don't think so," insisted Günter.

"Nothing's changed," added Joska. "Bombs are still falling from the sky. You could be dead at any second. The war's almost over. And there'll be a reckoning of who helped and who didn't. I tell you, you can't afford to pass up this chance."

Günter had a lot to get off his chest. "You cursed Hungarian. You come out of nowhere and you turn everything upside-down."

"Hitler did that, my friend. We're just trying to get it back right side up."

This stopped the angry Austrian cabbie. For one thing it made him even angrier, because he couldn't think of anyway to defeat it. All he had now were complaints, instead of arguments. He sighed and looked down for an eternity. Finally Joska spoke in hushed tones.

"Come on Günter, let's get a good night's sleep."

The man slowly reached for the key and hesitated.

"Joska," he slowly began. "We could die tomorrow. Don't give me that bombs falling on me stuff. I mean we could really die tomorrow."

"Alright, that's a possibility. But…" Günter cut him off.

"So, if this might be our last night on Earth, I'd like to get laid if it's all the same to you."

Joska was so content to have his comrade back he would have agreed to anything.

"So, you want to visit your wife?"

Günter looked a little shy, "Well, all cabbies know where to take tourists, besides museums, if you know what I mean."

Joska understood perfectly, but let Günter do the talking.

"So, if you could afford one more slight splurge…"

Now, it was Joska's turn to do the cutting off, "You're the driver."

And so, Günter drove into the night, bound for a taste of normalcy not even war can interrupt.

After an extremely sound sleep in the safe house Günter woke Joska up. Joska couldn't have been more surprised, and was grateful that he wasn't abandoned after Günter's big night. A rooster had already crowed twice so they put the dresses in the car and drove to Haydn *Strasse* and parked. In spite of Günter's exercise in relaxation the night before he was now extremely tense, and chain smoked to fight it. Joska reassured him, and hopefully himself in the process.

"It'll be alright. Those three girls will run like the wind, you'll see. And look, there's nobody on the street. And besides everybody's been paid off. So, calm down. Before you know it, you'll be sipping coffee and feasting on your wife's pastry."

The mention of his wife made him feel guilty, but Joska decided it better for him to think about his marital misdeed than the Nazis.

As it was, there wasn't time to think about anything, because the first truck passed before their eyes. Günter looked at Joska, but he dare not look back, lest he lose count of the trucks. Truck two. Truck three.

"Start you engine, Günter."

Truck four.

"This is it," said Joska, and he got out and opened the rear doors.

They heard the sound of down shifting gears and the fifth truck slowly emerged into the sunlight at the end of Haydn Strasse. Another second and three frail girls in prisoner uniforms jumped out, and looked around in confusion. But Joska, gallant tall Joska, made even taller from standing on the running boards, was waving them over. They covered the distance just as quickly as Joska had predicted, and dove into the car.

"Let's go."

Günter already had the car in gear with his foot on the clutch. He just released it and they were away. As the car moved Joska gave orders.

"These are your dresses, ladies. Change quickly, please."

They ripped the ragged uniforms off their emaciated frames and pulled on the dresses. Joska didn't even know which one was Rachel Giller as he addressed them all.

"Stephen Seredy sent me. My name is Josef Cséh. Here, put these on."

Joska handed them crucifixes, and they likewise donned them without question. But it was hopeless. If they were stopped they were doomed. The girls looked like nothing more than what they were. Papers wouldn't help these girls. They were disheveled beyond anything Joska had ever imagined. They were as thin as skeletons and filthy. Their hair was matted and they stunk. But the skeletons spoke.

"Bless you. Thank you. God bless you. Thank you, sir. Thank you. Food. Food."

"We'll be at the safe house in a few minutes," said Joska. "We have food for you there."

The mention of food and their new freedom made the girls sob and cry. Joska felt so sorry for these creatures he would have cried himself but for his resolve to stay alert. Günter, on the other hand, was in shock. He was getting a crash course in what the master race did to people, and before they reached their safe house in the suburbs he allowed himself the release of tears.

The girls huddled throughout the entire drive through the city. When they got to their refuge Joska got out first and looked around. He leaned into the window and whispered.

"Get out slowly and act calm. Just follow me into the house. Günter, you follow us in. Make sure the car's secure."

Once inside the girls fell on the food. Joska had put out some bread and Weiner schnitzel and wine. Fact was, it would have been a feast for anyone. Schnitzel was nowhere to be found, and fresh bread was a luxury few Wieners knew any more. Thanks to the money that Stephen Seredy had provided to finance the operation, he and Günter had lived higher on the hog than most Austrians had for years. It was this opulence that dragged Günter along for the ride. So, they splurged on the last gourmet meal in Vienna, a brothel, and some sausage. It was worth it.

To look at any of the three girls it was impossible to imagine his friend back in Hungary, or anyone else, being in love with any of them. Certainly, months or years before, when they were plumper and healthier, they must have inspired passion. But now, all they inspired was pity and compassion. It made Joska wonder what Rose might look like after months or years of such treatment. While they ate, Joska told them about the shower in the bathroom. The girls looked at each other in glee, and then started to cry again. Who knows what they were remembering at that moment. What relative shot before their eyes, or what humiliation and torture they had endured? Günter hadn't come in yet, and Joska was glad to go out in search of him, allowing the girls the dignity of the first privacy they might have known in God knows how long.

He found Günter sitting on the hood, smoking a cigarette. His hand was trembling as if it were freezing outside.

"We were lucky, Günter, we got out of there before anybody noticed anything."

"Yeah, we were lucky, alright." Then he fell silent.

Joska sensed that Günter had been talking to himself. Was he in shock over seeing the condition of the girls, or was he getting cold feet about his fledgling resistance activities? In any case, Joska thought it best not to dig too deep. He might just work things out for himself.

"Did you see those girls? Can you believe our own countrymen could treat anyone that way?"

No response.

"Doesn't it make you feel good to help them?"

Just the wind blowing through the suburban streets.

"So, we'll let the girls eat and rest to get their strength up for the trip back home. And tomorrow we're on our way."

That finally hit a nerve, and the Austrian opened up.

"Joska, what you're doing is great. I really admire you for it. But I agreed to drive just one girl out to the suburbs for four hundred, and it turned out to be three girls. And now I'm supposed to drive them all the way to Hungary. Don't get me wrong. I'm not asking for any extra for the other two girls. But I think you better just pay me the balance, and I'll be on my way."

Joska didn't bat an eye. He was half expecting it.

"But you will be getting more for driving the girls to the border."

Günter looked ashamed and remained still. Apparently his bargaining tactic consisted of stating his position, then clamming up, and Joska felt best to respect it. Besides, the shame he obviously felt over abandoning the project would just grow inside him if was left alone with his thoughts.

Joska lit himself a cigarette and looked out at the landscape. He had been through this part of Vienna countless times, and it looked miraculously the same. Bombs hadn't fallen here yet, and it was as quiet as prewar peacetime. But conscience dictated that it was no longer a pastoral tranquility, but a morbid silence. The land, the buildings, the streets, had all witnessed the changes as passively satisfied with the chaos of war as it had been with the serenity of peace. The goose stepping Nazis and their triumphant entrance, the mobilization for combat, the people dragged out of their homes and herded into trucks. The city witnessed it all, and said nothing. And now Günter was like one of the myriad statues that adorned the public plazas. He saw it all and remained silent. Was he aghast at what he saw or merely indifferent? But the statue could remain stoic, and rely on its stone soul to excuse its apathy, whereas Günter could not. He must decide. Certainly, it was dangerous. But Joska was right. The danger was all around him anyway. And maybe the same luck that protected him from allied bombing in the city might also protect him in the open country. Joska felt enough time had elapsed to mellow their confrontation.

"Look, Günter, let's look at it as military strategists. Right now our armies are at either the Eastern or Western fronts. They're either off trying to keep the Russians at bay in the East, or driving the Americans back to the English Channel. There's no challenge or threat to the Third Reich here in the heartland. Trust me, I came here from western Czechoslovakia on a public train, and we had not a single encounter with the enemy. There's practically no soldiers there at all. It makes sense. Think about it. Why would they concentrate any troops in Eastern Austria or western Hungary? It's true there are still soldiers committed to this senseless war on civilians, but they're not committing fresh troops to it. It's just the same units of the Gestapo and SS for years, and they're in the cities and rail yards and the camps. The countryside is open now. No fighting. No armies. It's the safest place to be right now. Safer than here, my friend. I tell you! It'll literally be a drive in the country!"

Joska spoke so convincingly he actually believed it himself. Of course, the theory did have a ring of sanity. And though Joska was just making it up as he went along, it really sounded reasonable. It was just the notion that anywhere in Europe could be safe that sounded ludicrous. But Joska left it up to Günter. He couldn't drag him. But the look of shame and guilt on his face told him everything he needed to know. He was too afraid to go any further. He just needed to hear its confirmation. And it wasn't long in coming.

"Joska, I'm sorry. I want to cash in now. I did my bit, and I thank you for having me do it. But I'm not up to any more. Just pay me and I'll be on my way. Good luck. I hope you all make it. I really do."

Joska was far sorrier than Günter. Where would he get another taxi driver he could trust in one day, especially with his funds nearly depleted? His mind was now so focused on this new wrinkle paying Günter was just a distraction. He mumbled, "Alright," and limped over to the house. He politely knocked on the door, and when he heard no reply he assumed the poor girls were cringing behind the door, expecting to be dragged out by the Gestapo.

"It's just me, Josef Cséh," he said in his most assuring tone. "I'm sorry, but I need to get something out. Are you decent?"

The civility with which Joska addressed the girls shamed Günter even more, and he was now absolutely desperate to get out of there. And when Joska came back with his money he was too self conscious to even look him in the eye. He just took the money, mumbled a word of gratitude, and left without driving so fast as to call attention to his cowardliness. Joska just sighed. He had to come up with a plan B, and he was underfinanced. He thought he'd already had plenty to do, having to come up with two more sets of papers for the cousins. Now this.

The first thing that Joska did was to arrange for an extra day at the safe house. The landlord couldn't have been less receptive to the idea. Three girls and three days, instead of the arranged one girl and two days. Joska was practically hoarse and broke when he left him. He was left with no alternative but to do one thing that he hated, and that was to borrow money. But he swallowed his pride, and visited a cousin he had in the heart of the city. The girls begged him not to leave them alone, but he assured them that they would be fine there, and that he absolutely had to leave to get things ready for their trip back to Hungary.

On his way to his cousin's apartment Joska became morose. He wondered if they would even be there, or even if they were alive at all. And if they were there would they help him? He was at the lowest point he had been in memory. He had gone to so much trouble to get Anci out, but it was impossible. And now getting Rachel out turned into a major logistics nightmare. He needed two more sets of papers, a vehicle, and cash, and had one day to do it. As he walked along he was looking all around him for candidates for selling papers, if only he could borrow some money. His head was swimming. For the first time in his life he was discouraged. A depression fell on him that brought guilt. Rose's husband came back to haunt him and it stopped him in his tracks. He was so despondent and close to tears that his vision became black, and he had to sit down before he fell down. He had gone to Auschwitz to try and free Rose's sister. He had purchased the correct document, secured funds, made the trip, but not once did he give a thought to helping Rose's husband. Rehashing these details tortured him. He had become so used to living with Rose as her de facto husband that he never even thought about her real spouse. And when he had announced plans to go to Auschwitz they were all too polite to bring it up. Joska had done so much for them already they'd have been ashamed to ask anything else. Rose had even done her best to discourage him from going at all. But how could he have been so callous? Was he so possessive of her that another man's life was inconsequential? Was he jealous of him? How could he have acted so thoughtlessly? He was racked with guilt and considered his failure thus far as punishment. He collected himself enough to stand up again, and began plodding along incoherently toward his cousin's apartment.

When they answered the half hearted knock on their door they discovered their old cousin Joska standing in the doorway wearing a smile every bit as weak as his knock. But after hearing the full explanation for his uncharacteristic melancholy, his cousins, in classic Cséh form, set about to alleviate as much of his anxiety as possible. They lauded his efforts on behalf of the Weisz family, and offered him two sets of female papers and a modest loan which, combined with a revived Joska Cséh's powers of persuasion, could probably negotiate a vehicle to the border. Joska was overwhelmed with both gratitude and guilt. He was more grateful than he had ever felt in his life, but shameful that he had expected anything less from his wonderful family.

After hugs, a toast of brandy, and a promise to not be such a stranger, Joska was his old self again, and on his way back to Rachel Giller and her cousins. In the taxi on the way he still had to consider where to secure a vehicle. The one he was in had a swastika on the dash board, so he decided it was no candidate. Actually, it so discomforted Joska that he had himself dropped off several blocks from the safe house and walked away in the opposite direction from it, just to throw a suspicious fascist cabbie off the scent. When he finally got back to Rachel and her cousins they cried in relief to see him. They were actually a little drunk from the wine.

"Now, which one is Rachel?"

One girl shyly raised her hand. "God bless you, sir. I owe you my life."

They all joined in, "We can never repay you. Thank you." But Joska cut them short.

"Well, we still have to get back to Hungary. It's not that far, and there aren't many soldiers along the way, but we do need to take some precaution. So, I have some peroxide to dye your hair. I also have papers for all of you. Learn your new names. Now, please tell me your shoe sizes. I need to go out and get you all some shoes."

The girls were overwhelmed. What with the joy of their unexpected escape, and the effect of the wine on bodies ill prepared for it, they were light headed and just fell to giggling over it all. The laughing gave way to tears again, and Joska left them alone to exorcise whatever grief had possessed them over the course of their brutal internment.

As a representative for a shoe company Joska knew all the latest styles, as well as their value, so it was easy to shop for the girls' shoes. The woman had never met a man who knew so much about ladies' footwear. Afterwards he stopped off to buy a scissors and comb, toothbrushes and powder, some make up, and the latest fashion magazine he could find. The girls were horrendous looking, but he hoped some judicious trimming and styling might restore them to presentability. He was also fortunate enough to find some fruit for sale. On his way back he thought about transportation, and he decided that the most economical thing to do was to steal a car. He had never done such a thing, but he was doing a lot of new things now. How hard could it be? Certainly, he could make up some story and distract the owner away long enough to make off with it. So, as he walked along he invented scenarios, discarding elements of some and combining the best into one solid plan. He could do it.

As he turned the corner he came upon a scene that was more than a dream. There was Günter, standing by his cab, looking a little sheepish. As a jubilant Joska approached, Günter opened the door and said, "Tours of the country side. Cheap. Just the way to spend the day with a lady friend."

Joska lied, "Günter, I knew you'd come back."

Looking even more sheepish, Günter confessed, "When I told my wife she almost threw me out. Called me a coward. Though, it might just be the coffee and sugar."

Joska laughed at this.

"You see how it all works out, my friend? It's a good thing we delayed an extra day. Come on in."

They entered their temporary refuge together to discover the girls were already blonds. They proudly presented themselves for inspection, and both Joska and Günter had to tolerate more gratitude, though Günter, unaccustomed to having unremunerated women gush over him, didn't mind it much at all. Joska gave the fruit and tools of beautification to the young ladies, and he and Günter sat down to plan the route for the next day.

The proximity of Vienna to Attila's old stomping grounds easily reminds one that the two countries once shared an empire. Indeed, it was the untimely death of its heir apparent that plunged the planet into the terrible abyss it now suffered. The first logistical hurdle to overcome was the fuel. Günter had already arranged for the extra cans, but with three girls in the back seat where were they going to store it? There really was no magical solution; they would just have to be uncomfortable for a while. Anyway, compared to what they had already endured it was nothing. He would leave with the car's tank full, and carry three cans. After the first fifty miles he would hide one of the cans along the way. And he would do the same with each of the other two cans at the same intervals. If nobody found the cans he'd make it there and back, assuming of course they didn't cross paths with World War Two.

The girls spent several hours copying the pictures in the magazine until they achieved a reasonable resemblance to typical war ravaged damsels. Nobody expected anybody to look like Jean Harlow, so they might be alright as long as they weren't stopped and examined closely. So, after a breakfast of bread and cheese and coffee with sugar, all the better to fatten them up and improve their appearance, the unlikely brotherhood left one safe house in Austria to travel through the middle of the Third Reich to another safe house in Hungary.

For all their trepidation they had an utterly uneventful trip. But when they got within a mile of the border Joska said the girls still might raise suspicion, and it'd be best to avoid regular border check points. As the two countries were ostensibly allies they hadn't installed the obstructive wall of barbed wire found between most European borders. So, Günter took a deep breath and drove off the road and across a field into *Hegyeshalom*, Hungary. Then he valiantly drove for another five miles until they came to a small town, blessedly free of any military presence. Their luck had no basis in reason, other than Joska's half supposed strategic theory. Apparently, soldiers really were needed somewhere more strategic than this as yet uncontested farmland. The car came to a stop, and Günter collected hugs from everyone. Then he turned the sturdy old taxi around and headed back west to retrace his route and collect his fuel.

Joska had almost no money left, so he traded his wrist watch to the only man in town with a car to drive them all the way to Rachel Giller's apartment, where Stephen Seredy was waiting.

Stephen was ecstatic. He liberated Joska's watch without hesitation and paid him something extra as well. Seeing Stephen and Rachel reunited reminded him of Rose, and he wanted more than anything to get back to her, even if it was in the middle of a horrific battle zone. He was happy to have denied the Nazis more victims. He went on his trip to free two people, but ended up freeing three. He was tired, but he felt good. So, he left at once for Budapest. Even if he had to hitchhike he wanted to get back as soon as possible.

There were no cars on the road, but after several hours a coal truck picked him up. Besides taking him within three miles of the capital, the soot covered man brought Joska up to date on the local scene. The Russians were already in Romania and Czechoslovakia, driving the Germans back, and Hungary was next. But the good news lost its meaning when he entered Budapest on foot. The city looked worse than he even remembered. The allied raids had not abated, and there were times when Joska couldn't even tell where the streets were anymore. They were now just huge piles of rubble, and whole neighborhoods were impassable. He tried to talk with anyone he passed about the situation, but everyone feared talking to a stranger. The news about the big picture of the war was good, but the immediate reality was hard to take. He hoped that 63 Hungaria Korut was still in one piece. Home is where the heart is, and as awful as this hellish battle zone was, he yearned to be by Rose's side, no matter where that was.

CHAPTER NINETEEN

JUDEO-CHRISTIAN

Protected by Thomas Molnár's birth certificate I had been brought back to the residential district on the east side of Budapest to live with the middle aged, Roman Catholic Debrecens. They were the superintendents of an apartment building that was designated for Christians. It had six floors with twenty five apartments on every floor, and every single one was occupied by devout disciples of Jesus, or people pretending to be. Mr. and Mrs. Debrecen had a son just my age that died from typhus, and they were thrilled to have me, as well as the extra forints. They were so lonely for their little Willie I think they would have taken me without the money. But they were nice. I was separated from my real family, so for now this couple was my family in every sense of the word. We endured the deprivations of war together, and prayed together, and shared what we had. Joska paid them, but they were risking their lives every day for a pretty pathetic sum. I came to care for them, and was actually as concerned for them getting caught as I was for my real parents.

As the supers of the building they could appoint whomever they wanted as concierge, and they found great joy in watching me play doorman. I loved it too. Back in those days large buildings like ours had a front gate which was locked at nightfall. When the tenants wanted to get in after that they rang a bell. That's when I ran out and opened up for them. I always bowed formally, and so charmed them with my manners that I always got a tip. I split the tips with my foster parents and they were proud when people commented, "This young man is as clever as a Jew." Life is odd.

One detail that worried Jews feigning another faith was the crucifix. Christians wore them, but not all, and not always. After all, they had nothing to prove. On the other hand, the Jews who wore them counted on them for protection, and never went out without wearing them. But they began to worry if they weren't being too obvious. They looked at everyone wearing a crucifix, and wondered if they too were really Jews. And they were afraid that the Nazis or Nyilasok were catching on to the trick as well. Perhaps they would crack down on people with crosses. Maybe they even decided that a sure fire way to recognize a Jew was if he wore a cross. Of course, if they did suspect us, we were constantly terrified of the most reliable way to condemn us, which was to pull down our pants and check for circumcision. More than one legitimate Christian had been sent off to a camp just for having had his foreskin removed in the name of modern hygiene. I had my foreskin off and my crucifix on.

One famous circumcised person was Jesus, and I went every Sunday with the Debrecens to sing his praises in Church. I sang all the hymns with gusto and genuflected with aplomb. The first time I went to the gentile house of worship I was terrified. My foster parents had told me not to worry, that I looked just fine, and that everything would be alright, but despite such reassurances I was convinced that I would be found out. Not that I wasn't prepared. The Debrecens had dutifully taught me every psalm and song a little Catholic boy should know. They taught me how to cross myself, genuflect, take communion, and pray. By the time I went to my first mass I was well tutored, but I was worried I looked too much like their savior, a real Jew. Another worry was the fact that I didn't resemble the Debrecens in the least. They had courageously made up a story that I was a nephew from out of town who had been recently orphaned. After all, they had come to this church for years, but never with me. I wonder now if the priest didn't figure it all out on the first day. Maybe half the church was really Jewish. Maybe the Priest was. Anything was possible.

Our building had a few extra tenants that nobody knew about. There were Jewish families hidden in the attic, and also in a most original hiding place, the elevator. The bombing raids had eliminated electricity, so the elevator at the west end of the building, which was trapped between floors, was of no interest to anybody. In it lived the Kovacks family. They were a young married couple with a four year old daughter. The elevator was just wide enough to lie down in. And the emergency trap entrance in its roof was how they received food. Not long after I arrived there I came to learn of the Kovacks from my adopted parents. They introduced me, because they knew I could help. I was small enough to squeeze through the half of the door that remained in the floor above the permanently stalled elevator, yet tall enough to handily step down to the roof of the Kovacks home and communicate with them through the trap door. I was the perfect size.

The original elevator had one glass side, but the Kovacks had covered it with plywood. There hadn't been electricity for months so nobody took much notice of the permanently stalled conveyance. The Kovacks had blankets, clothes and candles. As World War Two refuges go it was better than some. Every night, at three in the morning I visited them. My apartment was on the ground floor, and the elevator was stalled between the third and fourth floors in the corner of the building. I made my way quietly up the stairs which circled the elevator shaft. Once there I had been taught how to open the door without making a sound. Then I lowered my little bundle by rope to the roof. Then I turned around and stretched my body down until I almost touched the roof. A short quiet jump and I was on the roof, while alerting the Kovacks at the same time. They handed me up their dirty commode, and I handed them down a clean one. Then I gave them their food and water ration for the day which another neighbor who was involved in the plot provided. We whispered greetings, and I gave them whatever news there was. The little girl, Havah, always had a big smile for me, and I always gave her one back and tried to say something especially cheerful to her. Then I closed the trap door and climbed back up and shimmied through the half open door. Next I hauled up the dirty commode, then snuck back to the Debrecens' apartment and emptied it in our toilet. At least we still had plumbing.

To this day I can easily live with the inconvenient aftermath of a hurricane, going for extended periods of time without electricity. I learned that plumbing is a superior utility. You can live far better without electrical power, but with plumbing, than you can with electricity but no plumbing. But the fact is we were lucky to have any plumbing at all. By now my real family was melting snow for drinking water, and thankful for the bountiful winter.

After I took care of the Kovacks in the elevator I visited two more families in the attic. One family was the Moskovics. They lived in a tiny cramped space with their two children. About a hundred feet from them lived Mr. and Mrs. Farago. They were in the same attic, but they were separated by several walls, and I had to go through separate accesses to visit them. The greatest difficulty in visiting and helping them was the need for absolute quiet. The Debrecens were wonderful people, and there were probably many more like them in the building. But it only took one person who wasn't to go to the Nazis or Nyilasok and complain of suspicious noises in the middle of the night.

It's surprising how quiet a human can be if he has to. I learned to walk, crawl, and climb without making a peep. But the three families I was helping by night were the true masters of quiet living. For most of my own existence at this point I could behave normally. I only had to be careful when I went to help the families in hiding. But they had to keep quiet all the time. Day and night. I don't know which was worse for them. In the day there were people walking up and down the staircase that wound around the elevator. And there were apartments that opened onto the stairwell. People came and went from their apartments all the time. And at night it was quiet, so any sound was magnified. I can't imagine the anxiety they felt if they sneezed or coughed. Probably the only time they could speak normally was during an air raid. And they probably spent that time praying. I felt sorry for them, and also a great camaraderie. My existence was completely at risk anyway, so taking another threatening burden didn't scare me. Besides, a bombing raid could kill us all at any moment. Life was one big risk, so I didn't hesitate to help them.

Though the Debrecens was a relatively safe haven nobody was immune to air raids. One night the eastern corner of our building was demolished. But our first floor apartment, as well as the elevator haven on the opposite corner, and the families in the attic, all went unscathed. War was like a crap shoot; you never knew what was going to happen.

By the fall of 1944 there were forty members of our family living in the apartment building at 63 Hungaria Korut. About seventy percent of the building was Weisz or Weisz related. They had Christian papers and wore crosses, but rarely went out. Nobody wanted to run the risk of confronting authority, even if it meant not going to church. So, only life's most basic needs urged the reluctant emergence into sunlight of the least Jewish looking among us. And that was to collect snow.

The water mains had been blown up in allied bombing raids, and the only source of water was the plentiful white crystals falling in the Hungarian winter of 1944. The duly elected would go out at night and bring back pails of it and dump it into the bathtub. Then they'd chop us some furniture and build a fire in the coal burning stove in the kitchen and melt the snow. If there was enough furniture for kindling they'd let the melted snow boil. If not they just prayed and drank it anyway. For now collecting snow was the only activity that dragged my family from their hiding place. They had considered shopping for food, but it seemed wiser to leave it to Rose or Joska. For members of the Hebrew tribe without a Josef Cséh of their own a simple shopping trip was like a well timed commando raid, with a terrified Moishe buying as much food as he could carry without making it obvious he shopped for a dozen others, and getting back as soon as possible.

Despite all the precautions there was still the ever present angst of being turned in by a suspicious neighbor. Or the Nazis just might decide to start going door to door to look for undesirables. You were never completely safe. And at 63 Hungaria Korut there was a presence that made everyone especially edgy. Two catholic priests lived together in a ground floor apartment, right next to my parents. Even running out for snow in the middle of the night made them pray that, upon returning, the young holy men would not be outside and engage them in idle chit chat which could evolve into a theological discussion about a long ago Jew, and expose their ersatz Christianity.

After a month rumors started to circulate that Nyilasok or Gestapo had their beady eyes on the building. It must have been the priests!

That's it! Real Christians saw right through them, and they were as good as on a train to the camps. In anticipation of the coming raid one of the relatives on an upper floor always kept lookout, peering through the curtains at the street below. Of course, seeing them coming wouldn't have done any good anyway. There was nowhere to run. And finally we did see them coming.

Those damn priests! They call themselves Christians, but doesn't being a Christian mean that you love your neighbor? What kind of hypocritical Christians were these? Clowns. Farces. Two more two-faced gentiles motivated more by hate and mistrust than by their so-called superior religion. The Nazis were headed directly toward our building. All three floors were alerted, and everyone froze in their tracks. There were only three or four Nazis, but they were armed, and capable of summoning more. The Weisz family was doomed. Looking down they saw the four fascists approach the front door. They grouped in front if it and started to knock. But, by some miraculous mistake, they were knocking on the wrong door. They were not pounding on any Jew's door at all, but the priests' instead. This was fortunate, but only a few seconds reprieve for the Weisz family. They had lasted through the entire war. Moving to Budapest, changing to a Christian building, getting false papers. And allied victory seemed so close. Why now?

The Nazis pounded on the door, but got no answer from the priests. Unaware of their mistake they now started to kick in the door. It flung open and they stormed in. Now they would realize their mistake and divert their wrath to my parent's door across the hall. But at that moment the two Catholic priests dove out of their front window and started to run away. The Nazis ran out the front door after them, firing their guns. The two priests hit the ground and stopped moving. They were dead.

As it turned out they were two young Jewish men masquerading as Catholic clergy. It seemed like a good disguise, but someone must have turned them in. Later Joska learned that someone had indeed informed the Nazis that Jews were living in the building. And maybe they really were coming for my parents. But when the two fake priests dived out that window the Nazis thought that they had found their quarry. The building was cleansed of Jews, and the case was closed

Naturally, my whole family was relieved to survive the visit from the Third Reich. But they knew that the death of the two young Jewish men was the price. Two dead meant the survival of forty. If they hadn't been home maybe the Nazis would have continued their search. And if the two young men hadn't panicked and run who knows what could have happened. But the Nazi blood lust was satisfied for now, and my family was spared. It is the greatest irony that two young Jewish men, pretending to be followers of another young Jewish man who died for the benefit of others, now did exactly that. There is no doubt that on that day they were our saviors.

It was a wonder that there was any normalcy left to life at all. But Hungarians love sports, so there was still the occasional boxing event or soccer match. And, on occasion, Joska would pick me up in his motorcycle and off we'd go. Once at the event I focused on the activity and blocked out the reality of our day to day existence. Doubtless, the same was true for everyone present in the arena. But at these events there were some in the stands interested in much more than good clean sports fun. One such time, completely absorbed in a soccer game, we were unaware we'd fallen under the scrutiny of some Nazis behind us. About midway through the badgering began.

"Excuse me sir."

The all too familiar ring of authority tinged with mock politeness caught me off guard, and I froze. Joska too recognized that tone, but he did not freeze. Rather, he immediately planned his counter attack. The first step in his plan of action was to ignore them. To further mislead them, as well as snap me to my senses, he gave me a playful swat on the back and said, "What a game, hey Tommy?"

This opening salvo of Joska's drew two salutary responses. First, it calmed me. A calm person looks innocent and becomes a less likely target for aggressive animals, like the fascists. The second effect was to infuriate our antagonists. At first sight this might not seem like a good thing to do. After all, they're powerful and armed. It's like throwing stones at a bear in the woods. But making them mad also makes them stupid. Winston Churchill knew that. When he bombed Berlin early in the war he knew the German capital was devoid of any strategic value. He didn't even think it would demoralize the German people or sap them of their will to wage war. What he did think was that it would infuriate Hitler. And it worked like a charm. Der Fuhrer did not give a militarily response. Rather, he reacted with a knee-jerk bombing of London, another site without strategic significance. The Royal Air Force, England's first and primary line of defense, was spread out in small units in the country side. So, instead of methodically attacking those vital little airstrips out in the boondocks Hitler committed his Luftwaffe to endlessly dropping bombs on city streets which were far from the real war. In short, making Hitler mad made him a poor general, and protected the RAF. And those Nazis behind us followed suit. They put their brains on check in order to strut their egos like arrogant peacocks.

"Excuse me sir. I am talking to you."

I followed Joska's lead, and kept cheering at the game. I felt safe with such a brave tactician as Joska in charge. If he was going to ignore him I was his willing and patriotic recruit. Of course, we couldn't ignore them forever. Three times with any Nazi is usually the charm. But I didn't realize at that moment that Joska was playing cat and mouse simply out of the joy of doing so. He was climbing a Nazi mountain simply because it was there. No relying on false German military documents this time. He wanted to play with these fascists out of his perverse sense of humor and love of peril. Such risky bravado would have infuriated my mother, but his peculiar love of danger took over. He left the ball in the Nazi's court and tempted fate to its maximum.

"I demand that you turn around at once!"

The jackbooted Prussian put his hand on Joska's arm, but Joska blithely turned around as if someone were stopping him for the time of day. He showed no fear, hardly even concern. He spoke to the Nazi, but never stopped sharing the fun of the game with me. He smoothly picked the German's hand of his arm, and, still smiling from the thrill of the event, spoke.

"Yes, *mein anfuhrer*. What is the bee in your bonnet?"

Bee in his bonnet?! Bee in his bonnet?! What kind of a childish innocent phrase was this to use to address a representative of the Third Reich?! This upset the Nazi so much he wasn't sure if he was angry or insulted. In short, he was caught completely off guard. Who was this guy? He spoke perfect German, and tossed him a phrase he hadn't heard since he was a child. Bee in his bonnet?! Nobody had ever said such a thing to him in his whole military career. He turned red and started to inarticulately sputter. And his compatriots were no less at a loss. They were simultaneously amused and shocked.

All of this, of course, took place in the span of just a few seconds. Meanwhile, Joska had already gone back to being jovial with me. He put his hand on my head and gave it a little rub in classic guy-to-kid fashion. Observing this the fascists fell thoughtlessly back on their usual tactic of intimidation. It was trite, but it had served them well a million times before.

"Papieren bitte."

Joska sighed, and did nothing to mask his annoyance.

"Papieren bitte. Papieren bitte. I swear you sound like parrots. If I show you some scraps of paper will you leave me and my nephew alone so I can go back to enjoying the first respite from my duties I've had in months? Huh, will you?"

Now, the man was challenged in front of his comrades, and he was starting to lose face. So, he tried to remember what motivated him in the first place. Oh yes, the boy.

"I'd like to see the boy's papers. He has a very suspicious appearance."

"Oh yes, He looks too Hungarian."

Joska picked me up like a rag doll and dug his mouth into the side of my neck, making a bear noise, and tickling me. Even though I was feeling truly afraid from the whole situation, I was physically obliged to laugh. As I giggled and jerked around my cross dangled. The little silver crucifix caught the eyes of the Nazis, and they scrutinized me differently. Where they had suspected me of being Jewish now they were looking at me in a new light, maybe even trying to convince themselves that I was not. Its like when you find out that some movie actor is Jewish, though you never knew it. You look at him and say, "Oh yeah. I can see it!" The Nazis were approaching that plateau, but with the onus on them to realize I was gentile. Joska charged ahead, pointing merrily at the field.

"Oh look, that forward guard looks Jewish. Wait! So does the goalie. He's blocking too many goals anyway. Shoot him. It'll even the odds."

He tried not to, but this made one of the other Nazis laugh. The main antagonist was speechless. But not Joska.

"I am assistant to *Oberst* Steiner. If you don't know him you can come in Monday morning and I'll show you my papers. He'll show you his papers too. Then you can show us your papers. And for the big finale we can all show each other our own papers. It'll be quite a merry party."

The other Nazis practically had to bite their tongues to keep from tittering. They had no idea who this Colonel Steiner was, but felt certain their careers would derive no benefit whatsoever from meeting him under such circumstances. Apprehensive about badgering some mysterious military adjutant the ringleader decided that reviving his interest in sports was the wisest course of action. But first he had to make amends. Why take any chances?

"Of course, adjutant...."

"Just call me Cséh. That's what Oberst Steiner calls me."

"Herr Cséh, I didn't mean to bother you. I was just doing my duty. I'm sure you understand. One cannot be too certain."

At this Joska hardly even took notice. He acted bored, as if he was doing this martinet a favor just to tolerate his feeble apology. The demoralized peacock's tail drooped and he tried to get back into the rhythm of the game, as if nothing had happened.

"Who are you rooting for? Can we give you a lift home after the game?"

"I prefer my motorcycle. Check it out after the game. Now, if you don't mind."

"Not at all. Enjoy the game, Herr Cséh!"

You can talk about mythological heroes, or heroes of the silver screen. But they all took a back seat to Joska. He was simply unbelievable. Some things however, even Joska couldn't change. Like the human nature of a kid. Normalcy invaded the life of my nephew John, and we had to deal with it on his terms. Since his parents went to New York he'd been haunted by feelings of abandonment, and it was now manifesting itself with extremely poor timing. Anyway, that's my amateur psychological analysis of his behavior. Because we couldn't understand why, with a war on, with him in hiding for his life, he couldn't control his impulses. Normalcy, unwanted and unwelcome, manifested itself in Mr. Harigtay's apartment.

Mr. Hargitay earned a few meager *forints* repairing watches in his apartment, but every time he repaired a watch John would sabotage it. The old man would open up a watch to work on it, and when he turned his back, or went out for a few minutes, John would undo his work. The poor fellow was beside himself. He wanted to help the boy, and he badly needed the extra income, but after about six weeks he reached his limit. So, when Joska came to pay him the usual periodic fee he told Joska.

"Mr. Cséh, I'm sorry. But you're going to have to take John with you. He's driving me crazy!"

Joska tried his level best, "But he has no papers, Mr. Hargitay. You know what that means!"

"He's destroying my business. Actually, I think he already destroyed it. Just take the boy, please!"

Joska's powers of persuasion were formidable. He convinced Gestapo agents to release prisoners, and chased off armed Nyilasok gangsters with his fiery tongue. He even cajoled total strangers into selling their precious papers. But he met his match in Mr. Hargitay.

It was a fact that John had no papers. He was born John Nonasi, and he stayed that way. Fortunately, that surname only identified him as someone from the town of *Nonas*, and not necessarily a Jew. And combined with the classically Christian first name of John, and his turned up nose and red hair, he was in no immediate danger of being stopped. Still, it was a risk for anyone to walk around without identity papers.

As walking around was out of the question, Joska just took him to 63 Hungaria Korut, and made him stay indoors. To this day I think it was John's plan all along. Anyway, the whole family was happy to have him. And happier yet were they that the Russians had crossed the border into eastern Hungary. Of course, this was not the flag waving, rejoicing kind of happy. It was more like going to the dentist. We were glad that we were getting rid of a bad problem, basic to our well-being, but afraid of the pain that accompanied the process.

CHAPTER TWENTY

THE RUSSIANS ARE COMING

The Russian and American bombing campaigns were turning Budapest into rubble, and the hapless Hungarians now enjoyed even fewer creature comforts than those of four score years before, when the Hapsburgs consolidated their imperial power. Those citizens had no telephone service, trolley, or electricity either, but they did stroll gas lit streets and read newspapers. The war weary citizenry descended from those carefree Magyars however, had come to depend upon the uninterrupted flow of electrons to power both their lights and printing presses, so they were now plunged into a state of complete darkness. Not that anyone ever considered our wartime media to be objective organs of truth.

Since Admiral Horthy had handed over our destiny to the Nazis the printed page and the radio airwave had been under the iron clad control of the truth shy ministry of propaganda, and we had been fed a strict diet of misinformation for five consecutive years. According to our government and their overseers our valiant boys had prevailed so consistently that victory was a foregone conclusion. And any subrogation of that absolute inevitability could only be attributed to the demoniac machinations of the international Jewish conspiracy. Oddly, normalcy managed to creep in once in a while with a soccer score. But that was when we still had power. Radio was just a memory now. But, whether it was the latest from truck drivers, the infrequent chatty German soldier, or the last stealthfully hidden crystal set in Budapest, we somehow knew that the Americans were pushing east, and the Russians west.

When Joska came back from his trip he brought some good news about Russian advancement into Czechoslovakia, so everyone was on the edge of their coal bins waiting to hear Soviet artillery on the outskirts of town. When I went to church with the Debrecens I prayed to Jesus to protect me from his followers and open the way for the Reds to come in. And over at sixty three Hungaria Korut my family did the same. Yet, for all the anticipation of the vengeful Russian tidal wave coming our way, the Germans would not relax their genocidal timetable.

Whatever well earned insult you may wish to hurl at the Nazis, you must allow that they were efficient. Despite the constant destruction of rail yards they continued to fill cattle trains with human beings and send them off to their factories of industrialized murder in Poland. They shipped half a million Jews there, with almost none making a round trip. But, there were a few successful rescue attempts.

In one case, a multimillion dollar bribe rerouted a train to Switzerland, and saved nearly seventeen hundred people. And the famous Swedish diplomat, Raoul Wallenberg, set up neutral 'Swedish Houses' to save tens of thousands. Motivated by an avarice that nearly matched his homicidal inclinations, Adolph Eichmann himself proposed a bribe of fifty thousand trucks full of much needed materials to ransom the Jews of Hungary, but the logistics were impossible to work out. And there were other Joska Cséhs as well. But, by and large, the Jewish presence in Hungary was rapidly vanishing.

As for ourselves, we didn't know many facts and figures. We were a handful of frightened people, afraid to peek out from our hiding places. What's more, that winter was rough on all Hungarians, regardless of whether they accepted Christ in their heart or not. We huddled in attics, elevators, basements, and phony Christian safe houses, waiting for Papa Joe. Then, finally, November brought snow and the blessed atheist Russians.

As terrible as the air raids were, they gave us just a sampling of Red wrath. Their bombers had only flown overhead occasionally, and when they did, the hell was relatively brief. But now, the warm up was over, and the fire of Hades was at hand for real. Their massive cannons sat stationary within range of our city, and issued forth an incessant and thunderous barrage fed by eager troops that fired as quickly and steadily as they could open the smoking cannon breaches and reload them. Tactically, their target was the same as before, the entire city. As long as the shells fell within town limits it was right on the money. They had enough ammunition to last until either every last molecule of stone in Budapest disintegrated, or the fascists surrendered. The deafening reports and constant explosions sent everyone, authentic adherents of the Prince of Peace or not, fleeing down to the coal cellars for the duration. And with the speed of an artillery round the rumor that the Russians were finally on the outskirts of the city spread to the inner city and the apartment of the Debrecens.

As soon as I heard it I became so anguished over my parents' vulnerable proximity to the onslaught I sped out into the streets, making a beeline for Hungaria Korut. Whatever sense my ten and a half year old head had acquired was completely forgotten over fear for my parents, and I found myself retracing the steps I had taken after the birth certificate robbery. Only, this time thousands of artillery shells were falling on the city.

I ran along whatever flat stretches of street I could find until I got to Liget Park, and then ran through the forest. Of course, the artillery was aimed just as much at the parks as anywhere else, so there were explosions all around me. If I'd have thought about it I'd never have run anywhere but down to the Debrecen's basement, but I ran through the woods as if isolation from the masses offered me some measure of protection. I ran in such a state of tunnel vision I didn't even notice that forest and town alike were deserted. All citizens, soldiers and police included, huddled down in the coal bins, trembling. And if anybody would have chanced to spot a kid running through the barrage it's unlikely they would have entertained joining me for an interview. So, I was safe from inquisitive Nazis for now. I just had to contend with the Red gauntlet of a million cannon shells. That I made it, and in one piece, is testimony to the insane unpredictability of this world.

When I burst into the ground floor of my parents' apartment it was empty. So, I ran up to the second floor to see if some other relative knew where they were. Finding the second floor as deserted as the first, I abandoned any thought of making a try for the third. I changed course and plummeted down to the coal bin and, as it turned out, my entire family. They were amazed and elated, even if a bit angry at me, for stupidly risking my life. They hugged and kissed me, and then we all hunkered down, prepared to, at least, perish together.

As dismal as this fearsome conflagration was, I never felt that I would actually die in it. I was too busy staying alive. Dying just wasn't on my agenda. To this day I don't remember a specific instance of getting sick, eating, bathing or going to the bathroom. All of those things must have occurred, but the sole activity for all of us was, simply, survival. It was full time employment, with no sick leaves, vacations, or time outs. Day and night our sole occupation was to withstand the merciless shellacking of Budapest. The Reds had taken four years to get this far, and they were here for the sole purpose of kicking Kraut *heinie*. The German war machine had laid siege and waste to Moscow and Stalingrad, killing millions, and the time for righteous vengeance was now at hand. They had one objective, to kill and destroy until not a hint of resistance remained. We of course did not take any of that personally. We saw them as our liberators, and had no fear of them directly. After all, we reasoned, the artillery assault was not aimed at us. It was meant for our common enemy, the fascists. No shell had the name Weisz written on it. The Nazis, Nyilasok, and Hungarian army were in their cross hairs. Not us. Our saviors were here to rid Hungary of its oppressors. We just had to keep our heads down and keep out of the crossfire.

About sixty people, all the inhabitants of 63 Hungaria Korut, were in the vast basement coal bin, as wide as the entire building. Three quarters of that rank was composed of the Weisz and Krausz families. And the others were too concerned for their own safety to worry about anyone's foreskin. Everybody's official religion was orthodox survival.

Joska, Rose, my parents, my grandfather, John, and thirty seven other relatives, were huddled with me, wincing at each whistling bomb. And it went on for over a month. No invasion. No soldiers. Just artillery shelling. If the Red Menace intended to wear down our will to resist it was most persuasive. And, if the uniformed members of our society still felt resolute before the relentless Russian onslaught, they certainly didn't speak for us civilians. We were more than ready to surrender. Actually, there didn't even seem to be a battle going on at all. The shooting seemed to be coming exclusively from the east. We heard no salvos from our side being fired in response. Later we found out the Germans had definitely gotten the message and were organizing a complete pullout, leaving Hungary to tend with the subhuman commies on its own.

Hunkering down in the basement very few rumors of Nazi strategy made its way to us. So, we just sat there, listening to the constant explosions. One thing we noticed was that the artillery shells seemed to be mainly passing overhead and landing within the inner city. Hungaria Korut was on the outskirts, and the Russians would logically be targeting the actual city, not its perimeter or suburbs. The realization that we may not be in their primary target zone calmed us a lot. Of course, they were firing thousands of rounds, and allowing that even one percent fell short, we were all in peril of being blasted to kingdom come at any second.

If you can get used to the sight and smell of corpses, you can indeed get used to artillery. After about a million rounds had passed over our heads we grew accustomed to live with the flash of the cannon, and the crash of its target. Normalcy crept into our well defined lives and we took up the only activity available to humans in such circumstances, the fine art of conversation, with a single topic dominating each and every exchange.

We were confident the war would be over soon, and we made plans to live in a world forever freed from fascists. All the adults took their turns describing what they were going to do when the conflict ended. When each person spoke they had the floor, and we all gave them our undivided attention. Of course, there was nothing else from which our attention could be divided anyway, but we were desperately in need of contemplating the return of our lives again. For years we had lived like escaped convicts, hiding and hungry. Finally, we could openly discuss anything we wanted. Even just talking about freedom was as nurturing as the real thing. It was, in and of itself, a blessing. Mostly, we would resume our former lives, which compared to the existence of the last five years, seemed heavenly. Grandpa would reopen his café. Mother would return to the jewelry store. Everybody would take up where they left off. Or would they? Before the Nazi threat we lived in the tranquil rural village of Gyonyos. Would we really go that far back? The changes in our lives had been forced upon us by the threat of violent death, and for better or worse, we were different people now. Returning to the quaint village of our birth was no longer an option. And when we discussed John the focus for our lives became clear, immigration to America.

Why would we want to continue to live in a country that would steal everything from us, and murder us? Maybe it would happen again? We were born in Hungary, but we were no longer Hungarians. The Nyilasok saw to that. Had we remained in the countryside our neighbors would have abetted our arrest and murder. Simply put, we no longer felt welcome in the valley of the Danube. So when we discussed how Yolie and her husband went to New York, and escaped the hell of the last five years, our thoughts and conversation turned West, toward the dreamed destination of all the world's wretched refuse. Of course, it was all just a lot of talk. Maybe America would not welcome us. Maybe Jews still carried a stigma. It was heatedly discussed.

"They let Yolie and Nick stay. They'll accept us too. John couldn't go! We couldn't send him. They'd have taken him though! Maybe we can go to France. Russia's not so bad! Sweden will welcome us. It's too cold! How about England? Anywhere they don't speak German."

Once the big questions, like immigration and business, were dispensed with, we took delight in the little things.

"When this damn war is over I'm gonna sit myself down in front of the biggest platter of sausages you ever saw, with plenty of mustard and sauerkraut, and just dive in. Don't forget the cold pitcher of beer! I'm gonna find a strudel a meter long and eat every crumb. With coffee! And sugar! And cream! Lots of cream! I can't wait to eat goulash again! Me too!"

It was madness, because we had almost nothing to eat. But we enjoyed it just the same.

Joska was strangely silent throughout all this. We were all eager to move on with our lives, but Joska Cséh was a citizen of a country that was on the losing side of a war, and its greatest foe was at this moment planning on an invasion based on not only defeating its enemies, but exacting a terrible revenge. We would be liberated, while Joska might be executed. But, just as he had helped us, we were prepared to help him. Life's so funny. Joska had to hide us because we were Jews, and now we might have to teach him to be Jewish to save him. These thoughts dominated our lives through the Christmas of 1944. Shortly thereafter, the rumble of cannon fire ceased, replaced by flesh and blood Russian soldiers and the ratchety squeal of their tanks.

As we had become accustomed to the artillery barrage, if that even sounds half sane, it actually took us a couple of hours before we noticed when it finally stopped. Imagine, being interrupted by quiet. The conversations were called to an abrupt stop. If anyone dared to even whisper they were shushed with extreme prejudice. Wide eyed, we all looked at each other, then around and around, until we were sure we heard nothing. We held our arms out like orchestra conductors between movements, waiting for the audience to calm down. The hint of smiles appeared on a few faces, and disappeared just as quickly. Should we rejoice? Do we even know what this silence means? Were they just taking a rest? Had they run out of ammo? Did the Germans sabotage them? Dare we stick our necks out? What next? What do we do? We were so used to following Joska's lead we just waited for him to do something. But all he did was motion for us to wait some more. He was the only one standing, so when he sat again it felt like a setback. There was a great stir, then nothing. Now mystery and disappointment were of equal portions.

I spoke up, "I'm going outside." But I was immediately subdued by a chorus of denial.

I had broken two rules, speaking above a whisper and daring to venture out. So, I changed tactics, suggesting action through the medium of a whisper, "Can't we just peek out?"

It was such new territory nobody even knew what to say. Sixty people looked at each other, immeasurably deepening the confusion. Finally, Joska counseled me.

"Tommy, wait a few more minutes."

My parents beamed with satisfaction at the clear vision of Joska. Again, he had saved their baby, this time from the unknown.

I would have done anything for Joska. We were pals. So, I obediently sat down again. But my timid inquiry served as the herald for a myriad of verbal bravado that grew and grew in our lonely black chamber. Consumed by curiosity over what could conceivably await them in the sunlight, everyone exorcised their fear and weariness through triumphant statements, emboldened by the recent overture of Soviet artillery shells.

"It's over. The Nazis have left, the cowards. No! They're all dead. The Russians will be here any minute. Why the Russians? Have you seen one? Maybe it's the Americans! The Americans! Oh, please God. Let it be the Americans."

People were crying now. Some were even vomiting. They could take the barrages, the air raids, even the brutal police. But knowing nothing was unbearable. Someone had to go outside. They even dared suggest it to Joska. Not that he should risk it himself personally. Just someone. But Joska finally relented. He stood, bade us remain seated, and walked cautiously to the short stairway that led to the street, and the world. We stared at him until he disappeared into the unknown. A door creaked, and a thin shaft of light invaded our space as we caught our breath. Would he be shot? Maybe they spread poison gas, and that's why it was so still. Oh no! Poor Joska will breathe it and die! After one excruciatingly long minute he returned.

"There's no activity out there. But I think I saw a soldier slowly walking like in a crouch."

We all looked around. What could this mean?

"What kind of soldier?"

"I'm afraid it looked like a German soldier."

We were outraged. "They're still alive? After that shellacking?"

Joska reintroduced reason, "I said I saw one soldier, not a regiment."

Several people were entertained by that comment, and nervously tittered. The laugh was so silly others laughed at it. Finally, the whole basement was in an uproar. And all the tension it relieved was immediately restored with the gunshot, and we all fell as still as death. For a brief moment wide eyed terror gripped us again. It had come. Not knowing wasn't so bad after all. This was worse.

It was a distinctive crack that broke the silence. Within five seconds that rifle report was answered with another. Then submachine gun fire. The silence was not just broken; it was annihilated, gone forever. Moment by moment, the full compliment of foot soldier military hardware on both sides made their entrance. Within a minute, we had a new din to contend with. But these shots were not intended to pass overhead. They were at our level. They were at every level. Soldiers were shooting at each other, right outside our door. But who were the Germans shooting at? Americans? Russians? Not even a curious ten year old would chance a peek now. Whereas we sat through the artillery barrage we now had to throw ourselves flat on the ground to avoid the stray bullets. To intensify our escape from the carnage we even closed our eyes. Unable to block out the sound of war, like panic stricken ostriches we shut out its image. If we couldn't see them, maybe they couldn't see us. Satisfied we'd done all we could to escape the flying death that filled the air above our heads, we hugged the ground as our only refuge. But our feeble attempts at deadening our senses were mocked by the explosive pandemonium that enveloped and permeated our crude habitat. Combat had come to our very door, and it wasn't going to go away until one side won.

But who was fighting who? For the moment, it didn't matter. Guns were going off a few feet away, and their politics were not of much concern to us. With nothing else to do but travel far from the battlefield to the quiet security of our minds, we contemplated the potential cast of characters.

There were German and Hungarian soldiers. Were they on the same side or fighting each other? Were the Nyilasok up to fighting armed opponents at all? Were there Russians up there, vengefully blasting the Nazis to pulp? Or were there Americans here, ready to take on the lot? If they were Russians or Americans how would they view us civilians? Did they not know we were the pitifully oppressed? Surely, they wouldn't consider us the enemy! The Huns no longer trusted Hungarians, so maybe they were attacking us? Or were they united against the allies, whichever ones were up there? Whether we knew or not could not possibly effect our situation. Yet, we ached to know. As no actual bullets had flown into our basement I could not resist the urge to take a peek. So, ignoring the shouted whispers of my family I crawled to the wooden planks that covered the coal chutes. There were tiny cracks between the boards, and I pressed my eye to one. In my narrow field of vision I saw soldiers running right to left wearing helmets that looked neither German nor Hungarian. They were firing guns I hadn't seen before either. All this foreign accoutrement made me think they were either Russian or American. A tug from behind removed me from my perch. It was Joska. He put me down, and took a look for himself. After a few moments he turned around and crept back to the main bulk of us to make his report.

"They're Russians, and they're fighting the Germans. There might be Hungarian regulars too, but I didn't see enough to tell for certain."

A few people, who had pulled for the Americans to be their liberators, looked disappointed.

My mother spoke up, "It's the Russians! We've been praying for them to get here, and they finally made it. Thank God, I say. Thank God!"

A general rumbling of gratitude encouraged us all that our deliverance was at hand.

Deliverance was not as imminent as we hoped, however. Though we rooted every second of the day for the tough Commies to wipe the Krauts from the face of the Earth, both sides gave it their all. The Russians would advance a street, and make first down. Once that was accomplished they brought in their tanks to blast away the defense of the next street. But sometimes the Nazis would counter attack and take back that street. Not until the Reds advanced enough to safely bring in truck loads of supplies was a street considered secure. But we were introduced to this military strategy over an agonizingly long learning curve. And after a few days of observing through the coal chute we got recruited.

We heard the Russians upstairs. There was no shooting in the building, but the clop of their boots grew closer and closer. Up until then the knowledge that a soldier was coming meant one of two things, neither of which bode well. But this was different. Or at least we hoped so. The door flung open, and a language I'd only rarely heard was yelling something. We all looked to Joska. He was straining to catch a word or two. The yelling was now more insistent, and then joined by a voice yelling the same thing in unison, only this voice belonged to a woman.

A woman? Maybe it's not going to be so bad. But they kept yelling. Surely, they wanted to see if we were friend or foe. Joska, brave Joska, called out, "*Tovarich.*"

The word came back, but not completely mocking.

Joska said to us, "I think it's alright. Let's show ourselves."

Walking forward Joska calmly added, "*Horosho.*" Later I learned this was Russian for good, alright, or okay. A *horosho* word to know.

The soldier couple walked down the stairs and I got my first glimpse at Russians. There was a specimen of each gender. Both were thin, but had fat fleshy faces. The woman was dressed like the man, and the only difference between them was her tightly corseted bosom, and a little more hair than the man. In countenance they were identical. They were humorless and demanding. They seemed satisfied that we were noncombatants, but wanted to know something. While we were relieved and elated that they were not going to shoot us down like the Nazis would have, we had no time to celebrate. We had to figure out what they wanted. After hearing them repeat the same phrase several times, each time less patiently, my father, to the surprise of all, spoke up.

"I think they want to know where the Germans are. Where they're hiding."

We all turned around, and smiling like idiots, we pointed outside in the general direction of Budapest. This only seemed to exasperate them. They rolled their eyes up, and then tried gestures. They pointed up, and said, "*Namath?*"

My aunt understood this and made a wide gesture with both arms encircling our cringing mob. She even dared to speak, "*Nyet Namath.*" 'No Germans in this building.'

Satisfied that sixty three Hungaria Korut was not a German military installation the woman changed course.

"*Dabe chasi.*"

Seeing that we were totally in the dark she pulled up the sleeve of her coat to reveal an impressive collection of wrist watches, and repeated the foreign phrase.

"*Dabe chasi!*"

This time, though, she brandished her submachine gun. Joska took off his watch and, smiling, handed it over. The woman received it, and like the pro she was becoming, assessed its value, and nodded her approval. Pleased, she lowered her weapon. Now we were panic stricken. Was this their routine, to barge in, steal watches, and kill anyone who had none? Many of us no longer bothered wearing them. Were we goners? She repeated her watch phrase, and gestured to her comrade. So, we had to cough up another one for her buddy! My father, shaking, removed his and proffered it to the eager private. He pulled it over his shirt sleeve to join the three others. The man and woman were neck and neck in liberated time pieces.

Content with their spoils of war, our liberators exited. We were safe. But were we saved? Were these just a couple of oddball Russians who accepted bribes to spare their victims? There were Nazis who did the same. We all looked around, bewildered.

"Are we safe?" "What happens when we run out of watches?"

As it turned out, these crude front line Russian soldiers, almost half of which were women, were indeed here to kill the Germans and, in the process, free us poor oppressed Hungarians. But make no mistake; their number one job was killing. Once they had taken a street they went house to house, room to room, looking for Germans, German sympathizers, Nyilasok, and Nyilasok sympathizers. If they thought you looked or smelled like a fascist they shot first and didn't ask any questions after. After the infantry and tanks accomplished their mission, the trucks arrived with supplies and a more sophisticated brand of soldier. There was more communication with them, but they wanted the same basic thing, to know where the Germans were. Some people were eager to cooperate, but many were afraid the Germans would just return and take over again, and kill commie collaborators. But there was one class of people who had nothing more to lose, and would be dead anyway if the Germans triumphantly returned, the Jews. Indeed, the Russians sought us out as reliable comrades. The second wave of Russian soldiers even had Jewish soldiers and officers among their ranks, and we worked with them to root out hiding Nazis. As the soviet soldiers fought their way into the interior of the city they came to the realization that their main foe had fled. Since the artillery shelling began the Germans had been making preparations for hightailing it back to the Fatherland. They had brought in all manner of transport to shuttle their troops to Austria. And, by the time the Soviet advance had made its way past the outskirts, where we had been living, and into the heart of Budapest, the German gewermacht had nearly totally retreated. The Hungarian army and Nyilasok, were left in the lurch, but they had been well brainwashed by their Aryan overlords into thinking themselves superior to the lowly Slav, and they determined to fight the Godless commies, even murdering some undesirable Hungarian civilians, just like the good old days. All of this only served to further incense the Russians, and if they had been vengeful before, they were now absolutely bloodthirsty. Word had also spread to the countryside where resistance fighters and communist partisans had been holding out. They now came into the city and pointed out any German sympathizers or fascists that were hiding or parading as normal innocent Hungarians. The Russians freed the few thousand Jews left in the ghetto, and set about to rid the city of every remnant of the Third Reich. If someone was pointed out as a German sympathizer they were shot on the spot. This fanatical process was not honed to a science, and many innocent Hungarians were killed by friendly fire. For example, there was a man in our old neighborhood with the unfortunate last name of Namath. He was just a Hungarian, and harbored no love for the Nazis. But someone called out to him, "Oh, Mr. Namath." They weren't identifying him, but the Russians heard the word Namath and shot the poor man down. The Russians didn't shoot everyone though. They arrested as many of the Nyilasok as possible, with an eye toward post war justice.

The bodies in the street were piling up deeper than from the air raids or artillery shelling combined. The Reds went through every building and cleansed it of any tinge of their fascist foe. They searched for swastikas or arrow crosses or things written in German. Depending on which soldier did the discovering, that apartment's occupants were either arrested or just taken down to the street and shot.

By the end of January Budapest, and all of Hungary, was completely liberated. After five years of Nazis and Nyilasok we were free. But there weren't many of us left to enjoy that freedom. The fascists had done their job all too well. Before the Russians smashed their way in, half a million Jews were deported and murdered. Only half that many were left alive in Hungary. It was a big success story for the Nazis, eagerly abetted by the enthusiastic collaboration of Hungarians who had fallen prey to the lie of racial superiority.

It's not just little children who like to think themselves better than their playmates. Far too many so-called adults fail to achieve any real measure of maturity, and persist in strutting like peacocks. They grow tall, and their voices deepen. They shave and menstruate and work, just like big people, but their egos and consciousness never surpass the psychological development of a little girl. They remain petty their whole lives, consumed by envy for anything that they can't have. They're even willing to kill over it. So, Hungary's war drew to a close, and five hundred thousand of their number were sacrificed to selfish pouting brats, who could not learn to work or play well with others.

Actually, when the Russians liberated us we were quite ignorant of the enormity of fascist crimes. Jewish officers in the Red army told us something about the concentration camps, but we had no real idea of the vastness of their villainy. Hearing about the camps filled us with dread for Anci. She had been taken away nine months earlier, and this news from our liberators kindled thoughts about her, yet extinguished any hope that she was alive. Nor was there any encouraging information about the possible plight of my brother Josef. That we were glad to be alive, but sad for our missing relatives, was the prevailing mood of every living Jew and Gentile in Europe, and practically the entire world. The conflagration had extinguished the lives of fifty million people, half of which were civilians. And the whole mess was fought over virtually nothing. Back in 1914, when Austria-Hungary declared war on Serbia over the death of just one of its citizens, the planet they both inhabited had enough food, land and water to share for a hundred times its population. But spoiled children must have their way, world be damned.

Everybody in Budapest turned scavenger. The Russians didn't hand out chocolate bars like the Americans did, but at least they made it possible for us to go outside and look for food without being afraid of getting shot. Hungaria Korut was relatively sparsely populated, so the competition for food there was less intense. The men all went out like Magyar tribesmen of old to forage while the women remained behind to clean up the huts.

My aunts all felt such gratitude toward Joska that they each offered Rose their best furnishings so she could fix up her place in anticipation of the return of her heroic husband. Rose was embarrassed, but the women insisted. Now that the war was over for her she delighted in putting order back in her life.

Before Hitler led Hungary down the primrose path Rose had been a fussy homemaker. She loved beauty and cleanliness and everything in its place. Once again, she was pleased to assume the life of an aspiring middle class woman. So, she accepted the trappings of her former, and now regained, life, and rolled up her sleeves to clean. With the donations of each apartment in the building she managed to organize a presentable sitting room. She had a few tables, and some objet d'arte with which to adorn them. There was a slightly worn settee with the aura of antique, and an odd dining room suite with just three chairs. Not disappointed with the odd number of chairs, she set two at the table, and one against a wall next to a low table covered in picture frames. At the center of the room was her piece d' resistance, a large luxurious Louis Fourteenth easy chair. She couldn't even imagine how such a fine piece of furniture had ever made its way to the industrial zone of Pest. She considered that it was probably a copy, but was glad for it just the same. It had a few stains on the velvet, and she spent a good hour gently daubing at it, careful not to disturb its delicate brocade. She then polished its arms and legs, restoring some semblance of luster to them. Satisfied she'd done all she could she beamed at her accomplishment and went off to scrub a few layers of dirt off herself, confident the men would soon return with dinner. She had to go out and collect some snow to melt for water to perform her ablutions, but, doing it in freedom, it was no longer a terrifying sortie.

While Rose was sweeping and mopping and scrubbing, the men were looking for something to eat. They had all gone off in different directions to increase the odds of finding something. Even Grandpa joined the foraging. He had stoically tolerated the austerity of bare minimum sustenance, as we all did, and now he was determined to fill his belly. Having fled here to survive, he had never really gotten to know the neighborhood, so this sojourn was an exploration into new territory. But the old gentleman was game. And soon enough his dauntless optimism was rewarded with the sight of an abandoned commercial bakery. He naively thought he might bring back some flour for bread. What a hero he'd be! But the bakery was one of the first places scavenged by the Russians, and then the Hungarians, so grandpa had little hope of being the breadwinner that day. What he did find made his well known sweet tooth salivate.

Cast off to one side in the cavernous facility was a barrel that had once held the glory of a hundred pounds of strawberry marmalade. There was still some left on the sides, so he scooped some off with his fingers and happily thrust them into his grinning mouth, greedily licking his digits clean. What a tasty treat after so long! He dragged his fingers around the inside and scooped up some more. A second delicious mouthful! He hadn't tasted anything sweet in months and he was in heaven. Leaning in, and scooping lower, he managed an even bigger glob for his enjoyment. And as he scrapped lower he could see that the bottom held a full inch of the irresistible sticky jam. But it was a deep barrel, and he was not a tall man. He searched in vain for a long handled ladle or spoon of some kind, but previous scroungers had stripped the place clean. So, he went up on his tip toes and reached down as far as he could. He was almost there. The fruity perfume drove his senses wild, and he strained millimeter by millimeter toward his savory grail. His feet stretched to an extreme degree, and the angle of his ankle would have made any ballet teacher proud. He was Nijinsky, totally elongated, one with the barrel. He fell in.

His hands sunk into the marmalade, but by now he was one of Peter Pan's lost boys, free of responsibility, guiltless in his gluttony. He slurped with one hand while holding himself aloft with the other, and then traded. He gobbled until he could no longer sustain his posture, so he kicked and kicked until he so disturbed the center of the barrel's gravity that he fell to one side.

He and the barrel lay supine, and the new angle facilitated my grandfather's jam gathering even better. He was Winnie the Pooh, covered in goo, and happier for it. And when he'd finally scrapped off and eaten all he could, he wriggled and squirmed until he freed himself from the last wooden container that would hold his body until his funeral.

Satisfied, and more than a little proud, as well as tired, grandpa made his way to 63 Hungaria Korut and the shiny new living space that the industrious Rose had wrought. As he walked along his tongue found remnants of his banquet imbedded in his large moustache, and he continued to savor the delicacy. He wondered if there was a comb back at the apartment so he could run it through his bushy jam repository and lick it clean. His quest had borne fruit, and he was ready to brag about it to all the young men of his brood. What if he were covered in jelly from head to foot? He had eaten, no small feat for a Hungarian in February, 1945. His belly felt full, and his dignity was intact. Had the others fared as well?

Joska was out on his motorcycle, cruising for food, with me in the sidecar. He said we'd better be successful, not just because we were all hungry, but because we were sure to exhaust the last of his gas doing so. Joska was smart. He had no faith in finding anything edible in town, so we were bound for the countryside, where they grow the food in the first place. As we were on the outskirts of the city anyway, it was closer. Of course, the Red army had spent a month on the perimeter of Budapest with their artillery, preparing for the invasion and collecting supplies, so they had probably gone through every farm in the area already. But we didn't need much. And with forty two mouths to feed, and half of them on the hunt for it, our hopes were high. Even though it was not a growing season Joska was confidant we'd stumble across something. If we found some herbs we could melt snow and make soup. It's not goulash, but it would be plentiful, and sustain us until something better came along. Hot soup to the hungry is a treat. If only we could find some beets or potatoes to sink our teeth into. Then we saw the farm house.

Living on a farm was probably the best way for Christians to avoid problems during the war. You grew your crops, turning over a significant portion to the government for the war effort, but hiding enough away to survive. Around Budapest the countryside was unscarred from combat, and the farmers had been lucky right up to the Red invasion. Even then, the Germans preferred to fight it out in the city, as opposed to an open battle in the countryside. They'd had enough of that in western Russia.

We didn't really expect to find much in this little farm house, but we knew it was worth a look. Besides, gas was running low. As we approached it looked deserted. The noise of Joska's bike didn't even draw anyone outside. We pulled up to the house, and all was still. Not even a barking dog. We walked inside and discovered the reason for such complete peace. The farmer and his wife lie on the floor dead, a pool of their own blood framing them. Scattered around them were the reasons for their executions. They were obviously admirers of fascism, and either hadn't the sense to destroy the evidence of that credo, or were just taken by complete surprise when the Reds came calling. A smashed dual portrait of Hitler and Horthy reposed in fragments on their bodies, and a swastika flag was tied tightly around the man's neck. The woman was also partially naked, with a wooden arrow-cross protruding from between her legs. They were riddled with holes. I felt very manly and mature that Joska didn't baby me and tell me to look away or anything of the kind. He knew all that I had already witnessed, and that I could take it. Besides, considering their politics, we didn't give them a second thought, and we went looking for food. Maybe they'd hid something for themselves that the Reds hadn't discovered. But we didn't find anything. On our way out of the house we stepped over the cadavers of the farmers, and Joska stopped cold. He turned around and stooped down.

"Look Tommy, there's something here."

Sticking out from under the man's bloody hand was the edge of a rounded piece of brass. In their wrath to execute their enemy they covered up the clue to something. The corpses hid at least part of what the Russians would have liked to find, a trap door. I got really excited. Without ceremony, Joska just dragged the corpses away, and I went for the large, round, brass handle myself. I pulled, but it was too heavy. Joska tried to encourage me.

"Come on, Tommy, you can do it!"

I pulled as hard as I could. But as feisty as I was I had been malnourished for months and could barely move it before it dropped down again with a clunk. Maybe no ten year old in the whole country could have lifted it. Joska gave a little chuckle and pulled himself. Now, it was I who had to provide the encouragement.

"I tell you Joska, this farmer must have been a brute."

Joska agreed as he finally got it open, and let his air out in a rush. To modern observers, what we found there might not have seemed worth such efforts, but to us at that moment we felt we had struck gold. In a small cellar the farmer had stashed about fifty pounds of potatoes and beets and onions for him and his fascist wife to enjoy. It was a veritable smorgasbord. Covetous of our find, Joska went to the window to see if there was anyone out there who might discover us loading our booty into the sidecar of the motorcycle. There wasn't, so we got busy. I found a large burlap bag, and we filled it with the valuable crops, and set it into the sidecar. With that full I climbed on the back and held on to Joska for the return trip to 63 Hungaria Korut, praying we had gas enough for the return trip.

As we were just a block from the building we passed my grandfather who was also just arriving. He was empty handed, but he seemed content. As soon as we pulled up Joska and I jumped down and each took a side of the bag and schlepped it into the apartment. Rose was ecstatic.

"The mighty hunters have returned. You are my heroes!"

We each got a big hug and a kiss, and I felt jubilant. Then we noticed the new apartment.

"Wow," said Joska. "Am I in the lobby of the Hotel *Zacher*?"

I didn't even know what he meant, but I was dumbfounded too. While I was oohing and ahing at the ornate, and wholly unexpected, opulence of our new living quarters, and while Rose was stashing the produce in the kitchen, Grandpa came in, mysteriously covered in jam.

"Oy! Am I tired!"

With that he flopped down in the Louis Fourteenth chair and let out a big sigh. Then he called me over.

"Boychik. Come here. What a day I had. I found a barrel of marmalade, and…"

But he was cut short by a spine tingling scream from Rose who was walking back from the kitchen.

"If the Germans didn't kill you I will!"

Poor old grandpa didn't know what the fuss was all about, and looked around in confusion. Rose was livid. I'd never seen her like that.

"Get out of that chair you old fool! Now! Get up!"

Joska took a good look at grandpa and understood. "Uh, sir, let me help you to another chair."

Rose was in shock. "Strip him. Don't let him sit down anywhere until he's changed his clothes."

We hesitated for a second, and she came back, "Do it!"

My father came in to see what the fuss was all about, followed by my mother.

"Just look at that chair," commanded Rose. "I worked on it all day. It was like new. And..and..and…"

Rose was too upset to talk rationally. My father walked over to inspect the chair. He dragged his finger across one of the smears, smelled it, and then licked it. Smiling, as if he had solved a puzzle he announced, "It's marmalade! It's good too!"

My mother was not amused. "You like it? Do you know how hard Rose worked on that chair? No, you don't. Because you didn't help. And where's the food you're supposed to be out finding? Little Tommy did better than you."

Father couldn't reply, and mother was just getting started. "Vacation's over, Ignatz. And there are no saloons left for you to carouse in. So, you better get used to putting food on the table. Do you hear me? Do you?!"

The war was over, and normal life once again established a beach-head.

After a few weeks the Russians moved on to Austria, so we decided to return to the inner city and our old lives. We still had a contract for our apartment at 57 Harsfa Street, and we intended to see it honored. War or no war, we had a lease, which we had not broken. Demanding our apartment back was the normal thing to do, and reestablishing normality was the order of the day.

On the way to Harsfa Street we stopped off at the Debrecens to thank them and give them a little more money. We saw the Kovacks, who lived in the elevator, and the Moskovics and Faragos who lived in the attic. They all made it. Then, we swung by Mr. Hargitay, and were pleased to find that he had made it too, and people were even letting him fix the few watches left behind by the Russians. Next, Rose went to see Mrs. Barna, who could now shout out loud that she was Abigail Unger. She too had survived, and she remained good friends with Rose forever. After catching up on everybody we went to reclaim our old apartment.

That our old apartment lease held up was proof enough to us that civilization was returning to Budapest. We were actually amazed to even find that our old apartment building was standing at all. Half of the buildings around it were demolished. When we opened the door to our old apartment we discovered a void. No furniture and not one window intact. But we weren't any worse off than anybody else. Maybe we were even better off.

When we first arrived and clomped up the stairs some of our old neighbors stuck their heads out. They were curious, and maybe more than a little shy about breaking the ice. After all, they might have turned us in if things had gone differently. No doubt they were glad for the way things did turn out, and were eager to forget the past. We all were. And Mother made it easy for them. When the first neighbor's head peeked out of a half opened door mother spoke right up.

"Oh, glad to see you made it!"

They were uniformly relieved and elated by such a greeting, and grabbed at the chance to renew acquaintances.

"Glad to see you're all in one piece too! Welcome back!"

Who knows if they collaborated or not. They never had the chance probably, so we just let it rest, and never said anything about it. The war was over. The anti-Semites lost, and Hungary seemed ready to go back to the way things were before.

It's a funny thing about anti-Semites. They always lose. That's not an opinion, or the gloating of the victorious survivor. It's just history. I'm not extrapolating any conclusion. I'll leave that up to the scholars. History is full of people or groups who periodically rise up with agendas to enlist support for their ideology through the age old scape-goating device of picking on a weak defenseless minority. Notwithstanding loud, massive, fanatical support by the misled masses, they unerringly end up embracing dismal defeat, and a situation worse than the one they had hoped to ameliorate in the first place through their aggressive campaign of hate. In short, bigots are losers, literally.

Sadly, despite such an unimpressive track record, high decibel prejudice still finds willing ears among the frustrated elements of society. Maybe, advocates of love and peace should take a tip from the opposing camp, and start yelling their tranquil philosophy. While there doesn't seem to be much synergy between a serene message and a hyperbolic presentation, so much can be said for the latter that peaceniks should seriously consider shouting in favor of tolerance and understanding. Sheer volume seems to attract a constituency. In Hungary, for example, the strategy of wide spread, strident vitriol had convinced our neighbors of a creed decidedly not pacific in nature. So, maybe if some operatic peace monger would have climbed upon a soap box, and ranted in support of love, as Hitler did for hate, maybe the whole sorry mess could have been avoided. People do seem to admire a loud talker. The Nazis spread their hostile message through a relentless campaign of radio broadcasts. It was so central to their success they even gave away radios to insure an audience. But now those radios were tuned in to the songs of the victors. And our old neighbors were exhausted from hate, and only too glad to tune it out.

As soon as we assessed the situation in the apartment we went to see if we had a business too. If the old jewelry store was still there we might be able to start things up again. And, by some bizarre miracle, it too was standing. It had been illegal for Jews to own businesses, so it had been boarded up. But our name was still on the door and everything looked alright. There was no merchandise for the time being, but we had somewhere from which to start. Meanwhile I kept my eyes peeled for any possible avenues of income. Soon enough my favorite nighttime pastime brought me an opportunity.

The Vesta movie theater, on the corner of Ference Korut and Dobutca, had sustained some bombing raid damage, but rumors abounded that it would soon be refurbished and back in operation. John and I visited its boarded up ruins, but rascals of slight stature that we were, it was easy to squeeze through a small opening and explore the depths of the neglected dream palace. Looters had stripped it pretty clean, right down to its projectors, but we found a cache of tickets and claimed it as our booty. We reasoned that we'd scalp them once the theater reopened. And that's exactly what happened. John and I positioned ourselves at each corner and accosted anyone who looked like they might be out for an evening's cinematic relaxation. All we had to do was undercut the box office and we closed the deal. Business was so brisk I had to hire two other guys to peddle our product. But it was hardly the perfect crime. Each theater seat was numbered, and they sold corresponding tickets to the same seats we were selling. Following a few contested seats they investigated and discovered our dastardly plan. A plain clothes Hungarian detective bought a ticket off me and I was busted. My partners in crime took off like greyhounds, leaving me to confront the authorities on my own. As they dragged me through the cold wintry night toward the police station I cleverly let the evidence slip from my fingers into the snow banks. But material proof was of minor consequence to these policemen. Once inside the station they had me empty my pockets. I had contraband cigarette rolling gizmos and lighters, but no tickets.

"Where are the tickets?"

"What tickets? I don't have any tickets!"

My interrogator let loose a right, and then caught me in mid air with a left. I went down like a ton of bricks.

"If I ever see you at that theater again I'll bring out my rubber hose and whip the bottom of your feet so you'll never walk again. Do you understand?!"

When I got back to the apartment my parents were there and they were aghast at my appearance.

"Tommy! What happened to you?!"

I stoically replied, "Oh, nothing."

"Nothing?! You'd better have a look in the mirror."

I went into the bathroom and beheld my bloodied mouth and nose, and blackened eyes. In five years World War Two had not done such damage to me as this policeman did in five seconds. Confronted with such carnage I was reduced to tears. Perhaps it was a release for all of the war years, but I bawled for a solid hour. When I emerged I was utterly relieved of the desire to ever commit petty larceny again. Far worse punishment awaited those guilty of truly heinous crimes.

The Russians started executing whomever they had arrested in their initial sweep through Budapest. Near Liget Park, which I had fled through several times, was a centrally located intersection of streets called the Octagon, and it was chosen as the venue for public executions. The Nazis and Nyilasok members, who had been clearly identified by their victims or their relatives, were taken there and hanged. For about six weeks, every Saturday, the public was invited to witness these public executions. Anywhere from five to twenty at a time were taken there in horse drawn wagons. These were the nastiest, most vicious and sadistic fascists, responsible for routinely murdering defenseless civilians. Once off the wagons they were led through the vengeful mob to a tree or lamp post which served as the gallows. The crowd threw rocks at them, spat on them, and hit them with their fists or anything they wanted. There was no sympathy for them from any side, and the Russians made no attempt to protect them from the wrath of the people who were there to see them die. By the time they even got to the rope they were beaten half to death. And they were left to hang for continued pelting. Even the teenaged *Nyilosak* punks were strung up. And while their bodies twirled at the end of the rope, copious amounts of warm saliva dripping off them, their victims' friends and relatives visited upon them every manner of mutilation imaginable. War crime definitely does not pay.

Little by little we furnished the apartment. And as soon as mail service was restored we got a letter from Yolie and Nicolas in New York. We were all elated to hear that John would be able to join them soon. But we had no further knowledge of any other family members. No news of Josef or Anci or Rose's husband, Nicolas. Joska went out to find Rachel Giller and her cousins, but it was a bitter experience. Apparently she was no longer his pal's girlfriend, but he did manage to locate them. He knocked on the door, and it creaked open a hair. He saw Rachel in the crack and smiled.

"Thank God you're alive."

But Rachel coldly said, "Who are you, sir? I have never seen you before in my life," and closed the door.

Joska was dumbfounded. He waited a few more moments, but the door remained closed. Shocked, he stumbled outside and sat down. After some reflection he realized the situation. There were instances in this war when the Germans looked defeated but fought back and regained lost territory. And whoever rejoiced over that momentary German defeat was executed. The most famous instance was Operation Garden Market. The allies parachuted into Holland and liberated it. A week later the Germans counterattacked and took it back. A lot of Dutch underground fighters were exposed, and they were sent to die in concentration camps. Even in Budapest there were instances when the Germans lost a street to the advancing Reds only to regain it a day or two later. People were terrified the Germans would be back. You don't forget six years in six days or six weeks. It was painful, but he accepted it.

Weeks went by, and the apartment was returning to blessed tranquility. There was still no electricity, but the water mains had been restored. Food was available and I was putting weight back on. We all were. Soon I felt strong enough to go out and play soccer. I was actually kicking the ball around with the exact same kids as before. A few had died in air raids and the recent street fighting, but most of them made it. I didn't want to speculate about what their parents did, or how they felt about things. They seemed sincerely happy to see me, and everybody wanted to put the war behind them, so we just kicked the ball and ran.

A few more weeks transpired and it seemed clear that Nicholas was not coming back. Despite the fact his parents pleaded with Rose and Joska to wait a full six months to be sure, they were married. Two weeks later Nicholas came back.

Rose was numb. She had been living with Joska as his wife for almost a year, and had accepted that Nicholas was dead. But she calmly explained to him what Joska had done for her and her family, and Nicholas graciously bowed out. Actually, he was extremely grateful to Joska and showed it. They even remained friends. Nobody in the family resented Rose's decision. At least Nicholas survived, and we were all grateful for that. Then somebody else came back.

I was outside playing soccer. It was a beautiful summer day. Everthing was *horosho*. We had food, freedom, and even nice weather. We had hid through a cruel cold winter, and now the sun shone down on our new liberty. As I was running along, close to making a goal, this disheveled woman walked up to me and spoke.

"Hello, Tommy."

I had no idea who she was. This lady was all skin and bones, covered in sores, with terribly matted hair. Her filthy clothes just hung on her. Who was this lady?

"Tommy, it's me, your sister Anci."

Anci had been liberated by the British. When they were getting close to Bremen the Nazis loaded all the prisoners on to a train to take them somewhere for liquidation. Fleeing as they were from the allies, who were in hot pursuit, they chose to simply abandon the train and leave the prisoners to suffocate inside the hot cars, as was so often their plan at that time. But British troops discovered the train and took Anci and the others to a nearby vacation resort where they kicked everybody out and housed them until they could determine what to do with them. Soon she was on another train, but this time a safe one, all the way to Budapest.

I couldn't believe my ears or my eyes. I stared and stared, and after a minute I finally recognized her. My sister was alive! It was a miracle, but she was alive! We hugged and cried.

"Is mama alive?" she asked.

I was happy to fill her in. "We're all alive! This guy, Joska, hid us all. Even grandpa's alive!"

I dragged her to the apartment house. She stopped me.

"You go up and tell mama I'm here. I'll be behind you."

I ran up the stairs two at a time and burst into the apartment. "Mama! Anci's here. Anci's here! She's alive! And she's here!"

My mother was stunned, and put her hand to her mouth. Before she could say anything her youngest daughter was standing in the door. Mother flew to her and embraced her. As filthy as she was she kissed her again and again. "My baby. My baby." It was the most emotional thing I ever saw in my life.

When they finally stopped hugging mother gave her a bowl of soup. Then another. Thanks to good allied treatment she had regained the ability to eat. As horrific as it might sound, there were liberated people who actually died from eating too much too soon, just because they weren't used to food. But Anci was merely skinny when she got to us, and not the emaciated human skeleton she had been before liberation. Mothers are mothers, and even when things turn out alright they want to pry and investigate, and make sure there are no more problems.

"Was it terrible my baby? Did they treat you bad?" Anci stared off into the distance.

Mother's question was so inconceivably inadequate it was unworthy of a response. Yet, as laughably clueless as Mama's meager interrogation was, and as desperate as Anci was to forget the entire last year, these trite questions still brought it all back.

In almost a whisper she said, "I can't talk about it now." Another dead silent second later she added, "Maybe never."

She'd been through an unimaginable man made hell, which words were too weak to recount. It was too unbelievable to tell, anyway. Of course, Mother would believe it all, but why torture her with the tale? Anci's silence restored to her something that had been torn from her, her dignity. For, in addition to the physical brutality, there was the utter dearth of respect for human life that reduced these afflicted beings to mere shadows of people. They were stripped of health, wealth, and ultimately even the nobility of character that elevates a person from among the beasts. Finally free to decide for herself, she chose to revive her lost individuality through silence. After uncountable days of subjugation she cherished her emancipation by embracing the sublime license to do or say nothing. Anci had groveled her way through unbelievable oppression. And whether anyone would believe her or not, was inconsequential. She wished never to be linked to that lost year again, and only her silence would grant her that wish. No external force would ever exercise its sway over her again, not even her adoring family's concern. Her refusal to talk testified to the restoration to her of that singular privilege enjoyed only by humanity, free will. And she would relish that freedom forever. And loving her as we all do, we let her live her life unfettered by the challenge of curiosity. Back in that drab kitchen in 1945 Anci reclaimed her dignity. And she never looked back. To this day we do not what they did to her. But what we do know is that she was one of the lucky ones. She survived.

We celebrated Anci's return, and Joska was especially glad to meet her. And when word got out that she was back the boy who had always accompanied Anci's shy suitor showed up.

His name was Robert Frater, and he had the thankless task of bringing her the sad news that Andrew, her betrothed, had died in Auschwitz. But Robert had made it, and now he wanted to marry Anci. Apparently, he had always been in love with her, but had been beaten to the punch.

It had been a year since Anci had disappeared into that black Nazi hole, but here she was, in the bosom of her family, planning on marriage. There was no actual wedding celebration. But, despite the lack of opulence, it was a lasting union. They would stay married for over fifty years. But it was a childless marriage. Auschwitz is just a haunting memory, but its effect was permanent, whether you discussed it or not. But I'm happy to report that as I write this she still lives. Into her eighties she has never spoken about what they did to her. And years later, when I sought compensation for her from the ever officious German government, just as millions of people already had, they explained their verification process, which consisted of two examinations. In reply to this, Anci simply stated, "Not if you guarantee me one million dollars would I let another German doctor touch me."

On the other hand, getting a refund from the German ship lines for the unused portion of Yolie's round trip passage from 1938 was not half so complicated. Years later I just sent it in, and they refunded the money. Whatever you can say about the Krauts you have to admit that they know how to follow rules, even if they make them up themselves.

CHAPTER TWENTY ONE

THE RUSSIANS ARE STAYING

Weddings, marital dispute, soccer. We had gotten our lives back, as meager as it now was. Before the war, we were Hungarians, and being at a sort of a European crossroads we were well accustomed to the ebb and flow of human migrations. In the big historical picture the Germans hadn't even lasted all that long. Then the Russians came and kicked out the Germans. We were grateful, and willing to give them every wrist watch we could find, but after a while we started wondering when they too would be leaving. After all, there wasn't anyone else to come and kick them out. Not that they were oppressing us. They just weren't leaving, that's all. I mean, after five years of Nyilosak and Nazis, we knew what oppression was, and the Red army presence hardly constituted that. But they weren't leaving. We weren't afraid of them, exactly. But everyday they got more comfortable and more entrenched. Once they'd rubbed out anything that looked half German or Nyilosak they stopped the killing. But they weren't leaving. They were restoring basic utilities and infrastructure. But they weren't leaving. Hungary had a long dismal history of seeing her borders shrunk as the result of ill advised military campaigns, and World War Two was the worst yet. We had to give back every inch of land the Germans had awarded us, and it was starting to look like our whole country was nothing but spoils of war. But the Russians weren't leaving. Even though they'd achieved a resounding victory by January the war was still not over. While they pushed on to Berlin there were still a few die hard fascist pockets of resistance in the Hungarian countryside to mop up. So, they had a legitimate reason to hang on. But when the Germans unconditionally surrendered four months later, bringing the Nazis just nine hundred and eighty years short of their goal of a thousand year Reich, we thought the Russians would surely pack up and go home. "Job well done, and we'll never forget you! Spaceba! Horosho!" By now though, they'd officially declared war on Japan, prolonging an official state of hostilities, and their presence, longer yet. And four more months later, when Japan surrendered, we were ready to bet, giving good odds, they'd be eager to beat a path back to Mother Russia. "Have a safe journey home, and don't forget to write. Oh here comrade, you forget my grandfather's watch! Dosvedonya." But the Russians weren't leaving.

Actually a few Russians did go home. The original, front line, Nazi killing, watch lusting soldiers were sent back to their communal farms, and were replaced by the more sophisticated occupation forces, who were more policemen than soldiers. With hostilities over they didn't bother toting rifles any longer, and their presence didn't bother us in the least. They were slow to learn Hungarian, but they were friendly and didn't harass us.

We had nothing to fear from the ubiquitous occupation forces, or reprisals for any animosity towards us over the war, because every atom of antipathy and revenge in their beings was one hundred percent dedicated to Germany. They loathed it *uber alles*.

Deutschland had wrought a legacy of misery in Russia that would never be forgotten. Even during the most antagonistic years of the cold war, whatever hatred Moscow felt for forces outside their nation was still reserved for the Germans. America had not caused death and destruction to Mother Russia, but Germany had, and on an unforgettable scale. The Russians might have begrudged Yankees their opulence, but they did not hate them for it. They didn't want to blow up Disneyland. They wanted to visit it! But if the world would have turned its back for a day, Russian would have vaporized Germany just to get even. In any case, Hungary was now in Stalin's pocket, and we would have to get used to it. Our leaders, true to form, had gotten in bed with losers, and we were now paying the price. For centuries Hungary had made these rotten choices, and seen her lands either disappear or fall under the sway of foreign potentates. Perhaps such geographical and societal uncertainty are contributing factors in the equation that gives Hungary the highest suicide rate in the world. You quite literally don't know where you stand. In any case, after a few months it became clearer than the Danube that Hungary had gone from fascist domination to communist domination. The Russians were here to stay.

If Europeans love paperwork then the totalitarians are the ultimate Europeans. Nazis delighted in reviewing personal documents, and the Reds, having made their permanent presence known, set about making sure that everyone had proper papers as well. Of course, being from the same continent and still delirious over our recently restored freedom, we basically took it all in stride. So, without looking back, I stopped being Thomas Molnár and went back to being Thomas Weisz forever. Actually, updating the paperwork gave us hope that it was a step toward the rebuilding of our country. But that was not to be. Allied bombing had reduced Budapest to Bedrock, and even the Russians had nowhere to go. With few buildings left intact the commissars were forced to move into the old Gestapo headquarters. In such cramped quarters neither the Third Reich, nor the Union of Soviet Socialist Republics found office space for The Department for the Beautification of Greater Buda and Pest. This town was doomed not to get a fresh coat of paint until the next millennium, long after the hammer and cycle came down the flag pole for the last time. The Bolsheviks called themselves Reds but their color preferences definitely tended to lean toward the gray palette. And, though they know how many holes it takes to fill the Albert Hall, nobody knows how many bullet holes remain in our great European metropolis. A pockmarked veneer blankets most edifice facade to this very day.

In spite of the fact that we were now under the influence of an ideology that condemned capitalism, its official banishment was slow in coming, and we reopened our petty bourgeoisie jewelry store without calling down Stalinist wrath. But it'd be a while before we actually dealt in jewelry. For now we were metal dealers. With the gold that we had left we became mid-level links in the retrieved metal business. We bought pieces of copper from low men on the metal totem pole, and resold it to bigger links up the chain, who in turn sold it straight to the smelters. And we paid for it with gold. The economy was just like our infrastructure, in shambles. And the only valued medium of exchange was gold. And not just coins either. We actually broke off tiny bits of the precious metal, grams and parts of grams, to buy things. And we weren't alone. As it took a suitcase full of *forints* to buy a pair of shoes, everybody became savvy in gold dealing. We all carried around scales and gold testing kits, complete with vials of sulfuric acid.

I was only eleven, but I ran the afternoon shift as metal buyer. Everyday after school I ran over to the family shop, stopping to get my daily cream filled napoleon from the bakery across the street, and weighed and bought bits of metal from junk dealers who roamed the streets loudly calling out for the sought after commodity. And we had walk-in trade as well. No amount of metal was too insignificant. We even bought tiny watch parts and fragments. If it was metal we bought it. Once a month, after we'd accrued enough to reach wholesale levels, I trucked it about six blocks away to the next biggest link in the chain, and sold it. We did this for months until our so-called jewelry business actually started to deal in jewelry. We hired a watch repairman too. Meanwhile, Joska Cséh's black market trade made him one of the richest men in Budapest. No longer bothering to keep up his shoe salesman front, he went back and forth between Austria and Hungary, providing the ever popular tobacco. Along with that he sold cigarette rolling machines, and an immensely popular product, the cigarette lighter. It wasn't the never fail Zippo that American GIs had introduced to Europe, but it still sold by the car load. And by now he did have a car, a brand new Buick. He also added two new motorcycles to his stable, including a BMW. He was wealthier than anyone I'd ever known. He also dropped the imitation military look, and fell comfortably into the persona of a well bred, soft spoken aristocrat. He was the Adonis of Budapest, respected and adored by everyone for his success, good looks and accomplishments. His wardrobe of nearly eighty suits filled racks along walls in our apartment. And, in spite of having four times as many clothes as Rose, they were a very happy couple. We all were. John and I were still sleeping on the floor of the cramped apartment, due to a total lack of inhabitable living space, but we were free and had plenty to eat. We were getting healthy too. With every critter for a hundred miles around long ago consumed, our unintentional vegetarian diet was probably keeping us all fit. The farms in the south had hardly ever stopped producing, even during the war, so we now enjoyed plenty of grains and vegetables and fruit. Even wine production was back. This made the Russians very happy, because they were big drinkers. They didn't have vodka, but they were content with the output of the vineyards of the Gyonyos region.

Even though electricity was still a while in coming, mail service returned, and we started getting packages from Yolie again. Cans of pineapple, jams, salamis, and other delicacies made our lives all the richer. We almost felt guilty for not only having survived, when so many died, but now we were thriving. John no longer suffered from feelings of abandonment either. His parents, Yolie and Nick, made arrangements with the Red Cross to pick him up and escort him to America. But before all that paperwork was done he and I had fun selling Ronson lighters for good pocket money. Joska had seen to it they we had our own supply to sell. He was still our special friend and riding in his Buick was a thrill we relished.

As 1945 drew to a close electricity returned and John left for the states, becoming the first member of our family to fly. It wasn't long before I missed my playmate. We had been together for six long and unusual years. We had grown up and gone through things together that must be shared to be understood. And as soon as he got to New York he sent me letters filled with fairy tale images of skyscrapers, trains running on top of buildings, and unlimited cowboy movies. Where I had previously been a survivalist, living from moment to anxious moment, I now luxuriated in visions of America. I could dare to dream once again.

John's departure called to mind the absence of Sandor and Josef, and cast a slight pall on our lives. For all us though, reflecting on the last five years, life seemed phantasmagorical. There was tragedy, and now wonder. It was awesome in the truest sense of the word. Life had become as bright as the war had been bleak. Some mystical power was rewarding us for having gone through hunger and fear, and survival. We had endured a frightening cosmic initiation, and unseen forces now seemed poised to insure that we'd never know want or oppression again. But wrinkles in that silver lining were around the corner, and unimaginable things were yet to come.

CHAPTER TWENTY TWO

NOT GO ON FOREVER

The return of freedom restored to us, among many other things, our right to be Jews again. Soviet doctrines, such as atheism, were still a ways off before official implementation, and Mother felt confident enough in our future to revive our heritage and plant thoughts in our head of my impending Bar Mitzvah, a mere year hence. Of course, we'd already seen what dramatic upheavals can transpire in just twelve months, so while we had the guts to make plans, we did so with fingers crossed. You never can be too safe, and in our case, a lot would indeed go down before I'd officially become a man. Despite a quantum leap in our quality of life index, and the relatively relaxed Russian regime, certain impositions did begin creeping into our society. So, before celebrating a Bar Mitzvah we'd have to celebrate May Day.

The universal observance of the rights of workers was once before an official Hungarian holiday. Back in 1919, during the glorious three month long communist rule of our country, everybody got a day off. But it had been quite a dry spell between parades. Another hint at Red things to come, besides old St. Nick, was my nonoptional invitation to join a little club called the Pioneers. It was sort of a commie boy scouts, though I'm not sure if troops in Ames, Iowa followed classes on knot tying with readings from Das Kapital. They filled our heads with all kinds of communist indoctrination, even including anti-American propaganda. But, after all I had heard from John about the wonders of the west, it was hard to swallow what my earnest teachers had to say. We were denied the Voice of America and the BBC, but I was already quite obsessed with crossing the ocean to see cowboy movies, so the only conclusion that l could draw from my Pioneer social orientation was that I was hopelessly decadent, and quite unlikely ever to aspire to any position of authority in the communist party.

After such strong doses of government intrusion into our lives, first from fascism, now from socialism, we were more likely than anything else to favor anarchy. But there was a member of our microcosm that was starting to look decadent even in our west leaning eyes. Joska was falling under the sway of too much money too fast.

By mid 1946 he was selling prepackaged American cigarettes and lighters, and the unabated flow of money made his head spin. The war had sent sense gratification on prolonged leave of absence, so, with the return of peace, it was only natural for its survivors to try and rekindle their taste for it. We all wanted to indulge in those things denied us for so long, but for Joska, and others like him, pursuing pleasures of the flesh became a full time obsessive occupation.

At first he took us all out to dine with him and Rose on a routine basis. It was exciting for us, and he looked more glamorous to us than ever. His clothes were impeccably tailored, and he looked as dashing as a matinee idol. My father especially enjoyed hitting the few open hot spots with him, and I was in dream land. But after a while we were invited less frequently, and it was just him and Rose. We didn't exactly feel left out. Experiencing a decent degree of success ourselves, we weren't desperate for a free night on the town anyway. And once the initial thrill of it all abated, my family was content to lead conservative lives. But Joska was not tiring of post war celebration. And, since he was our savior, we hardly begrudged him a good time. Even when Rose opted for a few quiet nights at home, Joska stayed in party mode, and he continued to go out even without her on his arm.

That Joska felt the need to be excited by life was not unique. There were men and women all over the world who had just spent six years dealing with the bad guys, fighting the most justified war known to mankind, living through the event of the century. And while most people were quite content to continue ordinary lives after the war, free of the daily threat of death, many found their peacetime identities too nondescript. They had been resistance fighters, spies, couriers, and smugglers, gambling their existence in a confrontation with the forces of evil, and now they were supposed to go back to selling shoes and teaching arithmetic, and liking it. For people like Joska Cséh it was not a smooth transition. Whatever they had been or done before the war was irrelevant. They probably didn't have any idea of any hidden special talents, but, once the war began, a side of them they never knew bloomed and flourished. Mousy librarians were imbued with the courage to carry messages to partisans. Commonplace office secretaries became documents forgers, and farmers broke their plowshares into bombs to take up the occupation of sabotage. Nine to five insurance agents, school teachers, and truck drivers were all transformed into Douglas Fairbanks. Whatever else it was, the war was the high point of their lives. They were heroes, and the equal of any. Waiters and dentists fought side by side, and there were no social divisions. Every moment was an adrenaline rush, and they knew in their hearts they were doing the right thing. They were brave, determined, and proud. And for most of these people that pride would sustain them for the rest of their days. But for a few, like our dear Joska, the peace was too sedentary. Perhaps that's why he continued with the black market. It defied the authority of a foreign presence regarded with suspicion, and fulfilled his need to continue covert activities. That it was lucrative was only a bonus. But when profit became the sole incentive a void was created inside him from which there was no refuge. The war did not go on forever, nor did the empowering challenge and righteous thrill of it. Selling shoes was out of the question. Convincing a store owner that open toed high heels would sell big brought little satisfaction to someone who had just spent half a decade outfoxing gun toting Nazis. A future generation would spawn some psychologist to categorize and name this behavior, but in 1946 Hungary, Josef Cséh syndrome would have sufficed.

With clandestine Camel and Chesterfield fueling his merry lifestyle 1947 saw no abatement in Joska's revelry. The most painful part of the fallout was his deteriorating relationship with Rose. She watched her gallant and beloved hero descend into some unknown drunken depths, and she was powerless to dissuade him. Now he was going out all night, and even for several days at a time. My mother tried to calm Rose, but excusing Joe's debauchery as relief from the tension of war only held so much water. As much as she loved him she was still a woman, and she did not take infidelity lightly. After over a year of turning a blind eye her dignity would suffer a faithless husband in silence no more, and she gave him an ultimatum. It might have straightened him out for a week, but his need to defy, whether it was armed thugs or conventional propriety, ran too deep to control. As agonizing as it was, by midyear Rose sued for divorce, and Joska was obliged to pack up and leave.

My mother cried like a baby over the shame of tossing out their savior, but Rose could not tolerate his present condition any longer. I was bewildered. Like so many younger members of households world-wide, we just observe marital disputes without being privy to too much inside dope. Also, their gratitude was still strong, and they did not want to risk dimming my image of the man. But, even if it was none of my business, I knew Rose was shattered. And for the first few days after he left she did little but cry. The disappointment over his inability to maintain his white knight persona was unbearable. He had fallen from the heights of divinity to the depths of debauchery, and her heart was smashed.

Three months went by and we didn't hear anything from Joska. My Bar Mitzvah was approaching, and I was resolute that he be invited. He was my hero, and I was not about to celebrate such an important day without him. They tried to explain to me that he was divorced from Rose and out of the family, but I wouldn't hear any of it. My father agreed with me, and he turned detective, tracking him down through the bars of Budapest. This wasn't exactly a sacrifice on his part. With the return of peace Papa had returned to being a social butterfly, and he probably had a thousand mutual acquaintances with Joska. He just had to ask. And when my big day came I stood on the *bhima* of our little synagogue that had somehow survived anti-Semitic Nazis and anti-religion commies, and looked for Joska. I combed the crowd, but saw no sign. I started to curse my father's incompetence when the rear door opened and in walked my hero, struggling to keep a yarmulke from falling off. I was so elated I cried.

After the service we returned to our apartment for refreshments, and Joska came along. Everyone was cordial, but my mother doted on him. I was so overjoyed that, at first, I didn't take notice that he was no longer dapper. In the three months that had transpired since the divorce he had lost his polished veneer of aristocracy, and now appeared ordinary, even shabby. But he was still my hero, and I clung to him all afternoon. We reminisced about some of our adventures together, and we even shared a drink, tasting my first wine in his company. And when he left he promised to see me soon. But it would be twenty one years before we'd meet again.

In spite of our newly restored religious freedom, we still lived under the sway of a dictator. Of course, going from Hitler to Stalin was an immeasurably enormous improvement. Under Adolph we lived in dread, and even with all the bureaucratic Bolshevik bullshit, Papa Joe seemed a benevolent despot by comparison. But yet another dictator was about to change our lives in a most unexpected way. And he came from somewhere we had never even heard of.

CHAPTER TWENTY THREE

THE WEST AND PEACE

If you study the history of the western hemisphere in the middle part of the twentieth century you're sure to come across the name of Rafael Trujillo. He was one of a cadre of Latin American dictators who grabbed headlines for decades in the forty's, fifty's and sixty's. There was Batista in Cuba, Somoza in Nicaragua, Duvalier in Haiti, Perón in Argentina, and Trujillo himself was absolute ruler of a tiny Caribbean country called the Dominican Republic. As it happens though, none of us back in 1947 had much academic interest in the history of the western hemisphere, so we had never heard of him, or that piece of the island of Hispaniola which he ruled with impunity. Whatever wild fantasies we might have dreamily discussed in our coal bins during bombing raids and artillery shelling, nobody ever mentioned anything as exotic as a tropical paradise. The closest any of us had ever gotten to such an image was the public swimming pool in Gyonyos. Palm trees and papayas were as foreign to us as the dark side of the moon.

With balmy climate and sandy beaches, the Dominican Republic was so fundamentally different from the landlocked land of my birth it defies comparison. But its iron gloved dictator, half way through his three decade rule, hoped to steer his little nation into the bold new future, and considered the pathetic survivors of the holocaust as the ideal element to give his country the oomph it needed to achieve that aim. So, he flew to Europe, went straight to the recently liberated concentration camps, and personally offered refuge to the Chosen

People. Thousands of Jews, desperate for a new life, immigrated to his tropic isle. There were so many refugees a small city had to be built to accommodate them all, Sosua. The wily dictator's plan bore fruit, and within months Dominican industry took off. Modern manufacturing hummed like never before, and some of her industry in specialized areas even led the world for a time, only to be outpaced by Israel herself.

Like most Europeans the Weisz clan also longed for a life far from the dominion of dictators. But fate cast its ironic shadow over our lives once again, and another self styled Caesar, this time though, with no malice in his heart toward Abraham's tribe, sponsored our immigration to the Promised Land, America. As we were not actually liberated from a concentration camp the red tape was slightly different for people like us. Yolie hired a New York immigration lawyer named Max Blecher to arrange for us to pay the hundred dollar fee for a Dominican visa for us, and it was all set. It wasn't exactly the part of the new world we had in mind, but it'd do for now. And, even less anticipated, we'd be learning Spanish, a language as foreign to me as Greek, long before English. But it would still take some doing. Though one dictator tried to liquidate us, and another was warmly inviting us to his country, yet another was exerting all his influence to keep us in limbo.

Daily, the Hungarian communist party was becoming more entrenched, imposing rules and regulations to rein in the near anarchy that had replaced the repression of the war years. Since being liberated from the krauts the Hungarians had run relatively amok, openly enjoying black market goods, and improvising their economy. But such disregard for order could not go on forever. So, the Reds, big fans of order, cracked down on the black market, and regimented legal tender. This meant a dramatic fall in the fortunes of those who thrived on it, like Joska. Besides being the end of Chesterfields and chocolate, it also meant big time travel restriction. Having a visa to be somewhere else was one thing, but getting permission to leave was another.

We were supposed to be living in a soviet dreamland. And I suppose that everybody was so eager to get to our worker' paradise they had to build an iron curtain just to keep them all out. Basically, the communist tried to discourage anyone from leaving, because it made them look bad to have their contented populace fleeing. So, when your visa to visit the exterior came through you had to apply for an exit visa. They made you wait for an indeterminate period of time, and then granted permission to leave with just a three day window of opportunity. That means just seventy two hours to pack up and get out. This prevented you from selling anything large, allowing the state to claim it. They got a lot of furniture, cars, and pianos like that.

At the end of 1947 Anci and her husband, Robert Frater, were granted a one month visitor's visa to the United States, pending their immigration to the Dominican Republic. They flew to Germany, and then to New York. After several weeks in New York City Yolie and Nick gave them a loan with which to start their new lives in the Caribbean, and Anci and Robert were off to the tropics. Flying, they leapfrogged to Atlanta, Miami, and finally Santo Domingo, where they were graciously greeted by government representatives, and whisked to their new home, a picturesque tropical villa.

Who could have predicted Anci's life? From quiet Gyonyos, to the grim life in hiding in Budapest, to the unspoken horror of Auschwitz, to sultry Santo Domingo, and later to the hustle and bustle of the Big Apple, and much later the elegance of Aventura, Anci's life was, and continues to be, remarkable. She lives down the street from me now, but has never spoken about that dark era in her life.

A year after Anci and Robert opened their five and dime in Santo Domingo Rose left Europe. She paid Abigail Unger a farewell visit, and turned west, never looking back. She was eager to leave Hungary. For as long as she lived there she felt that she lived in the shadow of Joska's betrayal. He had been her hero, but had broken her heart, and irreparably tarnished his image with her. With every click of the railway track, and every foamy white cap, she did her best to put the old country behind her. She docked in New York, determined to start a new life. Then, after one afternoon of shopping for her tropical wardrobe, Yolie introduced her to a confirmed bachelor named Martin Buchwald. She never made it the Caribbean, and in 1999 Martin and Rose Buchwald celebrated their fiftieth wedding anniversary.

A year after Rose left Budapest my parents and I took a train to Le Havre, France from which we sailed west to America. On the voyage I was so full of anticipation I almost burst. So, when we hit Ellis Island it was a huge disappointment to find ourselves knee deep in a pile of red tape even the Soviets would've admired. Instead of going to a cowboy movie we had to spend five days waiting in endless lines and filling out equally endless paperwork, all the while looking out across the bay at New York City, aching to taste its pleasures.

When we finally made it in Yolie and Nick received us with nothing less than regal pomp. We were treated to a meal that has not been surpassed to this day, and, in spite of years of John's build up, New York did not disappoint. He was my eager guide, and I had the best time of my life, free in the greatest city in the world with my childhood playmate. We explored daily for four weeks, until I knew the City almost as well as he did. Then my parents and I took our first airplane flight.

Anci greeted us at the airport in Santo Domingo, and we settled into a life we'd never have imagined, not in a thousand years of daydreaming down in our coal bins. We were the elite of a tropical paradise, with live-in servants and private schools. Of course, there were a few problems getting the other kids to accept me. But my soccer skills, as well as my willingness to duke it out with anyone who badgered me over my past, won them over in the end. I even made their semi-pro soccer team.

As exotic as the Dominican Republic was, we always considered it a stepping stone. The United States was our real goal. So, after two years of privileged gentility, we were all granted visas to the U.S. We sold the five and dime, said adios to the island of Hispaniola, and flew to another island, Queens. We had gone through so much, and now we were so lucky to finally become Americans. From the moment the war began it had been our dream destination, and now we were finally realizing it. But, as much gratitude as we felt, what happened next exhausted our ability to express it.

After just a month in New York we received a letter that actually caused both my parents to swoon. My older brother Josef had survived Siberia and was in Budapest. So, with the continued labors of Max Blecher, visas were applied for. By now the line to immigrate to the United states had become so long it was a two year wait for Josef and his family. But the desire to escape totalitarianism was so strong they just abandoned everything they had and made their way to the Austrian border. Underpaid border guards were thrilled to accept Josef's bribe and they bid them good luck in the west. Once inside Austria their status changed to that of refugees fleeing soviet dominion, and they were able to fly to Idlewild. So, by 1951 none of our family was left in our native homeland. Elizabeth, Vera, and brother Josef, back from the dead, came home. Words fail me, so you'll just have to imagine my parents, my sisters, yours truly, and a ghost named Joe, all together for the first time since 1944. I'll just add that we stopped and said a prayer for Sandor, the only member of our family to die as a result of World War Two and the holocaust.

Better equipped with *español* than *inglés*, I struggled through my first few years of studies in America. But I became a regular Yankee and worked in Max Blecher's firm while I studied for a law degree. But my studies were interrupted in 1959 when conflict in Lebanon caused me to be drafted. Fortunately I did not have to fight, and I served out my brief military tenure completely inside the safe confines of the States. When I got out of the army I decided to switch careers and try my hand at trading stock. I did so, because I had a plan. I needed to make a lot of money to repay a big debt. I was determined to locate and, if necessary, help Joska.

We could not risk traveling to Hungary, because the government might not have let us leave. But, after a long letter writing campaign I finally heard back from him. Deprived of the freedom to travel, and with the black market long since eradicated, Joska had little alternative but to live the humble Hungarian life of a soviet citizen. Much later I learned how profoundly he regretted his years of revelry after the war. It had cost him Rose, the greatest thing in his life. Without her he had almost no will to go on. His own family provided him with emotional support, but he was already a shell of his former self, and he would never fully recuperate. He missed Rose and their life together so much he felt he could never find such happiness again. Nor did he try. He never remarried. And to her dying day Rose kept in her heart the image of her gallant knight who defied the Nazis and saved her and her entire family from certain death. And she joined me in my efforts to repay Joska. As soon as I could arrange it I started sending money to him. Communist bureaucracy made it a bit bothersome, but the funds finally got to Joska. And from that time to the present I am proud to say that I have continually supported him. He's in good health, living in Pécs, where he got the papers that saved my family.

Finally, in 1968, when the communists eased travel restrictions, I flew to Budapest and reunited with my savior. He was overwhelmed to see that the little *pischer* he had taken around on his motorcycle was now a grown man, with children of his own. And every few years since then I return there to see how he's doing. I also visit the scenes of our war years.

Our old apartment is still there, as is the Debrecens', though they long since passed on. Liget Park flourishes, and as of my last visit in 2007, they finally put a new coat of paint on the old buildings. Hungary was almost coming into the new millennium.

A coat of paint can beautify something, but it doesn't mask what it is. The bullet holes are still there, and seeing them, and Joska, brings back the war years to me. I had witnessed those bullets ripping into the stone facades of the Christian designated and Jewish designated buildings. I played soccer outside of them with a yellow Star of David on my chest. I ducked those bullets, running through the war ravaged streets, dodging Nazis, *Nyilosak* and Russian front line troops, all on a killing rampage. I hid in these buildings, and brought food and water to the war's victims, hiding in elevators and attics. I myself hid in the coal bins of these buildings, with those bullets whizzing just overhead, and bombs exploding just outside.

Sometimes, when I share these memories with others, I'm asked if I can explain my survival. Why, when so many in identical circumstances perished, did I make it? Millions were mechanically shipped off and murdered. Thousands were discovered hiding. How do I account for coming through it all without a scratch? Is it fair? Is it right? Do I feel guilty? In response to all this deep philosophical speculation I can only say that I see no grand cosmic design to any of this. I don't understand things like fate and karma, or even luck. As for the holocaust, I feel as any decent person should, regardless of faith, that it was a tragedy and a crime. And my only explanation for surviving it is one which my more philosophical friends inform me is called existential. Simply put,

I survived because somebody saved me. Some say I should thank God. But I don't think I'm more deserving of God's attention than those who died. Why would the Supreme save me and not them? It makes no sense. What does make sense to me is that I was saved. I had nothing to do with it. And when I remember the war, and not a day goes by when I don't, one image stands out above them all. It isn't a fearsome soldier or gun toting hooligan. It isn't one of the uncounted victims. Instead, it's the visage of an elegant gentleman, offended by the cruelty of our oppressors, and determined to turn the tables on them and deprive them of their innocent quarry.

Josef Cséh stood up to the fascists and lived a long life to tell the tale. He's ninety five and has outlived all those bastards. In his youth he risked everything to help total strangers, a family of Jews whom he never met. He was brave and dauntless, and worthy of praise, more so than I can tell. Of course, I know he was not alone in challenging the Nazis. There were many like him, who also took a stand and defied evil. There were real Christians, like the Debrecens, who helped hide the Kovacks, Moscovics, Faragos, and me. And there were many others who hid Jews, both adults and children, and they deserve thanks and praise as well. But I leave those acts of gratitude to those who were rescued by them. I do my duty, and I thank the courageous individual responsible for my own salvation. I thank Joska and try to repay him over and over again. But how can I really? He saved my life. He saved the lives of my parents, and my sister, and nearly forty other relatives. If he had done nothing but rescue those three girls from the Vienna ghetto he'd have earned his fame. He is a hero, and I proclaim it to the world. You cannot imagine the fear in which Europe lived. Ninety nine percent of the people who lived under the heel of the Nazi boot trembled in terror. But Joska looked in the face of fear and spit in its eye. He would not hand over one victim or cooperate with them in any way. They could go to the hell as far as he was concerned. No submission to tyranny. No kowtowing. No surrender. He did not tremble before their threats and their guns. He stood toe to toe, unarmed and alone, against the worst bloodthirsty scum that has ever crawled on the Earth, and backed them down over and over again. Grateful I am he saved me, and proud to know him and be able to help him.

The Nazis are a grim memory, but Joska lives still, victorious in his longevity, ready to dance on their graves. And it makes me happy that he enjoys a simple life in his homeland, in the company of his nieces and nephews, all of whom honor him. I thrived in America, and raised three children of my own. I have three grandchildren as well, and they are all here thanks to him. So are over fifty descendents of the rest of my family. On their behalf, and in the beloved memory of my parents and Rose, I dedicate this to our hero, Joska.

THE END

Made in the USA
Middletown, DE
10 January 2024

47433957R00156